SPIRITED OASIS

TALES FROM A TANZANIAN VILLAGE

Jeannette Hanby
David Bygott

SPIRITED OASIS

TALES FROM A TANZANIAN VILLAGE

 FriesenPress

Suite 300 - 990 Fort St
Victoria, BC, V8V 3K2
Canada

www.friesenpress.com

ISBN
978-1-5255-7627-0 (Hardcover)
978-1-5255-7628-7 (Paperback)
978-1-5255-7629-4 (eBook)

1. BIOGRAPHY & AUTOBIOGRAPHY, CULTURAL HERITAGE

Distributed to the trade by The Ingram Book Company

DEDICATION

We dedicate this book to two mentors who inspired and encouraged us:

"All life is about relationships and the art of living is getting those relationships right."
Ernest Neal

"The brook would lose its song if we removed the rocks."
Wallace Stegner

TABLE OF CONTENTS

CAST OF CHARACTERS

Home crew—Athumani, our esteemed cook and advisor in all local matters; Pascal, our "Man Friday" who did many different jobs; our three foster boys, Len, Sam and Gillie; Gwaruda our night watchman; Ali, our head gardener.

Margaret Gibb (British) and husband **Per Kullander** (Norwegian)—Owners of Gibb's Farm, a small lodge near Karatu town that welcomed tourists, researchers, photographers and all manner of transients, including us.

Hans and Leoni Schmeling (Germans)—Managers of the Karatu farm known as Shangri-La. They also established Mangola Plantation and Kisimangeda Farm in Mangola.

Matayo—A Hadza hunter living in Mangola who became a dear friend.

Saidi Kimaka—Gorofani Village Chairman, a Sambaa elder.

Athumani and Zaharia Omari—Sambaa cook and wife who worked at Mangola Plantation.

Njovu—Manager of Mangola Plantation, a Ngoni man, descended from Zulus of southern Africa.

Kaunda—A Hadza man, Njovu's helper and an important part of Mangola Plantation operation.

Stefan—A German farm manager who left Mangola soon after we arrived.

Kampala and Onkai—Two Hadza brothers who worked on Mangola Plantation from time to time.

Mama Ramadhani—An Iraqw woman central to the village of Gorofani.

Issa—Iraqw young man who worked for Mama Rama, also a worker and guard of our vegetable farm.

Adam Chorah—A Sukuma elder, leader of the Muslims, the village "sheikh."

Julius Meruss—Gorofani Village Chairman 2, Datoga elder.

Jumoda—Datoga young man with ambitions.

Ruth—A young Iraqw woman with a dream to become a nurse.

Flycatcher Lodge—Felista, housekeeper, Tido, tour guide, Dominic, butler, Tseama, cook, and others.

The Builders—Kefti, headman, Pius, helper, Ibrahim, block maker, Pili, block maker assistant, and others.

THE FOUR MAJOR MANGOLA ETHNIC GROUPS

Genetically, historically, socially, linguistically distinct people—all living in Mangola during the time we lived there:

Hadzabe: a small and unique group of traditional hunter-gatherers speaking a click language.

Iraqw: a lineage of farmers who also kept some livestock, migrating over centuries southwards from their origins in Ethiopia region, speaking an Afro-Asiatic (Cushitic) language.

Datoga: herders of livestock displaced by their relatives the Maasai, who also migrated south along the Nile, speaking Nilotic languages.

Bantu: a major group with many subgroups, farmers originally from central and western Africa speaking Bantu languages—Swahili being the major one and used as lingua franca by all these groups.

MAPS

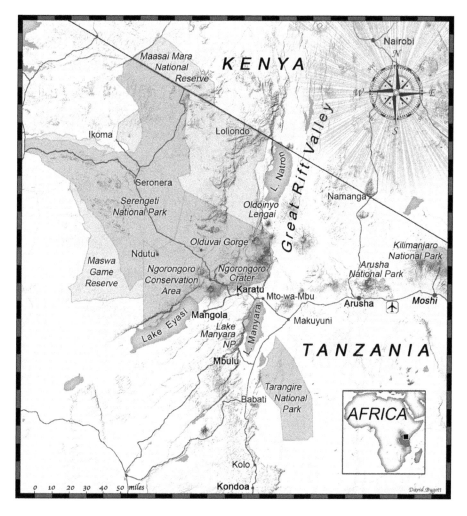

Map of Northern Tanzania. The Mangola area at the east end of Lake Eyasi is surrounded by famous wildlife areas. Serengeti and Ngorongoro lie to the north with Lake Manyara and Tarangire to the east, both on the floor of the Great Rift Valley. Further east, a string of volcanic mountains culminates in mighty Kilimanjaro.

Map of Eyasi-Manyara area. This shows most of the locations described in the stories. Near the center, Gorofani was our "home village" and Mikwajuni was the home that we built, after a sojourn at Flycatcher Farm near Oldeani. Karatu and Mto-wa-Mbu were sources of supplies. Supportive friends lived at Gibb's Farm and Kisimangeda. For wildlife experiences, it was easy to visit Ngorongoro Crater and Lake Manyara National Park.

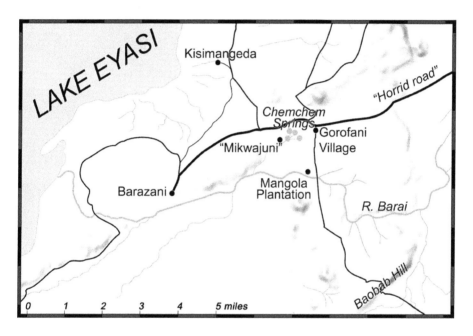

Map of Mangola area. This is the loose name of a cluster of villages including Barazani, Gorofani, and Kisimangeda. Groundwater springs such as those at the Chemchem oasis are the lifeblood of these farming communities. Away from the springs and the Barai flood-plain, the terrain is arid and rocky. Mangola Plantation was the farm where we first lived before building at Mikwajuni alongside the stream.

PROLOGUE
SCORPIONS AND ONIONS
WILD WEST TANZANIA

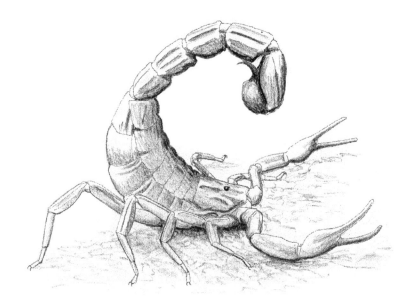

Adapted to Africa, a worldwide story goes like this: A scorpion asks a hippo for a ride across the river. "No, you will sting me, and I will drown," the hippo replies. "If I sting you, then I will also drown," says the scorpion. So, the hippo allows the scorpion to crawl onto her back. Halfway across the river, the scorpion stings the hippo. Before they both drown, the hippo asks the scorpion, "Why?" The scorpion answers, "This is Africa!"

The cautionary tale reminds us that no one can expect things to be as they seem or as promised. Life is full of surprises and topsy-turvy events. The uncertainty of life was part of what attracted the two of us to live in Tanzania. This book is about the stings David and I got and possibly gave as we rode on the eastern part of Africa's back. And what a view: vast skies over extinct volcanoes and glistening dry soda lakes rimmed with palm-studded oases. We were in for the ride, choosing to live in a foreign land with people of many different backgrounds. We wanted to immerse ourselves in the life of a particular place and the people there. The stories in this book are the harvest from nearly two decades of learning.

We tell these stories to share some of our insights about an unusual setting called Mangola, a place with stings, but also a place that grew onions, dreams, and schemes. From 1984 to 2003, we lived in Mangola, a vast area where indigenous tribes were being squeezed off the land. Where all manner of wildlife, from hippos to hornbills, were also losing ground—literally.

The village we chose to live in was no ancient dream of Africa; it was a modern creation. The Tanzanian government was making a deliberate attempt to get people to settle and farm an area just south of the world-famous wildlife areas of Ngorongoro Crater and the Serengeti National Park. Ancient peoples in Mangola were still living their traditional ways of life—the hunter-gatherers and livestock keepers. They mingled with newcomers, mostly farmers, who came to grow cash crops of onions, plus the inevitable shopkeepers, teachers, thieves, politicians, and bureaucrats.

Mangola was the Wild West of Tanzania, a place where we became immersed in the daily struggles over land and water, illness, cattle raids, robberies, and bootlegging. The nearest clinic was 40 miles away along what we dubbed the Horrid Road. The government was a distant rumor, except when it arrived toting guns, official forms, open palms, or, confusingly, help and good sense. Add to the mix the tourists, students, missionaries, researchers, and aid workers who were mostly privileged people from countries driving the juggernaut of Progress through Africa.

And who were we? Two pale-skinned persons with layers, like the purple onions grown in Mangola. We were ordinary folk with practical outer layers; we could sow seeds and sew clothes, help heal people, maintain equipment, build, and improvise. Professionally we were primatologists who'd studied chimps (David) and monkeys (Jeannette), then turned to studying lions. We were drawn to Africa by the animals but became deeply enmeshed with the people, growing to respect and appreciate them. We had deeper layers too and our innermost selves were escapists, withdrawing from the societies we were born into, from their complexity, commercialism, and materialism. And at our core, we were hedonists wanting to experience life fully, deeply, daily.

We had to trust we had enough smarts and talent to earn some money on Tanzanian terms. We'd put our small inheritances from both sets of our parents in the bank. But that was insurance, not income. Building a business of our own was mandatory. As artists and writers, we produced paintings, greeting cards, and books.

We also got small contracts producing educational materials and displays. Giving lectures and leading tourist safaris as professional guides were the most profitable.

To earn both income and status, we needed to build relationships with local people and learn our way through local customs and national bureaucracy. We had to discover how to make our way in a country recovering from a failed socialist experiment and under threat from the wider world's failing capitalist experiment.

We laughed and we mourned as we struggled and learned. We fostered children and animals, made friends and enemies. We were overwhelmed with awe at the beauty of wild nature and intrigued by human nature. We were passionately involved and distanced observers all at once.

We've made two books of stories from our experiences. In this first book—*Spirited Oasis*—we tell how we got to Mangola, what it was like to live there, and the people we came to know. In the second book—*Safaris of Song and Stone*—we tell stories about visitors, events, and adventures. The stories peel off layer by layer, hopefully letting you smell, taste, hear, and feel what life was like in a distant part of Africa where onions thrive, rocks sing, people mix, and scorpions sting.

Jeannette and David

CHAPTER 1
FIRST VISIT TO MANGOLA
OUR INTRODUCTION TO AN INTRIGUING PLACE: 1984

"Hey, look, that's the tree on my map," I said to David, pointing to a giant baobab tree that balanced on the edge of a rocky ridge at the side of the road. "That baobab is opposite the track leading to the springs. Turn here." He pulled the car off the main road, and we puttered downslope through a grove of tall trees to emerge in a meadow of grass grazed short by livestock.

The quality of light changed from the harsh glare of the open road to hazy golden sunlight filtered through feathery green leaves. We were enchanted. Shaken and tired, we emerged from our cramped car at the edge of the forest. We'd arrived at the source of Chemchem Springs, an oasis of cool shade in a dry thorny land. It smelled heavenly, the acacia blossoms soft and sweet, wild gardenias intensely fragrant, and fig trees added their spicy scent. Best of all was the sound of fresh, bubbling spring water, the liquid treasure of Mangola.

What is this place called Mangola? It's a cul-de-sac of the Great Rift Valley, that vast cracked trench running down the east side of the African continent. In the mid-1980s, Mangola was a remote niche in northern Tanzania, semi-arid bushland along the eastern shore of the mostly dry soda lake called Eyasi. Why we'd arrived there requires a bit of background.

During our years as researchers and educators, we'd made countless trips from Serengeti National Park to the safari town of Arusha, passing the road that led to Mangola. People had extolled Mangola's dramatic scenery, unusual environments, and fascinating tribal groups. But even after living 12 years in Tanzania, we'd not taken the sidetrack into the Lake Eyasi Basin.

What finally tempted us was our desire to experience another part of East Africa and the time to do so. There was also a more urgent push: we were homeless, and some friends offered us a place to live on their Mangola farm. We were jobless, too. We'd been banned from doing our lion research and also from teaching university students. This enforced break allowed us to do some deep thinking about our roles as field biologists and educators. While we waited anxiously for the bureaucrats and politicians to rescind the ban, we wanted some distance from our foes.

We were searching for the right spot: a quiet, remote, interesting place to live. In May 1984, we decided to check out the Mangola area. To get there required becoming acquainted with a terrible, rocky, eroded track that shook us to bits and chewed up vehicles. On our first visit, what I came to call The Horrid Road led us into the unknown, tickling our sense of adventure, luring us into wildlands.

Off we went, as David put it, "A woman who always wanted to know what lay round the next bend, and a man resigned to helping her get there and repairing whatever damage ensued."

We set out in our compact white Renault 4, a "tin-can-on-wheels." Such cars were known locally as Roho, meaning "spirit" in the Swahili language. We could only hope it would be undaunted by the 35 kilometers of dirt and

Erosion gully by Mangola Road

rocks ahead. David had painted on its tailgate "Roho ya Pori"—*Spirit of the Bush.*

The car had been useful to us in our recent city roles, but it was soon to get the shock of its life in the wild west of Tanzania.

We departed from Gibb's Farm, our temporary base. Gibb's Farm lodge sat above the town of Karatu on the long highway that led from the coast of Tanzania to Lake Victoria. Our enduring friends—Margaret (British, born in Tanzania) and Per Kullander (Norwegian)—let us stay while we sorted ourselves out.

Their German neighbors, Leoni and Hans Schmeling, learned that we were looking for a place to live. The Schmelings managed a huge farm nearby, where they did everything from smoking hams, growing vegetables, and keeping livestock, to maintaining vast areas of productive coffee, equipment, and roads. They also managed a new farm in Mangola that had an empty manager's house where we could stay.

We passed through Karatu town with its few shops, a bank, post office, outdoor market area, fuel pump, and not much else. The wind seemed anxious to push us westward. Rust-red dust billowed up through the thin metal of the car's floor, filling our eyes and noses and coiling in our throats, making us cough. We had to go slowly over the increasingly rough track with the wind swirling dust onto the windscreen, sometimes making us stop to let it pass so we could see the way ahead.

We tried to take in the landmarks as we bounced along. On the northern side of our route, we looked up to the extinct volcano called Oldeani, named for its dense stands of light green bamboo growing on top. Darker forest trees lower on the slopes marked the boundary of the forest reserve and below that were distant farms with whitewashed buildings. Avenues of red flowering trees lined the deep green rows of coffee bushes. Lower down were blankets of honey-colored wheat and stunning carpets of bright yellow safflowers and sunflowers.

The road turned abruptly through stony banks and plunged into a valley with a muddy stream. Rows of coffee bushes followed the watercourse, guarded by tall trees carrying large bouquets of orange flowers. People stood talking or bathed in the stream while others walked alongside the road carrying loads on their heads or backs. This refreshing green scene was to be the last such spot on our journey until we reached the oasis called Chemchem in Mangola.

We chugged across the stream up a slope to an open ridge where the road turned downhill. In the distance, a smear of blue marked the Eyasi rift escarpment. We paused to admire the grand view, took in some dust-free air, and pushed on, descending the mountain slopes, winding in and out of the folds. The fragile volcanic soil was fine and dry, easily swept up into dust devils. They swirled across the land, rattling the dry maize stalks that etched the outlines of cultivated fields. The few squat stick-built houses lacked trees or bushes to soften their desolate shapes.

An Iraqw (pronounced ear-rack) man trudged along the road, his hands clutching the ends of the traditional cudgel he carried across his shoulders, his black clock whipping his thin legs, and his rubber tire sandals stirring puffs of dust. We recognized him as Iraqw because of his stance, his shoes, clothes, and Ethiopian features—long face with high cheekbones. Iraqw people had settled the surrounding highlands after migrating slowly down the Rift Valley over hundreds of years. They were a large part of the population around Karatu and Oldeani.

Further along, we had to go at the pace of a tired tortoise, picking our way down staircases of stones. Roho complained as it jolted, bumped, and bounced. Our stomach and buttocks were clenched as we drove. We thought about the road's jagged teeth below the Roho's rusty floorboard.

Charcoal bags

We crossed several ravines and clambered back up ridges, finally reaching a broad plain where red dirt gave way to a more desolate grey. Shacks plastered with mud seemed planted near scarce acacia trees. There were scratched-out farms, skinny cows, herds of goats feeding on thorny bushes, and stacks of sooty colored sacks. We knew what was in the bags—charcoal.

Seeing the bags stirred an uncomfortable mix of sadness and anger in me. Making charcoal meant cutting down the trees that protect the soil from heavy rains as well as provide shade, cover, and moisture. The loss to the environment was tremendous. And charcoal making was very inefficient; most of the energy disappeared in the burning of wood. People stood by their charcoal stacks while others loaded bags of charcoal on top of a truck. They stared at us. I sighed, wishing they made a living doing something less destructive. Although charcoaling was illegal by government decree, the only laws down this road seemed to be those of supply and demand.

Trucks coming from the regional town of Arusha used the Horrid Road to Mangola to fill up with onions. They picked up sacks of charcoal on their way out. Mangola produced almost half of the onions in Tanzania. With irrigation, onions, a desired commodity everywhere, grew well in Mangola's dry climate. Onions endured transport over rough roads and were the major cash crop drawing farmers into the area. Trucks came from all over Tanzania, even from Kenya, and picked up loads for export.

We swerved to pass the truck as it started on its return journey to the city, spewing diesel fumes and covering us in a thick pall of dust. We emerged to climb a hill, at last able to see a distant cluster of buildings and trees. This, we reckoned, was the settlement called Gorofani (gore-o-fahn-nee), Mangola's first substantial village.

I checked the map I'd drawn when Leoni Schmeling had given us directions. It showed the main road crossing along the outer edge of Gorofani. About a mile further west were wavy lines labeled Chemchem, the name for the oasis beyond the village. We decided to visit the springs before looking for Mangola Plantation. We needed some shade and a break from the wind and dust.

As we slowly passed along the main road with its scattering of houses, we saw many people out and about. Some were carrying sacks or sticks and even spears. Children ran across the street, waving at us. Several adults stopped to stare, their faces expressionless or filled with curiosity. They might have been more amazed by our inappropriate vehicle on the rutted road than the two *wazungu* riding in it. Wazungu (wah-zoon-goo) is a Swahili word for Europeans. It amused me to know that *-zungu* was the root word for "wander" or "go around": so apt for the white tribe in Africa, so apt for the two of us.

We stopped our current wandering at the verdant oasis called Chemchem. The luxuriant vegetation was a welcome sight after our long drive. We looked up the tall yellow trunks of the acacias with their fern-like leaves then down over sycamore fig trees standing like leafy buildings. Turning towards the springs, we faced a fantasy, an animated Egyptian painting. The plumed tops of the papyrus tossed and swayed in the vigorous breeze like a crowd of green stick women with bouffant hairdos.

Vines crawled and lounged on tree limbs, snuck through the papyrus, making the place appear a jungle, prehistoric. Spooky. You could easily imagine dinosaurs lurking within. Indeed, a dinosaur shape startled us as it leaped off a branch. We caught our breaths as the monitor lizard dropped into a stream with a splash and was gone.

Laughing at our momentary fright, we soaked in the beauty and mystery of the place. An oddity caught my eye. Poking out of a marshy patch near a running stream were white funnel flowers with yellow candle-like spikes in the center. They had to be calla lilies, a garden plant. I was puzzled. Were they native to this land? If not, what were these snobbish-looking domestic flowers doing here among the tangle of wild, marshy vegetation? I was later to learn the answer after forgetting the question.

Nile monitor lizard

As we gazed around the grassy glade, we could see seeps and springs all around where water emerged and trickled into deeper streams. I put my hand in the clear water and was surprised how cold it was. The water burbled, pooled, and murmured to itself before taking its silent, secret journey into the patches of papyrus. Sitting quietly on boulders with our bare feet in the water, we scanned around.

Colors and sounds of animals living in the oasis caught our attention. Scarlet and blue dragonflies flitted in the beams of sunlight. Glossy-winged hadada ibises flew overhead, emitting screeches matching their names, *ha-da-da*. A shrill chittering came from a woodland kingfisher, azure and gray, motionless on a bright yellow branch. Vervet monkeys swung and hung like fruits in a fig tree whose thick boughs bore clusters of small green figs. Baboons shrieked from the depths of the papyrus thickets and hippos honked from hidden pools.

We heard a murmur of human voices from the village side of the clearing and heard the clank of metal buckets being filled. Between the main village water source and ourselves was the grassy meadow. On the edge, in the shadows of trees, we spied a tall man in a black cloak with several rows of white buttons sewn on it. He was almost invisible as he stood near his flock of goats. We reckoned he was a Datoga herdsman, the Datoga being the main livestock owners in the area.

Matayo at Chemchem

Then came a most remarkable sight—a small, sturdy figure emerging into the sunlit clearing. The man was nut brown, lean, and muscular, carrying a large bow and a handful of arrows. A knife sheath bounced from a belt that barely supported his tattered shorts. We stood staring at what we recognized was a quintessential Hadza (hahd-za) man. The Hadza people were foragers; only about 1,000 still roamed the Eyasi Basin. They called themselves the Hadzabe in the plural, but worldwide they were called the Hadza, and we will use that for individuals and well as the tribe.

We'd heard a lot about them but never expected to see one at this oasis. He turned his eyes to look at us, not at all surprised to see two strange pale people. We rose as he approached us, his deep brown eyes dancing and amused. We greeted him with hello and smiles, using simple Swahili, the lingua franca of East Africa.

"Hello, my name is Matayo." He seemed happy to sit on a stone and talk, telling us he lived in a Hadza camp behind the sentinel baobab on the little escarpment above the springs. His Swahili was simple but understandable, about on a level with ours. We shared names of researchers we'd met who'd told us about the Hadza. Matayo nodded at each one, knowing most of them. He then taught us the proper greeting among the Hadza. "*Shayamo,*" he said. We repeated: shy-ah-mo. The word had none of the clicks so characteristic of many Hadza words. Shayamo slipped easy from our tongues. We smiled at one another, pleased; we were now mutual acquaintances.

Suddenly Matayo stood up and said in Swahili, "I'm going to hunt baboons!" With a big grin revealing brown-stained teeth, he strode downstream towards distant baboon screams, turning to call over his shoulder, "Bye-bye," in English.

After Matayo left us, we decided to walk to the village side of the necklace of springs. We passed by the dark-cloaked Datoga man with his livestock and watched Iraqw and Bantu women and men clustered around the village pond, filling white and blue buckets, loading braying donkeys with containers of water. Standing in the shade at a distance, we tried to take in the variety of cultures living in the area. They were all dependent on the water from these Chemchem Springs, mixing here like paint in a pool, a pool we could observe and learn from.

We wanted to know more about these Mangola people, their lifestyles and histories, the springs, and the wildlife too. So much to absorb.

Chemchem invited us to linger, but we had another destination on this visit: Mangola Plantation, the farm the Schmelings had told us about with its empty manager's house. If we liked it, we could stay there for a year or so until they found a farm manager. Would we like it? We set out to answer that question.

Dragonfly at Chemchem Springs

CHAPTER 2
MANGOLA PLANTATION
THE FARM, DECISION MAKING: 1984

Mangola Plantation farmhouse

Reluctantly David and I left the green shade and burbling water at Chemchem Springs. We climbed in our spirited Roho car and set off to find Mangola Plantation. According to my map, it lay on the south side of Gorofani village. A whirlwind swept towards us as we backtracked to the settlement on the main road, covering the windscreen with dust. We were aware that the thoroughfare was not only for vehicles but for the wind. It rushed down from cool Ngorongoro (nn-gore-on-gore-o) highlands to mix with the low, hot air of the Eyasi Basin, sweeping up the fine grains of soil from the old volcanoes along its way.

When the dust swirled onwards and we could see again, we chose the nearest track going in the direction of what we hoped was Gorofani central. A partly-built mosque and several houses made of mud and sticks formed the outskirts. Most roofs were thatched with faded palm leaves, while others gleamed with corrugated metal.

The track intersected with what we presumed was the main road through the village because huts, half-built barns, and half-built houses lined both sides. Roho bounced in and out of erosion gullies as we made our way along the track, passing people sauntering along, dogs crossing the road, children running. We slowed near a shop selling goods like soap, kerosene, salt, and matches. Above the noise of our car, we could hear the rattle of a diesel engine at the grain mill.

"This must be downtown Gorofani," David said with a laugh. "Where's the local bar?"

I lifted an eyebrow, saying, "And now where do we go? Where exactly is Mangola Plantation?" We weren't sure what to expect by the word "plantation." Leoni Schmeling had told us the farm was on the far side of the village. We wished we'd asked more specific questions. Would there be trees outlining the farm? Fences? What might be growing there? Sugar cane? Maize? Onions?

I opened the window, breathing in the strong smell of onions. It was not the savory smell of cooking onions, but a nose-wrinkling smell of the drying vegetable with an underlying stink of rot. The odor seemed to come from some long, thatched, open-sided barns where onions waited for a lift to the outer world. We puttered past huts and tin-roofed hovels crouching alongside the road, avoiding shabby-looking figures fighting their way against the wind. People hunkered in doorways, and skinny children threw rocks at starved dogs. Our first view of Gorofani village was a rather dismal one.

We continued, trying to keep our dust trail down, searching our memories for the name of the chairman of Gorofani village. The Schmelings told us to try to meet him. But where was his house or office in the maze of shacks? I checked my map,

Mzee Saidi

where I'd scribbled his name: Saidi Kimaka. Alas, his home wasn't on the map. But as if conjured from the dust, a compact, well-dressed man with a startling white Muslim cap stepped into the road. He flagged us down.

Saidi introduced himself, his open face wearing a broad smile, head tilted back. It seemed uncanny the right man should appear when we needed him as if he knew that we were coming. I suspected he did, though this was long before any phone service was available in Mangola.

Saidi looked like the local mayoral figure he was, confident and imposing. He spoke excellent Swahili in deep, rich cadences, as if addressing a council meeting: "Welcome. You are in the right village. You are on the correct road."

We got out of the car to shake hands while a small crowd of youngsters gathered around to giggle and stare.

"Sorry, I can't accompany you to Mangola Plantation," Saidi told us. "But Njovu, the farm manager, and Athumani Omari are there. Athumani takes care of the main house and visitors. They both know you're coming."

"Please tell us, where exactly do we turn off to the farm?" I asked.

Saidi gestured towards a distant line of trees marking the route of a seasonal river. "Head for the bridge. Before the bridge, turn right. There's a track through the bush. It's muddy, but the main house is easy to find."

We thanked him; he waved us on, the children waved too. The houses diminished in number and size as we left the village. They'd almost disappeared by the time we got to the large bridge over the dry river known as Barai (baa-rye). Scraping through thorn bushes and squishing through gooey mud puddles, we reached a barren clearing surrounding a small house. We reckoned the building belonged to the farm and wondered if it was the one on offer. We didn't see farm manager Njovu or anybody else there.

We decided to explore further. The track went westwards through a green tunnel of umbrella acacia trees. We emerged onto an open stretch bordered by grey-green cactus-like trees with ruffled ribs edged by thorns. These imposing succulents were a kind of euphorbia, obviously planted as a screen or fence. The avenue led us to a little clearing around a majestic tree, the biggest umbrella acacia we'd ever seen. It was so impressive that we parked under the tree and stared before we finally noticed the house nearby.

A short fellow wearing an apron emerged from the side of the house. He came towards us slowly, smiling and nodding, greeting us in Swahili: "Karibuni sana. Jina langu ni Athumani." *You are most welcome. My name is Athumani.* We introduced ourselves, then Athumani politely asked about our journey and invited us into the stone-built house. He brought us to the front where three steps led to a covered porch.

We stepped inside. While our eyes adjusted to the dark interior, we looked around the large main room. A wall separated the living room from two bedrooms. Between them was a small room for toilet and shower with louvered windows sandblasted to opacity by the constant gritty wind.

Athumani brought a thermos flask of coffee, placing it gently on a big table in the central room where two cups on saucers waited. The blond wood table was the room's centerpiece, flanked by four straight-backed chairs as rigid as sculptures. Clunky wooden armchairs filled more of the space, and in one corner stood a notable stereo system with a guitar propped against a speaker.

A scattering of pelts covered the flagstone floor. I noticed one in particular, an impala skin. I leaned down to stroke the warm rusty brown fur and caught a whiff of musk. The scent glands on its heels still gave off a wild animal fragrance, although the pelt had been lying spread-eagled on the stones for several years. The Schmelings had built the house for a foreign-born farm manager. They also used it as their base when friends came to hunt in the wilds of the Eyasi Basin. Hunting was still a tradition with many Europeans living in the area.

A cupboard full of glassware caught my eye. Delicate dusty wine and sherry glasses stood shyly next to sparkling clean and bulky beer and whiskey shot glasses, clearly indicating the drink preferences of the occupant. I went to scan a bookshelf, hoping for other insights. There were novels in German, English, and French, plus a Swahili dictionary.

Kaunda and Stefan

On one of the shelves was a picture of two men, one of them the man who was leaving this house, leaving Tanzania, leaving Africa. His name was Stefan, the son of one of the owners of Mangola Plantation. When we first met tall, cigar-smoking Stefan, he told us he was disenchanted with farm work and wanted to leave. "This farming, I do not enjoy it; it is hard work. Mangola is a lonely place. No woman, no friends, no one speaks German. What is there for me? Often I need to go to Karatu or Arusha town where I have more chances to meet people."

Stefan wanted to leave; that is why we'd been offered the free house until the Schmelings found another farm overseer. Stefan was leaving a lifestyle behind as well as one of his closest companions; we knew his name already, Kaunda. The Schmelings had mentioned him as being an integral part of their hunting safaris, a valuable tracker as well as farmhand.

I looked at the picture carefully, struck by the contrast between the two men. The photo spoke of their differences as well as their friendship: Stefan—tall, pale, from an aristocratic Bavarian family, unhappily transplanted to the African wilderness; Kaunda—short, dark, a Hadza hunter-gatherer, firmly rooted in a line of people who'd never left Africa. The two were great pals; they hunted, smoked pot, and laughed together. Stefan was going; Kaunda was staying.

Athumani stood waiting while we looked around the room, a kindly expression on his face. Somehow his presence made me feel relaxed. We told him we would like to explore before having coffee. He nodded calmly and disappeared into the kitchen.

Going back outside, we wandered around the compound, looking at the bare and weedy garden space lined by sad-looking trees. They were called flamboyants after the masses of bright red flowers they show off at year's end. But now the trees had no flowers and few leaves, their long seedpods hanging down like dry brown tongues panting in the hot wind.

We turned to look at the magnificent acacia and noted some stunted orange and lemon trees with leaves as curled as arthritic hands. Having been raised in a citrus grove, I could see that the circular basins around the trees were too small and too close to the trunks. Stefan obviously had not cared much about the trees.

From the citrus plot, we walked through the bush to the edge of the Barai River. We stared down at the dry, sandy-bottomed riverbed bordered by cliffs of grey-brown silt where fig trees and acacias clung with desperate roots. You could easily mark out a football field across the riverbed's width. Some youths were making use of the space, playing soccer, kicking a ball made of rags bound with string.

Though no water was visible, we knew that runoff from the highlands could sweep down the Barai channel, carrying sand, silt, rocks, and trees to the shores of Lake Eyasi. On the other side of the dry river, slopes covered with scrubby grey-green vegetation struggled up to rocky summits. Yet another range of mauve-colored hills, fuzzed by dust and distance, led our eyes further on. The scene was at once wild, beautiful, grand, and intimidating, beckoning us with its mysteries.

We stood on the cliff, then turned back towards the stone house. It looked tiny against the backdrop of distant Oldeani Mountain brooding in its cloak of purple under a haze of rust-red dust. We stood in awe, then a playful gust swept dirt and grit into our faces, reminding us to return to the shelter of the house.

Athumani, standing on the porch smiling, made us feel welcome. He brought us a plate of cookies. As we sat to drink our coffee at the blond wood table, in the stony Germanic house, David and I discussed the place. While the questions inside

turned and twisted, we decided we'd take a look at the farm that went with the name
Mangola Plantation.

We asked Athumani, "Can you tell us where the farm manager Njovu is?"

"Yes," he answered, leading us out the kitchen door, past our car, and the big
acacia to the edge of a vast field. He pointed at some distant figures shimmering
in the heat haze. We thanked him and headed off, squinting against the bright sun,
towards the silhouettes.

Mangola Plantation was big and mostly bare. We saw only a few planted crops,
no sheltering trees, no windbreaks. Irrigation pipes, about as thick as your leg, were
lying silently in shiny lines linked together. Some sprinklers were flashing water in
circles over a distant patch of plants.

The water that escaped the thirst of the hot midday wind was showering a small
plot of knee-high green plants. Beyond were rows of taller, fully grown sunflowers
bending and dancing with the wind like they were listening to a rock concert. We
crossed the open space to the far edge of the farm with its wavering images of people.

Njovu and Kaunda

Two figures turned towards us, a tall, dark man with a cap and another short
man dressed in an odd array of garments. The tall one had to be Njovu, the farm

manager. He waved. The shorter man just stood with a bright grin, barely taller than the hessian bag full of onions he leaned on.

Njovu greeted us, and we chatted in Swahili. He told us, "We're in the middle of the harvest. We grow onions now, as well as the sunflowers." He gestured at the fields around. Njovu introduced his short helper, "This is Kaunda." I repeated the name out loud: ka-*oon*-da. The lively man eagerly held out his calloused hand and pumped mine.

"Shayamo," I said proudly. His handshake paused briefly, in surprise, I hoped, because I used the Hadza greeting. He cheerfully replied, "Mta-ana mama!" *Hello mama*. Kaunda was full of pep and energy, and we liked him immediately.

All around Njovu and Kaunda, we could see onions gleaming in the sun; fist-sized knobs of purple spread out on the ground. Hot-looking farm hands were piling them into sacks. We tried to take in the size of Mangola Plantation; it was huge, about the size of 200 soccer fields. Irrigation was critical here. I'd hauled big pipes around alfalfa fields to earn money as a teenager and knew how much work it was. Luckily, if we took the chance to live at Mangola Plantation, we'd be resident caretakers only, not workers or managers. We didn't want to be part of that team. We appreciated just how hard Njovu, Kaunda, and the laborers needed to work to keep the farm going.

Njovu

We were glad Njovu was in charge. His name was Bantu for elephant, and it fitted the man like the elephant fits its skin—strength inside a loose, wrinkled hide and a trunk with a delicate touch. He seemed to know what he was doing, preparing the soil, planting, setting the irrigation pipes, as well as trying to keep the workers, generator, and water pump going. Njovu wasn't a local man; his people, the Ngoni of southern Tanzania, were descended from Southern Africa Zulus. His tribal status gave him a degree of impartiality when hiring or firing locals. And he needed many workers to process the crops grown on Mangola Plantation.

Most local farmers lived on small plots and relied on family members and neighbors at the harvest. The bigger farms had to bring in helpers, older school children, or gangs of temporary workers. Since onions were the main cash crop throughout Mangola and they matured around the same time, there was a high demand for laborers when the onions were ready. To avoid competition with other growers, and get enough workers, Njovu relied on Kaunda and the Hadza. Kaunda did his best to entice them to work, then tried to keep them at it.

In a flurry of dust, we turned away from Njovu and Kaunda, who went back to supervising the filling of the onion sacks. Shielding our faces from the grit, David and I returned to the stone house by the umbrella acacia. We had been slapped silly by the wind, scoured by the dust, stretched by the immense views, pleased by the people, and generally overwhelmed by the place. We entered the dim room, sat at the big table, and drank more coffee.

We talked. When we make significant decisions, we list pros and cons, then weight each one. The procedure slows us down and gives us the illusion of conscious control over our lives. Now we laid out the positive and negative reasons for living on Mangola Plantation.

On the positive side:

Mangola Plantation would be a place where we could weave our lives back together and develop our fledgling business. We'd be free from farm duties. The Schmelings had made it clear Athumani was to be our housekeeper. We'd never had a servant but were glad he was going to continue to look after the house and us. Athumani would be a valued resource, knowing the place, customs, and people. Plus, we liked him already.

Chemchem oasis was a wonder, the Eyasi area worth exploring, and the variety of people especially fascinating. But would local people accept us? Would they see us as respectful and helpful or just as privileged white people indulging their curiosity? Such thoughts led us to the drawbacks of living in Mangola.

On the negative side:

Mangola was far from anywhere: there were few shops, no post office, no fuel pump, no doctors, no clinic, no police, no fire department, no bank, no phones, let alone a library or village hall. We didn't know anyone in Gorofani village. No one spoke English well enough to help us in distress. We'd be outsiders.

There was no public transport; we'd have to depend on our car and David's ability to keep it running. We'd need to invest in a more robust, more expensive car. To live here would be risky, cost us some of our precious savings, time, and energy. All of these factors were serious challenges. Already we had lived over a dozen years in East Africa, mainly in the wilds. We were used to living rough, but *this* rough?

We discussed alternatives.

"What about applying to do another research stint with lions or chimpanzees, or even birds, here in Tanzania?" I proposed.

"We wouldn't get permission right now," said David. "And think of the trauma involved in getting a grant. All those papers we'd have to write. Groan."

"Maybe we could live in Karatu? Or become lodge managers at Ndutu Lodge? Or maybe a camp in Serengeti?" I offered.

"Been there, done that, don't want to do it again right now," said David. "How about Kenya?"

"Too many people; too much corruption."

"Maybe Zimbabwe?"

"No, we know no one and nothing about the country."

"How about Europe or North America?"

"Find jobs in those crowded places? Good grief!"

We rejected each idea.

In the end, we weighted each point's importance to us on a 10-point scale and added it all up. There were more negatives than positives; it was clear we should not choose to live in Mangola. But we didn't want to go anywhere else, either.

Thus, the decision rose out of deep, unclear feelings, not our rational minds. When we chose to live in Mangola, we persuaded ourselves that the move was temporary, time limited. We'd give in to our curiosity and desire to be in a rural setting, not in a lodge, not in an embassy, research, or "helpful" project. We disregarded the disadvantages and took on Mangola Plantation, Gorofani village, the Horrid Road, and the unknowns, along with the promises.

We held Mangola like an onion and started to peel off the layers.

CHAPTER 3
SETTLING IN
GETTING TO KNOW MANGOLA, TAMING TRAUMA: 1984–1985

Fig trees in Barai River

Going to Mangola was like stepping out of an airplane and mounting a mule. Our recent lives had been busy, stressful, even traumatic. We looked forward to a gentler ride at a slower pace in Mangola. We settled in, getting to know people and the land while building our young business.

Both of us were happy to take time to catch up with ourselves, tackle projects, and explore. David launched into painting for an art show. I planted the vegetable garden and trees for fruit and windbreaks. I photographed my collection of kangas, the colorful printed cotton wraps worn by many African women and me. Mangola stretched around us. Our spirits stretched to accommodate the space and opportunities.

On foot, we quickly found favorite places, such as the sandy bed of the Barai River. We walked in the dappled shade between high banks inlaid with the twisted roots of fig and acacia trees. Soft-feathered eagle owls tilted their eared heads from perches in the tree canopies as we strolled by, listening to the laughter of children playing ball in the riverbed and the lilt of invisible golden orioles singing.

Sometimes we strode quickly across the dry and wind-scoured fields between Mangola Plantation to the fresh waters of Chemchem Springs. There, out of the wind, we could hear baboons barking, ground hornbills drumming, and people talking and banging their buckets as they collected water at the village pond. We wandered the meadow to check out the patch of white calla lilies and catch glimpses of brilliant blue and red kingfishers or drab brown cisticola birds darting through the vivid green papyrus stems.

"Triffid"

"Geometree"

The nearby hills held surprises, like the odd bulbous plants we called "triffids" for their many thorn-studded arms, like some alien from space. And there were the spiny plants we called "geometrees" for their angular zigzag limbs. We discovered mysterious mounds of rocks on top of hills that we learned were old graves.

We sold our unsuitable Renault Roho, our Spirit of the Bush, and bought a used Land Rover. We named it "Herbert" after the researcher who sold it to us. Herbert was like a pony, trotting up hidden roads when we explored the steep slopes of Oldeani Mountain that dominated the landscape. Where the track ended, far below the forest boundary, we had impressive views over the seemingly endless stretch of the Eyasi Basin. The soda lakebed stretched sere and white for 75 kilometers between the distant purple Eyasi rift wall to the west and the mauve brown Yaeda hills to the south.

Near the top of the mountain grew a band of pale green bamboo forest that gave the ancient volcano its Maasai name—Oldeani. The bamboo and the undulating green and silver-leafed cloak of the mixed forest below captured the water that wandered through lava conduits to feed the underground springs of Chemchem. Climbing the upper reaches of Oldeani, we often saw russet impala bounding away and sometimes a group of shy grey eland, graceful antelopes the size of large cattle. On one safari, we were thrilled to find a whole pride of tawny lions.

Coming down the slopes to the flats, we bumped our way over ditches and irrigation canals to the edge of the usually dry expanse of Lake Eyasi. There we saw remnant herds of dancing grey gnus or families of striped zebras. Finding hippos and many varieties of birds near the small sets of springs that entered the lake delighted us.

In the opposite direction, we discovered the wildlands to the south. We named our favorite destination Baobab Hill. To reach it, we crossed the dry Barai riverbed on a decaying concrete bridge that felt as safe as going over rotting logs. On the other side were eroded tracks passing sad, abandoned huts and corrals surrounded by bare land. At a deep gulley, we headed into the hills. Sometimes while we lurched slowly up the staircase of rocks, we'd pass a goatherd. More interesting would be a slender Iraqw man guiding a laden donkey downhill. The molasses in the panniers was destined for the makers of spirits in the Chemchem oasis. Happily, for us, the hill was usually luxurious with silence, empty of humans.

Baobab Hill was our magic place. Rosy-colored and silver-flecked rocks stood proudly among thorny commiphora and impressive baobab trees. These massive outcrops sheltered hyraxes, lizards, and snakes as well as offering us viewpoints and caves.

Baobab flower

In the dry season on Baobab Hill, the baobabs' bare limbs hung with velvety gourd-like fruits. We broke them open to eat the tangy foam and hard, nutritious seeds inside. During the wet season, the swollen, fleshy pink trunks lifted limbs decked out in swathes of green leaves. Their white flowers, the size of my two hands cupped together, opened at night to attract bats. In the morning, the blooms fell to the ground to be eaten by diminutive dik-dik antelopes and impalas. We loved this hill of gigantic boulders and guardian baobabs, a place of rugged beauty and peace.

Baobab Hill

One day when we'd been living for a few months at Mangola Plantation, we felt the need to visit Baobab Hill. We wanted to escape to a remote spot where we could absorb a new sting from an old adversary. We needed to take stock and figure out the implications of a letter we had received, a summons that scared us. The letter was from Solomon Ole Saibull, the conservator of the Ngorongoro Conservation Area (NCA). He wrote a short message on official stationery: "I would like to meet you in Karatu soon. We have matters to discuss."

Please stop here and consider skipping the following. The complicated backstory about why we feared the conservator is not essential to enjoying our tales about Mangola. Suffice it to say we did meet the man and survived. You are welcome to carry right on to the next chapter and meet Athumani.

Ole Saibull had caused us a great deal of trouble. He was one of a few powerful bureaucrats who banned us from our research and teaching work. Those office men were so vindictive that we'd been in turmoil about whether to stay or leave the country. So far, we hadn't been expelled—yet.

The conservator was in charge of the Ngorongoro Conservation Area, a famous tourist destination that also had many archeological sites, mountains, and forests. It was a powerful and lucrative position. A significant part of our motivation to live in Mangola was to escape people like the conservator, to avoid politics and conflict with authorities. We hoped the problems (being accused of spying and other misdeeds) would evaporate in time. But this letter made us apprehensive. Would we be forced to leave Tanzania?

Tanzania was in a paranoid state with a failing economy, ever since the East African Community fell apart in 1977. Tanzania, Kenya, and Uganda closed their borders, impounding vehicles, ships, airplanes, and trains. At the time, we were in the Serengeti studying lions. When the borders closed, we had the park mostly to ourselves.

Only daring people like filmmaker Alan Root could fly in and out, alone or with celebrities like Robert Redford, who was filming "Out of Africa." A few safari groups wandered in, but nothing like the stampede before the border closed. Tourism collapsed, and the borders stayed closed until negotiations started up in 1983.

During border closure, we left Serengeti to write up our lion work in Cambridge, England, did a lecture tour across the USA, and committed ourselves to do conservation work in Tanzania. It was to be a way of "paying back" something of what we garnered from our exciting years as wildlife researchers.

David took a two-year local contract with the University of Dar es Salaam to teach wildlife biology. I decided to help establish a conservation education project. I raised meager funds and support in the USA. The authorities in Tanzania welcomed me, and I set out with my work permit in 1981.

We had little money but were dedicated. I had an income so low I didn't have to pay taxes, and David's job at the university earned barely enough for fuel for his car. We were doing these jobs because we cared deeply about Tanzania's wildlife.

My project was called *Malihai*. The word was composed of the Swahili words "mali," meaning wealth, and "hai," meaning alive. The name referred to the living wealth of wildlife, very fitting. I learned that Ole Saibull coined the name. When I started working with Malihai, he was supportive, even helpful, and friendly.

Malihai started in Arusha town. The Headquarters of Tanzania National Parks and the Ngorongoro Conservation Area Authority existed there. Both these organizations supported the Malihai project by providing me and my coworkers an office and supplies. Our team was under the wing of the politically powerful Ministry of Wildlife. The wildlife division dealt with lucrative hunting areas in Tanzania, as well as overseeing parks and reserves. I was naïve. I assumed most of the people in these agencies shared my concerns about protecting the wildlife heritage of Tanzania. It was a time of paranoia, however, and certain people questioned my motives and activities.

A warning came when an accountant at National Parks accosted me one morning. "Look at this!" he shouted, standing outside his cubicle, catching me in an awkward stance, my arms full of posters and books. He waved a magazine in front of me, shouting, "So this is what you think of us? Is this the sort of thing you are telling?"

I stood still, feeling as though I'd stepped on a hidden puff adder. Finally, the man calmed enough to let me take a glimpse of the offending article. The article was in a British magazine, written by a well-known biologist who cared about Tanzania and conservation education. Thinking he could help Malihai, he wrote a report about what we were doing. In the article, he made a plea for supplies, such as sleeping bags, blankets, binoculars, and camping equipment for the children. He put my name and address at the end of the article. That was a big mistake.

"Why have you been doing this behind our backs?" snarled the accountant who grabbed the magazine back. "We did not let you in here to say bad things about us. We do not need the British to send us their soiled blankets."

His hostility—so fresh, so nasty—affected me deeply. I couldn't summon any humor about the situation. The best I could do was appreciate that Mr. Accountant had made me vividly aware of the sensitive nature of aid.

I became ultra-cautious but couldn't just quiver in fear. Funds and logistical support required at least a bit of boldness and numerous requests. My counterparts and I needed supplies to refurbish youth hostels in the parks, books, films, and teaching materials. My colleagues were more familiar with the dangers of standing out, so they pushed me in front to do the negotiating, the requesting, the demanding. I became a target.

I took on the challenge and got zapped.

A couple of examples:

Films: I found an unused stash of the famous movie, "Serengeti Shall Not Die" by Bernhard Grzimek, in both English and Swahili versions. Perfect for school visits. We submitted a proposal to the German organization that had contributed the films to get a mobile screen on which to show them. The local German rep of the organization was furious that he hadn't been consulted and caused us trouble ever after.

An office: Swarms of school children, dignitaries, and assorted visitors did not fit in the tiny office given us by National Parks. We needed a more accessible and spacious place for Malihai. I went to Dar es Salaam to see the head of National Museums. He was in charge of an old German fort that became the British colonial headquarters during colonial times. It was in the heart of Arusha.

The museum head was delighted to give us access to a big, unused space where we could work. When I told an administrator for National Parks, the response was, "Why did you go to National Museums without consulting us? Aren't the offices we gave you good enough for you?"

I took the stings and arrows of displeasure as best I could. But eventually, I, the target, got hit in the bullseye. It was a shock to realize that some people thought I was a spy.

A man in the National Parks office snooped among my things. Mr. Snoop found an unfinished letter to my closest friend. I used our joking salutation based on a humorous incident with canned beans: "Dear Mr./Mrs./Ms. Bean." This opaque form of address led officials to think Bean was a code name. In the letter, I spelled out all my difficulties and frustrations. The authorities who read it jumped to the conclusion that I was intent on exposing and publishing demeaning articles about Tanzania's wildlife managers. I knew nothing about the theft of the letter.

One day I received a summons to the office of the director of National Parks. After waiting anxiously and fidgeting for what seemed an eon, a nervous man handed me a sealed letter. It said National Parks were suing me for defamation of character. The lawsuit demanded millions of shillings. Aghast, I tried to get in to see the director for some explanation. After being brusquely refused, I stumbled out of the office and walked a long way to see some Americans who ran the tire factory in Arusha. They knew well the twists and turns of local politics and also an excellent Tanzanian lawyer.

He told us, "There are no grounds for this complaint. I suspect the director wants to get rid of you because he thinks you have observed too much, like seeing all the illegal cattle in the park, and airplanes picking up rhino horn and elephant tusks."

Whatever the underlying motivations, I faced a long process of clearing up mis-understandings while the lawyer resolved the case. Oddly, I wasn't even asked to terminate my project but told I should take a period of leave. This sidetrack was a typical Tanzanian solution, the lawyer told me. If you screw up or find you're the target of displeasure, you disappear for a while. Eventually, you get transferred or promoted, depending on whom you know.

I asked for a month off and got it. David also got time off from the university. We did a safari with friends and managed to contract hepatitis. This debilitating disease meant months of physical rehabilitation. We thought it an opportune time to hand over Malihai to my counterparts. When I regained physical health, I resumed research on lions in Serengeti National Park, hoping to regain my emotional equilibrium in Serengeti's embrace.

David was close to the end of his contract with the University of Dar es Salaam. He decided to end with a final field trip for his wildlife ecology students.

A month of relative peace passed. Then, at dawn one morning, loud knocks came on the door of the Lion House in Serengeti. A Tanzanian colleague blathered at me: "You have to leave. Right now. They are sending people to kick you out. Go now." He repeated again and again, "You must leave; right away. Go now."

The threat disoriented me. Pulling out would upend all our plans. David and I had worked hard to secure transport, money, and supplies for this field trip. I'd made preparations for the students and teachers to stay at the park's hostel and hear talks from resident researchers. Convinced I couldn't do much until I understood what was going on, I fled to Karatu and our friends at Gibb's Farm.

During my eviction from Serengeti, David was driving from Dar to Arusha, blithely unaware of the tumult. He dropped in at the Ngorongoro Conservation Area office and cheerfully greeted Conservator Solomon Ole Saibull.

"Hello sir, I just wanted to check in with you. Is everything OK for our field course? We do want to spend some of our time in the Conservation Area."

"No, it will not be OK," growled Ole Saibull. "You are banned."

"Huh? What? Why?" David stammered.

"I said you are BANNED! From the entire Conservation Area. All the parks, too. Ask your wife."

Ole Saibull strode out of the room. End of conversation.

David and I met at Gibb's Farm. He told me about his encounter with the conservator. We were shocked, bewildered, and perturbed about what to do. Ban the students? Whatever could I have done that would make bureaucrats stop Tanzanian students from visiting Serengeti and Ngorongoro? We struggled to make sense of the situation, visiting people, and making phone calls.

We were pleased and surprised when the regional warden of National Parks told us the power play was indefensible, even silly. He told us to ignore the ban and gave us special permits. We boldly went back to Serengeti to meet the students and instructors. The field course was about as much fun as a safari in the dark, on foot, surrounded by hungry lions. But the students were happy.

After the students' safari, we still felt vulnerable and puzzled. We retreated from all our research, conservation, and educational projects.

Searching for a place to recover from the furor, we chose to live in Mangola and await developments.

We did our artwork at home, but our tour leading exposed us to view and led to a showdown. The employee who stole my private letter to Mr./Mrs./Ms. Bean insisted I was a spy and continued to stir up trouble. He wanted me banned from all parks and kicked out of the country. When he saw me on a safari with my guests at the Serengeti Park entry gate, he made the guards refuse me permission to enter. The embarrassment stung.

At last, the powers-that-be decided all the spy stuff was nonsense. A new director of National Parks replaced the former. He sent us a letter saying we were most welcome in all the parks and commended us for our educational efforts—what a relief!

The letter from the conservator of Ngorongoro caused that relief to evaporate. We left our calming sojourn on Baobab Hill with apprehension and went up the Horrid Road to Karatu to meet the former conservator.

David meets Solomon ole Saibull

Solomon Ole Saibull sat in a comfortable chair on the lawn at Gibb's Farm. He looked every bit the plump, princely, authoritative Maasai elder he was. His smile was smug and brief as he extended courteous greetings. We cowered, cringing inside, waiting for the final blow. Instead, he told us he wanted to explain some of the nuances of the situation when we were banned. We were appalled to learn of the involvement of the sport hunting faction in Tanzania, the influential people in the wildlife division, the suspicions, and power plays. Intriguing as it was to learn of the politics and strategies, it was way over our heads.

Finally, he turned to me, and in unexpected gesture of reconciliation, said, "I apologize for my part in all this." He then turned to David and said, "And to you, too, I apologize for the trouble. It was all a sad mess and shouldn't have happened." While I sat amazed, he went on to express his gratitude for all our efforts to educate Tanzanians about conservation, ecology, and wildlife.

We sat in shocked silence, letting the balm of his words and smiles settle into our souls. The session helped restore our faith in reason, sanity, Ole Saibull, and Tanzanians in general.

That was not the end, however. The thief of the purloined letter continued his efforts to sabotage our reputations by doing such things as sending immigration officers to bother us and have our residence and business permits examined at length. Months passed. One day I saw him at a lodge in Serengeti National Park. I was tempted to hide, wondering if he would make more trouble for me. Imagine my surprise when he strode over and said, raising his eyebrows, "Well, we did have a conflict, didn't we? I honestly thought you were a spy and would publish bad things. I was wrong." I stared. He said, "Can I buy you a beer?"

Tanzanians are good at forgiving and letting the past recede. It took me longer to forgive that man than I like to admit, and I haven't yet forgotten. And heck, all the trouble toughened us up for future stings, led us to Mangola, and prompted me to write funnier letters to Mr./Mrs./Ms. Bean. She laughs about it all to this day.

CHAPTER 4
ATHUMANI
OUR COOK, BUTLER, ADVISOR, AND SUPPORT SYSTEM: 1984 ON

Athumani

One cloudy night, a man came to our house at Mangola Plantation. I was alone, feeling new and vulnerable. David was away, and no neighbors lived within shouting distance. The man pounded on the door. My heart pounded, too. I was scared and stayed in bed. The pounding continued—*bang, bang, bang*. Irritation and a surge of courage forced me to get up. I wrapped kanga cloths and courage around me and crept to the window. The man pounding was a farm worker I'd seen carrying onion sacks. I reckoned he wasn't a threat, so I opened the door. He stood there for a moment as though I was a ghost, his eyes wide. Then he babbled in rapid Swahili, repeating a message over and over, "Msaada, tunahitaji msaada." *Help, we need help.*

"Slow down!" I begged him, "Explain what you want."

Taking a deep breath, he blurted, "We must take a man to Karatu. We need help." He repeated this several times. When he paused for breath again, I asked, "Why does this man need to go to Karatu?"

"He is dead," he answered.

My eyes opened wide in amazement. A dead man? I could not understand why taking a corpse to Karatu town was so urgent. Couldn't it wait until morning?

"The dead are dead," I said in my most careful Swahili, trying to make myself understood. "If someone is sick and in need of a clinic or hospital, maybe I could help. But if he is already dead, can't he wait?"

The man ignored my question. He continued his requests, trying to convince me to take the dead man to Karatu. I tried to think of a way out of this impasse. I did not want to take a corpse to Karatu in the middle of the night. Cult horror-movie scenes flashed through my mind. The man opening his eyes as he is loaded into the car and rolls off onto me. Another scenario: halfway up the Horrid Road, the dead man decides he is undead and sits up, screaming. I drive off the edge and crash.

Athumani rescued me. His keen ears had heard the knocking and talking. When he appeared at the porch, I felt a wave of relief. Athumani listened patiently to the anxious visitor. He quickly dealt with the situation, saying in his soothing Swahili voice:

"Ahh, I know what you can do. Bwana Schmeling returns from a hunting safari tomorrow morning. Then he's going to Karatu town. Schmeling is the boss. This Mama is just a guest. Truly, the boss must be the one to deal with this situation."

The man accepted Athumani's reasoning, nodded, and mumbled something. Athumani escorted him away.

I was soon back in bed, still nervous and puzzled, as well as appreciative. Once again, I'd seen how Athumani buffered situations. I considered him my personal Sancho Panza. Like Don Quixote, I would rush at projects and problems head-long. My dragons and worries would often turn out to be mere "windmills" when Athumani gave me his practical insights.

Athumani took care of us in a way only the mythical English butler could, the cool minded, warm-hearted, insightful, polite butler—a Jeeves or a Carson. But in Mangola, Athumani was neither valet nor butler; he was our cook. Not just a person who cooks, he was The Cook. He did not always prepare fantastically creative dishes out of meager supplies, though he could do so on occasion. Besides cooking, Athumani ran the household, as a Tanzanian cook was expected to do. He also dealt quickly with problem people, like the man who wanted me to deal with a corpse in the dead of night.

The morning after the event, I asked Athumani, "Please help me understand last night. Why was the worker so bothered? Why did he want me to take a dead body to Karatu late at night? Why couldn't he wait until morning to ask about transport?"

I could hear David in my head, telling me that asking "why" questions was always a mistake. But Athumani cocked his head as he searched for explanations. What he said in Swahili, I summarize as:

"Mama, here in Tanzania, a dead body is a dangerous thing. If people are sick, they get better, or they die. If they die, Mama, their spirits may stay nearby. Those spirits can influence us, the living."

Athumani paused, obviously thinking his words were not quite enough to explain the situation. He continued, "Unless a dead person is laid to rest properly, the spirit can cause all sorts of problems. It is best to deal with dead bodies right away. That man who died yesterday, he does not come from here. His body needed to go to his real home."

Athumani was a deep well of such local wisdom. I'd consult him often, on how to entertain or avoid a politician, peddler, drunk, beggar, or intruder. He was a superb receptionist. Because he worked mostly in the outdoor kitchen, he was strategically placed to receive the people who came selling fish, eggs, allegedly precious stones, or antique coins. He deftly handled villagers wanting jobs or medicine. Catching, deflecting, or dealing with all sorts of people was a significant part of Athumani's role. That he was good at it made life in rural Tanzania feasible, even enjoyable for me.

How can I describe Athumani? Perhaps the pictures of him help show some of his essential qualities. He had a round guileless face, purest Bantu, a descendent of the Wasambaa people who

Athumani and lungfish

lived mainly in the Usambara Mountains near the coast of Tanzania. For many generations, Athumani's ancestors farmed in the cool remote uplands. Then the German explorers found the highlands, introducing Christianity, pear trees, and school education.

As a young man, Athumani came to Karatu town. He got a job as a "houseboy" with the farmer, Hans Schmeling. Schmeling was a keen hunter, for the sport of it as well as for providing virtually free meat for his companions and staff. Athumani often worked as a safari cook for the Schmelings on their hunting trips. Athumani told me, "I didn't like safari work. Being a camp cook wasn't difficult, but I didn't like being in the bush. I like going home to my family at night."

When he was asked to take on cooking for Stefan, the amiable, hard-drinking Bavarian who lived at Mangola Plantation, Athumani agreed. He was content to work at the Mangola house, cooking European food for the young farm overseer. It was a steady job. He and his family lived in a small tin house a hundred meters away.

Stefan's departure from Mangola Plantation had allowed us to move into the vacated house. The Schmelings told us that they wanted to keep Athumani as the housekeeper. Although we felt uncomfortable as employers, we were allowed to pay Athumani's wages as a contribution to our mostly free stay.

When we showed up at Mangola Plantation with our boxes, planning to live there for a year, or two at the most, we fell into the habit of letting Athumani take care of us. At the start, he regularly cooked the same kind of meals for us as he had for his German bosses. He served pork chops and roasted potatoes, overcooked vegetables, and thick desserts. We tried to cope with the fatty fare but started to bring home anything but bacon. Not cooking pork was a relief to Athumani, a Muslim, who didn't like handling pig meat.

We brought fresh fruits and vegetables and whatever produce we could get locally. I planted a garden so we could have fresh vegetables and remade the basins around the citrus trees, so they got appropriately watered. Gradually Athumani modified the food to suit us, including more salads and raw vegetables. He also made good whole grain bread and stews. His forte was a family-sized meal called *pilau*, composed of chunks of goat meat cooked slowly with rice, onions, and fragrant spices.

Athumani did many household chores, such as cleaning and washing clothes and dishes. He was at his most indispensable when three abandoned boys came to live with us. He helped teach them manners, good habits, how to cook and clean, and settled disputes. But his most important job for me was Chief Advisor. Without his common sense and local knowledge, we would have been even more lost floundering through the social swamps of Mangola.

For example, after living in Mangola for a few years, we hardly noticed an influx of swaggering young men around the area. We'd heard neighbors commenting about the incomers but ignored them. Alert Athumani carefully pointed out what was happening.

"You'd better hire a night watchman," he told us politely in Swahili

"Why?" I asked.

He took a deep breath and said, "These days, many young men are coming to the village to mine for gemstones. People say there are emeralds and rubies in the hills, but I wouldn't know." Athumani retied his apron strings and continued.

"You understand these are poor youths who want to get rich quickly. They dig in the ground, and all they find is how hard this work is. They drink and take drugs to endure it. When they find no gems, they have to get money somehow, so what do they do?"

"They steal?" I suggested.

He nodded and looked at me directly, saying, "Who will they rob? Who do they think has wealth and possessions?"

"Us?" I said, following his train of thought.

"Yes, Mama," he beamed at his promising student. "So, you should hire a guard, someone local who is well known to be fierce; who knows how to use a spear or poisoned arrows."

We hired a night watchman, Gwaruda, a local herdsman with a sharp spear. Whether it was his alleged ferocity, his spear, or connections with villagers we never knew, but the marauding miners never raided us.

Another example of Athumani's useful local knowledge was when Hans Schmeling and other hunters brought in game meat. Schmeling usually shared out the meat from his zebra and buffalo kills with the Hadza, who flocked to Kaunda's mysterious summons. Athumani would carefully distinguish the real Hadza from the fakes. The imposters came wearing their grubbiest rags, pretending to be part of the Hadza tribe and grab a share. How were we to know who was who in the throng clustering around the hung carcasses? Athumani knew.

Athumani had a few endearing quirks. He was afraid of chameleons. He'd been raised to think they were poisonous or evil. He was also able to sit patiently, stoically, in a detached way. That was a fascinating quality to me, who can seldom keep my monkey mind still. Athumani would prepare a meal, deal with sundry household chores, then sit on a bench and stare away for a half-hour or more. When I walked by, he would sometimes nod or sit there motionless, wholly present yet somehow absent, too. Raised with the Puritanical "work ethic," I felt I should be busy doing something every minute when awake. I envied Athumani's ability to stop and relax wholly, attentively.

Athumani was a friendly guardian, always kind and generous with his time, staying on if we were late in arriving after a trip, opening up the house before we came home. He loved his family and was hap-

Chameleon

piest among them, so was usually home and willing to help if needed during his off-work time.

His wife had been born Zaharia but went by the name of Mama Furaha, "mother of happiness." In the Wasambaa tradition, and most local tribes, the name of the firstborn becomes the name of the mother. Another daughter, Shakila, followed Furaha. And Mama kept going. Over the many years, she produced Munila, Khalifa, Chausiku, and the boys, Yasini, Bashiri, Omari. She stopped with Islam. All were healthy and happy.

"Mama Furaha" was a perfect name for Zaharia. She was a jolly, warm, smart, and loving person. She liked to fish by the river; she was comfortable tilling the soil, pulling weeds, or arranging a wedding. Anyone would have been happy in the Athumani family.

Both Zaharia and Athumani believed in the value of education, sending each child to school. Mama Furaha herself could write and read well. I started out calling her by her local name of Mama Furaha, but at some point, when I knew her better, I asked her if she liked being called by her first name. I asked because I wanted to show her respect as a person in her own right, not just a mother of many children and the wife of our cook. She beamed, saying, "Yes, I would like to be called Zaharia!" She twinkled when she added, "But many won't know who you are talking about!"

I enjoyed Zaharia's insights, humor, and casual friendship. We also had a bond because of an inconsequential emergency. (See Chapter 6, *Where There is No Doctor*) She was a gentle matriarch and also befriended many single women who sought her out for company. I'd often find women from our and farther villages, sitting on her porch helping her pick stones from rice or shell peas while they chatted, the children playing around them.

After living in our compound for many years, the family wanted to move. They bought a small plot in the village where they could build their own house. In careful Swahili, I questioned Zaharia about the move when I visited her on their chosen spot.

"Zaharia, pardon me for asking, but I am puzzled by something. Why did Athumani choose this place to build your home?"

She looked puzzled and I chastised myself for asking such a bold "why?" question. I tried a different approach, saying, "This plot is rather far from your farm. There aren't any shade trees. The wind swirls the dust around over bare ground," I said, pointing at the dust devil whirling behind her.

I added, "And there is the noisy and dusty grain mill right near you. We could have helped you get land nearer the mosque and your friends. Why did Athumani choose this spot?"

She smiled, tilted her head, and swept her gaze towards the distant green patch of trees at the Chemchem Springs where the family's farm was. Turning back towards me we both got a blast in the face from windblown sand. We looked at the skinny goats nibbling at bushes festooned with windblown plastic bags. Her eyes settled on the dilapidated buildings close to us. The slight lift of her eyebrows wordlessly conveyed her mystification for the choice. She shook her head.

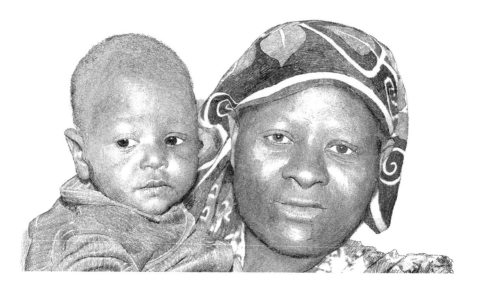

Mama Furaha and Yasini

"Athumani does all he can for us," she said. I interpreted that statement to mean she loved and supported her man, no matter how strange his choices might seem. Zaharia wasn't one to question or demand. She added, with a laugh, patting her rotund belly, "Maybe he thinks I need to be near the maize mill."

In all the years we spent in Mangola, I can honestly say that Athumani and Mama Furaha were among the dearest people I have ever known. If Athumani had a fault, it was that he put too much salt in the food, but the salt he added to our lives was just right.

CHAPTER 5
ARCHERY CONTEST

THE CHALLENGE, THE GOYCH, THE CHAMPION: 1985

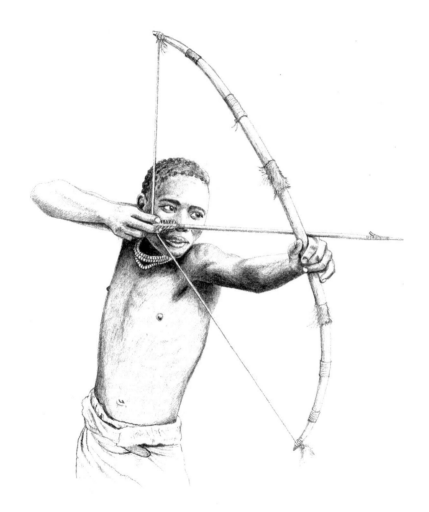

Hadza youth takes aim

Soft sunlight settled on my face. I kept my eyes closed, feeling a deep peace. Several months of calm had allowed fears and worry about our futures to drop like leaded weights in deep water. Free of dread, my senses could open up to the day. Sounds of Athumani fussing in the kitchen and the wind hissing through the louvered windows made me stir. What got me out of bed was the rich smell of coffee brewing.

I went outside on the porch and gazed through the haze at the purpled bulk of distant Oldeani mountain. The plaintive whistles of mousebirds tickled my ears, the sounds matching the powdery fuzz of light poured over the landscape. I breathed deeply, sneezed, and coughed, feeling as though I'd swallowed a drought. Having senses wide open didn't always lead to delight, I reminded myself.

Mousebirds and madabi fruit

In Mangola, the constant whisking of the wind as it broomed its way westward across the dry land sucked out moisture while whirling sand and dust into the air. On this particular morning, the wind was in a relatively gentle mood and only caused the leaves to flicker and boughs to bend. But the boughs of the bushes lining the edge of my garden plot were tossing about, making a rustling noise.

I looked at the bushes. They bore clusters of delicious reddish fruits, called madabi by the Hadza. The small round berries were sticky and tasted like persimmons when ripe. They attracted humans as well as the birds.

When the mousebirds in the madabi bush thicket flew off abruptly, I had a suspicion as to why. Then came the snap of broken branches as brown bodies tumbled out, laughing. They were Hadza children, their faces smeared with sticky orange pulp from the berries.

I watched the adept youngsters as they clambered back into the bushes, chattering in their click-punctuated language. Slowly we were getting to know our Hadza neighbors. They'd been one of the main attractions luring us to Mangola. Even so, we were reticent about intruding upon their lives.

There were three Hadza camps nearby, one close to our house and two across the Barai River. Men, women, and children came over to our side of the river to help harvest sunflower heads or onions, eating a lot of the sunflower seeds grown for sunflower oil.

Kaunda, our local Hadza resident, came across the yard and headed towards the children. They giggled and scattered when he came close. I realized that sitting outside on the porch staring at the fruit pickers might make Kaunda think I disapproved of the children being close to the house. He'd already shown an unusual sensitivity to situations, and mostly I was grateful. But now I wished he'd not scared the children away.

Kaunda embodied, for me, the best Hadza qualities. He was alert, knowledgeable, capable, and had an irresistible charm. He was also vital to the management of Mangola Plantation. Kaunda did all kinds of odd jobs on the farm, from bagging onions to organizing Hadza labor. Through him, we slowly met more of the Hadza who played, picked, and plundered around the farm.

Kaunda

At the time, I did not realize how rare it was to have so many of these special people living nearby. The whole tribe numbered less than a thousand individuals, yet about 100 of them were staying around the plantation. Most could neither read nor write, but they were highly skilled. They could start a fire with a stick, find bush food, make sandals, adornments, bows and arrows, hunt animals, and gather honey. They also did an excellent job of looking after their kin.

The older Hadza twinkled with humor. They taught their grandchildren their stories and songs, as well as where to find water and food. I loved hearing the loud, shrill voices of the women as they teased, scolded, soothed, and sang. The Hadza were a joyful people; to be among them lifted my spirits. I liked them, admired them, and wanted to know them better. How?

Dark skies and singing offered me some chances.

The dark of the moon was the time when the Hadza danced. The men sang and acted out scenes, the darkness supposedly cloaking their identity. Of course, dim light did not fool the women. The Hadza sang often. During song nights, women sat swaying in a semi-circle around the dancers, children in their laps. When enough courage overcame my shyness, I could creep up to the edge of these groups. No one seemed irritated when I slipped into the ring of onlookers.

Listening to the singers, watching the dancers, smelling the dusty fragrance of my companions were precious moments. One of the most memorable was when a floppy breasted woman handed me her child as she went to her hut. I felt honored and managed not to give the baby back when he peed all over me. Holding the child while the group sang under the starry sky was an experience that molded and melted me.

I loved these short, lithe people; these free spirits, who came and went as they liked. There seemed to be little jealousy, envy, or greed in their natures. They shared everything. Once I gave a woman who treated me like a member of her family one of my favorite boldly-colored kangas. The next day Abeya's son had the kanga tied around his waist. The cloth disappeared for a while, then re-appeared on the shoulders of Abeya's husband. The tattered cloth ended life torn in half, one piece on a baby and the other on another woman's head!

The Hadza were so accepting, so tolerant of us that I wanted to do something special with them. I invented an event: The Hadza Archery Contest. I had several motives. First was to get the Hadza to come to our place so I could get to know them better as individuals. Having them together, I might be able to sort out who was who and watch how they interacted. By nature and training, I love to observe social beings.

My second motive was to see what skills they had at archery.

The Hadza are famous hunters. I hoped to observe them in action without having to invite myself along on one of their hunts. The contest would be for the men. It was a whole lot easier for me to imagine an archery competition for men than a root-digging contest for women. I envisioned a game that would let the men prove what they could do with their big bows and long arrows.

I reckoned that if enough men assembled, the women would come to admire or mock. And children would come with their mothers. I came up with the idea of a contest simply because I couldn't think of any other way to assemble the Hadza outside the context of work. Not being an anthropologist, I didn't have the skill or will to follow them about in their daily lives. I wasn't a disinterested bystander; on the contrary, I wanted to interact with them and build more reciprocal relationships.

Inviting the Hadza to an archery contest meant asking them to submit to some sequencing and organization. Being directed and getting prizes were an imposition of my Western ideas. Still, the Hadza were already being organized, working as crop hands, submitting to rules dictated by the farm manager. As for the competitive angle, I'd seen Hadza men and boys shooting arrows at targets and playing a gambling game. So obviously a contest was something they understood. I started to prepare the archery contest with that in mind and let the Hadza decide to participate or not.

When? The turn of the New Year seemed appropriate. I would have some weeks to get everything ready. The contest would be on January first, a holiday when there was no work in the fields.

Where? I wanted a neutral space. The empty expanse near our stone house seemed perfect. It was bordered on one side by the dejected-looking row of flamboyant trees. All around were the fruiting madabi bushes like a living fence. Some little acacias at either end of the field would be useful for shade and as targets.

Targets? Yes, what would I use for targets? My first thought was to get cardboard boxes and paint bull's eyes onto them, traditional for archers in the Western world. Okay, but not very prey-like. Then I got a bright idea—sunflowers. I could hang sunflower heads from the branches of trees. I could also tie them to poles at specific distances from the shooting line. They would swing and sway in the wind, requiring skillful aiming.

Shooting line? I chose a place a few paces in front of a shady acacia and made a long line of rocks for the lineup.

Scoring? I contrived check sheets so I could keep track of names and targets hit, or not.

Inducements? The Hadza would win prizes. I had to assemble a range: tobacco, soap, maize, sugar, honey, matches.

Participants? I began this project with solely the Hadza in mind. Gradually it occurred to me that others might want to try their hand at shooting and getting a prize. Should I encourage it? I reckoned it best to let what happened, happen. After all, this was to be a fun event for all. I ran my scheme past my beloved and tolerant spouse. He knew he wouldn't be home for the contest, so let me carry on into what could be a disappointing or even disastrous situation.

Kaunda helped me rake and weed the field, measure distances, find where to hang the sunflowers, and set out the bull's eye boxes. He also visited the camps to tell the Hadza about the contest set for the morning on January first. All was ready by New Year's Eve. I did not stay up late because I anticipated the gathering of the archers early in the morning.

Athumani met me in the kitchen as the sun rose through the haze of the new year's birth. He was happy to take his holiday another time, so he agreed to help during the archery contest. He drank tea and I drank coffee while we waited for the participants. Nobody appeared on the archery field. No one came all morning except dust devils. When the sun reached halfway to noon, two Hadza men drifted by, but they did not stop. They headed to the camp on the edge of the Barai River. They were wobbling, bumping into each other—drunk, stoned, or hungover. I should have known.

To plan, hope, and wait for something that didn't happen is a classic "goych." A goych is a promise or expectation without a satisfactory resolution, leaving one frustrated. Indeed, I was very frustrated and blamed myself for not anticipating the goych. New Year's Eve had been a time with dances, drumming, and drink freely available in the village.

Kaunda came by in the afternoon to confirm that many Hadza men had taken advantage of the occasion. They were in no shape to hit a target or anything else, except maybe their beds.

Undeterred, I talked to Kaunda. "Let's try again. Do you think some might come tomorrow?"

Kaunda bounced on his toes and pursed his lips, actually having to consider this idea. Anxiously I awaited his reply. He said carefully, "Labda." *Maybe.* It was worth a try, so I asked Kaunda to send out the invitation again to the Hadza encampments. I also begged Farm Manager Njovu if he would give his Hadza workers another day off for the competition.

He agreed but warned me, "Some onion lorries and smaller trucks are coming tomorrow to collect the bags of onions. So, after the contest, we will have to have some help loading."

By the next morning, most of the Hadza had sobered up. Also, the word had spread widely, so even the onion truckers were around, eager for diversion. Several drivers, Athumani, Njovu, and others assembled by our house, surrounded by bull's eye boxes and dancing sunflower head targets. The Hadza men strode in, carrying their exceptionally long bows and bunches of arrows. Women clustered here and there and little children skittered around playing, some of the boys holding their toy bows and arrows.

It was chaotic. I wasn't sure how I'd organize the crowd. With Kaunda's help, I managed to get some individuals lined up at the firing line. I tried hard to get their names down on my score sheet. Unfortunately, the Hadza wear names like other people wear scarves, a different one to match their mood. They had family names, parental names, random names; names after towns, events, years. All those were changeable on a whim.

After the contest, I was dismayed to find redundancies, mistakes, misspellings, invented names, and missed names. I don't know why this surprised me—local people called me Mama Simba or Mama Kanga. I also had a variety of monikers from friends and family, including Jeannette, Jan, Jenny, Janet, even Patsy. My favorite was Genetta. I gave up on Hadza names.

Adding to the chaos of the contest was the complete disregard of rules. Men lined up or didn't line up, kicked away the starting line rocks, and fired their arrows out of turn. I couldn't keep track of who did what. The Hadza were to be the primary archers, but other men grabbed the bows and arrows and tried their aim. I was impressed by one drunken lorry driver who staggered over the line of rocks, lurched out onto the field, stood tall, and aimed. But he started falling backward, sending his arrow twanging high up into the sky. It fell back almost at his feet. Everyone laughed and gave him a big round of applause and cheers.

Athumani was taunted into trying. He was a hilarious failure, all the while smiling and apologizing about his inability to shoot. Njovu wasn't much good, either. I was further amazed and amused by one tipsy driver who did almost as

Learning to shoot

well as the best Hadza man on the box targets. Some of the youngsters did quite well, too. A couple of the more confident women tried their luck but could not pull the bowstrings back far enough to launch the arrows much more than a few body lengths.

Overall, the Hadza men did excel. They certainly had a better stance, could pull their bowstrings back further, send arrows longer distances. A tall, wiry Hadza, with the name of Uganda's capital city, Kampala, had remarkable strength when aiming at the boxes. He hit one with enough power to make it bounce and roll across the field. Another Hadza, named after our village, Gorofani, shot his arrows high and managed to hit the tops of the boxes. He didn't seem to understand the idea of aiming at the bull's eye.

After the full range of target shooting, especially that of hitting the distant swaying sunflower heads, I concluded the Hadza men were best. They could shoot further and more accurately than any non-Hadza. As I expected, there were differences among these hunters: some were good shooters, some not. When hunting wild animals, endurance as well as skill would make a difference. Also, maybe the poison they put on their arrows during a routine hunt was as crucial as their aim.

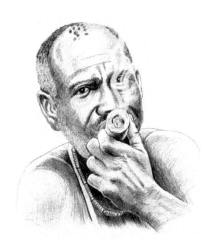

Matayo the champion

Adding up my "Chaos Scores," per nameable person, I found Matayo won by a large margin. I was inordinately pleased. Matayo was the first person we'd met when we came to Mangola—he of the hand-made knife in a skin sheath banging on his buttocks as he walked around Chemchem Springs.

Matayo smiled as he puffed on his odd stone pipe, using the lighter he won. Choking on the smoke, he said, "Ah, Mama Simba, mimi ni bingwa!" *Yes, Mama Simba, I am the champion.*

CHAPTER 6
WHERE THERE IS NO DOCTOR

VULNERABILITY IN THE BUSH, HEALTH CARE, A VALUABLE BOOK: 1985–1996

Kaunda hurts his foot

Dust rose around a gaggle of sweaty young men playing soccer on the open field at the side of our house. Most were playing barefoot. I watched them from the front porch as I sewed, wondering how they could kick the ball without shoes. It hurt me to look at them.

I recognized Kampala in the crowd. He was tall for a Hadza man, lean and fast. As usual, he was talking, gesturing, and playing soccer at the same time. Going full tilt, he miscalculated. I cringed when he kicked a sharp rock as well as the ball. He let out a yell and hopped around, holding his foot.

I stood up, intending to leave the porch. I didn't want to see any more. But Kampala turned and hopped towards me, baring his teeth and lips in a grimace. He collapsed on the steps, gasping. He held up his leg to show me his gashed, bleeding foot. The wound was deep and filled with dirt. I made Kampala sit in a chair with his foot on another chair while I went to get a pan of clean water and some cloths.

Holding his calloused foot to inspect it, I asked myself: Can I clean it properly? Does this wound need stitches? Did I need to give him an antibiotic? Who could help?

No help was near or accessible. I had no car. David had gone to the town to get supplies; he wouldn't be back for hours. And where could I take Kampala anyway? There were no doctors, nurses, hospitals, nor clinics within many miles. The Flying Medical Service visited our village's bush airstrip once a month. What could I do? I told Kampala to sit still and let his foot soak. I brought him some juice to drink then went to get my book, *Where There Is No Doctor*.

I checked the index for "bleeding wounds" and dutifully followed the book's directions, carefully cleaning Kampala's foot, washing the wound with a syringe full of boiled water, and plucking out grit with tweezers. I pulled the sides of the gash together, deciding I couldn't risk sewing the cut shut. The risk of dangerous infections and gangrene was too high. Instead, I put on butterfly bandages I made from adhesive tape and wrapped the foot with clean gauze.

When done, I told Kampala. "Come every evening, and I'll bandage you up again." I added half-jokingly, "I will send spies to find you if you don't return tomorrow. And you won't get to eat the honey sandwiches I'll make for you." He laughed, then nodded, still smiling. I trusted to Kampala's youthful health for rapid healing. He was soon kicking balls barefoot again.

Kampala's injury wasn't the first time I'd consulted my valuable health guidebook. Living in the bush with no local medical help, I found the book indispensable. Another example of its use involved Adam Chorah, the respected leader of Gorofani's Muslim community. He came to ask me for medicine for his third wife, who was eight months pregnant. Her symptoms were terrible headaches and swollen feet. "What sort of medicine has she been taking?" I asked the worried husband.

"I don't know, the women might have given her some concoction," he replied.

I mulled over his words. Giving his wife "modern" medicines on top of some "concoction" was adding insults to her innards. Even a pain reliever to help take down swelling would not be advisable for a pregnant woman. *Where There Is No Doctor* confirmed my conclusion that no painkillers should be taken in the late stages of pregnancy. The text also alerted me to signs of a danger that might occur in the last three months: toxemia.

I explained in Swahili what might be wrong and translated the advice to him: "Get your wife to stay quiet and in bed, give her meat and eggs and such foods with a minimum of salt. Keep her off her feet to take the weight off her legs and back."

"Yes," he responded in English, "I will ensure she will rest. I will not give her any medicine, just good food." He switched back to Swahili when he looked me full in the face to say, "I know you want to help when people come to you for medicine. But you must be extremely careful."

I knew that Tanzania's government had laws about ordinary people practicing as doctors. If I wasn't conscientious, I risked jail or banishment for trying to help sick people. Chorah had an added caution. "There is another big danger in helping people here. For example, when a child is born deformed, people often accuse someone of bad or evil intent. When they believe it is witchcraft, they accuse a person; they never blame the medicine."

That was ominous; to be thought of as a witch worried me as much as being put in jail. A foreign "witch" could be shunned, even killed. Amply warned, I was even more careful. Within a few weeks, Chorah was back to announce the safe birth of a healthy son. I was relieved, glad for him and his wife.

Until our area got clinics and doctors, I often had to rely on the No Doctor book and common sense. Many people came for medical help. Mothers came with children who had rolled into fires, horribly burnt. They brought children who were sick with ailments of the skin, stomach problems, coughing, and undernourished.

MAHALI PASIPO NA DAKTARI...

Kitabu cha Mafunzo ya Afya Vijijini

David Werner

The Daktari book

Mysterious fevers came with people of all ages. People arrived with sores, aches and pains, sexual diseases, genital warts, and knife wounds. We saw women in labor, pregnancies gone wrong, babies dehydrated and near death.

Some of the cases were unusual, such as the young man with a lion bite, a girl bitten by a rabid dog, a little boy coughing up worms, and one who put seeds up his nostrils and into his ears. I was no doctor, but in each case, when I needed a source of medical treatment, I consulted my book.

When Chorah came another time to get medical advice, I realized I could give a transfusion of knowledge. I fetched my last copy of *Where There Is No Doctor* and gave it to him. His English was good enough to make use of most of the advice in the book, but I knew the information on medicines, dosages, and precautions would be easier to understand if in the local language. Not for the first time, I wished I had a Swahili version to give away.

I decided to write the author and publishers of the book—David Werner of the Hesperian Foundation. Initially developed for Spanish speakers, the book was translated into many languages, including Arabic, Bengali, Chinese, Creole, Dari, Korean, Nepali, Thai, Urdu, Portuguese, and Vietnamese. I had nothing to lose by asking if they would consider translating it into Swahili.

I wrote, they answered, others helped. They organized and financed the translation of the book. The Rotary Club of Dar es Salaam sponsored a printing of the Swahili version of the book titled Mahali Pasipo Na Daktari. All these negotiations took a couple of years.

I was thrilled to receive two bundles of the translated book at long last. Then came the joy of handing them out to villagers, to border guards, to health workers in remote clinics. I gave them away at every park, reserve, and hidden corner we ever visited in Tanzania. Friends and colleagues got copies of their own; used and distributed them.

I was at home when I learned firsthand how useful was the translated version. One night, Athumani awakened me, knocking at the door. He explained he'd come to me for help: Mama Furaha, his wife, was giving birth again. This would be their fifth child. Athumani looked tired and worried, saying, "It is not going well."

Grabbing some cloths and rubber gloves, I ran. I thought as I sped across our compound and up the slope to their house: First, I'll find out how she fares. If she is suffering, I'll get her to our nearest hospital. But it's so far away! If I'm lucky, I can solve the problem by consulting my book. Maybe she's already given birth to the baby.

I was breathless as I pushed open the door and looked into the gloom at Mama Furaha in her cozy bed. She smiled at me, though quickly the smile became a concentrated frown as she suffered through another contraction. I sat on the edge of the bed as she strained, then relaxed. Wiping her sweaty forehead, I looked around the small, clean room lit by a single lamp. As my eyes adjusted to the dark, I could see a low table nearby covered with a kanga. On it was a basin of water, a sterile razor blade ready to cut the umbilical cord, clean cloths, and wrappings for the baby

She saw me looking at this array and said, "The book." She pointed to the Swahili copy of *Where There Is No Doctor* that I'd given her. She'd followed its instructions perfectly. I complimented Mama Furaha on her preparations; she rewarded me with a weak smile. I held her as she gave the last strong push, bringing forth her new son.

Giving her the baby, I helped clean up, cut the cord, and stayed as she cuddled her newborn. A squirm at my bottom startled me. I hadn't noticed her other son was curled up asleep at the foot of the bed! So natural was the birth of his baby brother; he had not even awakened. As she held the baby, I marveled at the competent way she had prepared for this birth.

"Why did Athumani think you needed help?" I asked her.

She smiled and looked down at her new baby. "Oh, I mostly sent him to you so I could have some peace," she said. "You know how men worry and fret when a woman is giving birth."

Mama Furaha's confidence and knowledge impressed me. Knowing that I was just a backup and reassurance for her husband tickled my fancy. I also was cheered when Chorah came one day to tell me about how his oldest boy had done well in school. We talked about the importance of education. Before he left, he grasped my hand. "I want to thank you for all the advice, food, and medicines you have given me," he said. "And the doctor books—they are a far greater gift than just medicine."

Over time Mangola did get clinics and doctors. The case of Onkai (rhymes with own-shy) illustrates how health care in Mangola changed over the decades we lived there.

Onkai was the brother of Kampala, he of the cut foot and lively disposition. Onkai was quiet, the opposite of talkative Kampala. This thin, short, puny fellow arrived at Mangola Plantation in a dreadful state, wheezing and coughing. Kampala helped his brother along to keep him from collapsing. He stood at our stone porch in his determined way and said, "He is sick. You help him." It was a statement, not a question or a request.

As usual, my first thought was I'm not competent to deal with this sort of thing. These were days when health care in Mangola was minimal. A sick Hadza man with no money had about as much a chance to get examined and treated as a stray jackal. I'd try to help, but I'd be a fool to think I could do so adequately. While I flipped from reluctance to acceptance, I told Onkai to sit down. He sank onto the seat with a sigh, giving me a weak, lopsided, gap-toothed grin. That was encouraging and made me smile in return.

I asked Onkai a question, but his only answer was a prolonged bout of coughing. Kampala filled me in with some details. His Swahili explanation went like this:

"He's been sick a long time. He only just came from the bush. He coughs all the time. He bleeds. He needs medicine." Onkai just sat mute, so I put a thermometer in his mouth. His temperature was above average, but not so high as to indicate an attack of something like malaria. I consulted the book and concluded he might have pneumonia. But whatever he had, he needed monitoring.

Onkai

I set up Onkai at his brother's hut in the nearby Hadza camp, provided a mat, a blanket, and food. My instructions to him were not to sneeze and cough on anyone. Kampala laughed at that because he'd already been smeared with Onkai's secretions. He insisted he was immune to his brother's germs.

Onkai improved somewhat but didn't seem to have much appetite. Kampala readily helped out by eating what Onkai could not. Onkai's ongoing condition included weakness and a lot of coughing, sometimes bringing up blood. He complained of chest pains. According to *Where There Is No Doctor*, all those symptoms suggested Onkai had tuberculosis. It was contagious, and therefore dangerous; I could not treat it.

Luckily, in a few days, the Flying Medical Service was due to arrive, a once a month highlight. The doctors and nurses flew in, did examinations, gave vaccinations and medicines, and held mother and child clinics. In the 1980s, the Flying Medical Service (FMS) was our primary source of local health care. FMS was a non-profit organization providing air transport for medical emergencies as well as regular mobile clinics.

The prime mover of the enterprise was Pat Patten, a pilot, priest, and doctor. Pat was a miracle

FMS logo

of energy and expertise: able to organize tricky rescue operations as well as rural health clinics, get planes donated, and fix them. He took in disabled, blind, and destitute people and fixed them, too. He was humble, an excellent communicator, and extremely likable.

It was always a pleasure when Pat passed over our place en route to the village airstrip. But more often, another pilot was flying the aircraft, bringing a nurse and a doctor based at the Endulen hospital perched on the rift wall near Mt. Oldeani. The hospital was about half an hour's flight away but took a day or more to walk or drive there. It was much easier getting to the village airstrip than Endulen. But we had to trust that the villagers had cleared the airstrip, or the Flying Medical team wouldn't land. They insisted on a clean landing field with no termite mounds, bushes, holes, children or livestock.

I heard the plane buzz over and immediately set out to walk to the clinic so I could consult about Onkai's condition. After over half an hour push against the wind, I arrived dusty and disheveled at a little shack built of poles and thatch at the end of the airstrip. This was the clinic. As usual, a long line of people of all ages and tribes straggled from the door. I went to the end of the line even though I only wanted advice. People in front of me beckoned me forward, stepping aside to clear a path to the entry. Embarrassed and muttering thanks, I moved quickly to the front of the line and into the hut.

FMS plane at village airstrip

Wiping the grit from my eyes, I ducked into the shade to wait for my eyes to dark-adapt. A Dutch doctor I recognized nodded to me and gestured to a chair in the back of the hut. He finished with his current patient, and his nurse called time out for a break.

I described Onkai's condition. The doctor agreed the symptoms could be due to tuberculosis. He looked me in the eye and said, "Onkai might need tests plus long-term treatment. I want to examine him here and make a decision. He may have to come to Endulen." I thought of Endulen, that little village high on top of the Eyasi rift wall. The isolated hospital would be an alien environment compared to Onkai's wild home in the Eyasi Basin.

I wasn't eager to try to persuade Onkai to come to the clinic but told the doctor I'd return with Onkai if I could. On my brisk walk back to the Hadza camp, I tried to think how to make Onkai go to the clinic. I found him lying on his mat in the gloom of his hut. He raised himself on an elbow to peer at me.

"Onkai, are you feeling better?"

"No, Mama Simba," he said, coughing and hacking. "But the food is good."

Such an answer always flummoxed me. Even so, I forged on.

"I want you to go with me to the clinic at the airstrip. I want you to see a proper doctor who will examine you."

"No, I will not go," he said. "I don't want to go. I am tired. I will rest here."

When Kampala peered through the entryway of the hut, I enlisted his help. Onkai couldn't resist; he was too weak. Between us, we put him in the car and drove him over to the airstrip. The doctor examined Onkai with concern and announced his verdict: "Tuberculosis. The disease is contagious; this man must go to the hospital. We need to take him for treatment today."

Oddly to me, Onkai, who had hardly ever been in a car, agreed to go in the airplane. Either he was sick of being sick, hopeful of being cured, was curious, or just acquiesced to our pressure. Whatever his reasons, I was glad he agreed to go. But as always, it wasn't easy.

The usual procedure for sick people at a local hospital was that someone—usually a relative—would come to help. They provided food and clothes and entertained the patient. Who was going to help Onkai at the hospital? Kampala refused to go with his brother, so I arranged with the doctor and nurses for Onkai's care. I contributed money for his stay at the hospital. Off they flew.

We got reports on Onkai's condition from time to time. The doctors and nurses told me that Onkai had become a sort of hospital mascot. He was the odd man in, and everyone loved him. The hospital was built in Maasai country, primarily for that tribe. People from other tribes, including the local Datoga and Iraqw, came somewhat reluctantly because they feared or disliked the Maasai. But Onkai was a small Hadza hunter without weapons, not threatening to anyone. He went freely around the hospital, meddling with all. No one minded. We awaited his return.

During the time Onkai was being treated at Endulen, there were many other medical emergencies beyond the scope of *Where There is No Doctor*. Our bond with the Flying Medical staff became stronger. When they came to Mangola, I'd walk over with flasks of cold peppermint tea and snacks like honey bread or scones with jam. Every so often, the plane would not be full of staff or patients when they left, and I'd hitch a lift. I'd get to fly to one of the other rural clinics, always a thrill and an adventure.

One of the scariest destinations was the airstrip near the hospital where Onkai was treated. The winds from the mountains made landing and takeoff especially risky. Despite the teeth-clenching flight, I liked seeing Onkai.

The work done by the courageous flying doctors impressed us very much. David, who enjoyed inventing lyrics to well-known tunes, even composed a song for them:

Ghost Doctors in the Sky

An old Maasai went striding out, one dark and windy day
He tripped and broke his leg against a rock along the way;
And as he lay in agony, he looked up in the sky,
And saw a Cessna 206—swiftly drawing nigh.

    Yippee-i-ayy, yippee-i-o-o, ghost doctors in the sky

The plane was held together by duct tape and baling wire
Its paint was old and peeling, and its engine did misfire;
And as this ghostly aircraft through the gloomy sky did sail
A flash of lightning showed the blood-red cross upon its tail.

    Yippee-i-ayy, yippee-i-o-o, ghost doctors in the sky

The plane it swiftly landed and out poured its ghostly crew,
They hurried to the Maasai and began their work to do;
They cleaned his leg and dressed it, with bandages and splint
Then swiftly climbed back in the plane—and vanished in the wind

    Yippee-i-ayy, yippee-i-o-o, ghost doctors in the sky

After many months Onkai came back to us at Mangola Plantation, much healthier. He needed to continue taking the medicines, and I tried to ensure he did. He stayed at our place for some months and took up with a local Hadza gal, but she didn't stick with him. Gradually, Onkai began spending more and more time out in the bush, staying in Hadza camps.

I wasn't too anxious when he disappeared; he belonged in the bush. But I worried that he probably wasn't taking his TB medicine. He might be contagious or suffer a relapse.

Over a year later, Onkai emerged from the bush. He was ill again. Pilot Pat Patten had helped us install a radio that allowed us to communicate with the outside world using a system developed for remote hospitals. Begging Onkai to stick around, I checked in and asked when the FMS plane was due to arrive. On the clinic day, Onkai and I went over to the airstrip.

While the doctors examined him, I talked to Pilot Pat. We discussed the way health care was developing in Mangola.

"Things have changed here since we started the clinics," Pat told me. "There are now lots more choices for local people. We're going to stop coming to Mangola soon." I was sad to hear this, but not surprised. The options for health care had increased, along with the continual rise in the population.

"Even though local people have more options now," I said, "think of all the emergencies you deal with: childbirth, heart attacks, drug-resistant malaria, HIV, TB, bilharzia, sleeping sickness, typhoid. And that's just the bad stuff. What about vaccinations and the mother-child clinics? How can we do without you?"

Pat just shook his head; we both knew the expense was too great to keep the service going. But on this visit, he was still able to accept Onkai as a valid emergency. Pat flew him back to Endulen hospital for more treatments, one of the last Flying Medical Service visits. Onkai returned from his second round of treatment just before the monthly clinics stopped. He seemed better but was also weaker and more reluctant to leave us. He was not happy either. No Hadza camps were nearby, so he hung around our place, restless.

Then Mangola had a cholera epidemic, and we were all told we couldn't leave. Since cholera is a world health disease, it had to be reported. Health officers and aid workers soon poured into Mangola. Gorofani village sat astride the main road into the area, so a police roadblock was set up. Mangola was shut down; schools closed, the monthly market ceased, permits were needed to go and come.

Eventually, people understood that to try to contain cholera with a barricade and guns was not sensible. Education about cleanliness and boiling water were better solutions. Officials finally removed the gate. It was then I realized that Onkai had vanished. He was somewhere out in the bush and healthy, I hoped.

Our reunion was unexpected. David, Gudo, our Hadza friend, and I were on a local safari searching for rock art. We came to a dry streambed bordered by big acacia trees. While David and I set up camp, Gudo disappeared into the fruiting madabi thickets nearby. He came back with some Hadza at dusk, moonlight shining on the faces of the hunters. Striding out in front with his funny grin was Onkai! We were as delighted to see him as he to see us. He looked much healthier and happier in his small group as they shared some meat around our campfire.

We were glad to see him fit and well, living in the bush. Alas, a year or so later, Onkai returned to our compound. He would come to eat with us but usually slept at the local Hadza camp on the ridge above Chemchem Springs. The group living there were alternately listless and restless, waiting for tourist handouts. They still hunted locally and were slowly but surely killing off the baboons, bushbucks, and vervet monkeys. They even resorted to catching rats and mice, hanging the little carcasses from their belts. There were no tubers to dig, and they started eating starchy, fatty foods.

Onkai did not have a resurgence of TB, but inevitably he aged. His crooked smile never left him. He'd come with his bow and arrow and any gifts he had got from tourists. I was expected to exchange them for things he needed, such as matches, knives, trousers, or a jacket. He did not reach the age of 45; he died in the bush where he was happiest.

Kampala sent the message to me because he knew I cared a lot for his brother. I remember Onkai with fondness, grateful to have known him as well as the people of the Flying Medical Service who kept him alive. I am also grateful to the Hesperian Foundation book. Even in this digital age, there is still a need for many people to have sources for health information that do not require electricity, telephone, computer, or car. For the millions of people who live where there is no doctor, there is help.

CHAPTER 7
MAMA RAMA
A LESSON IN RELATIONSHIPS, THE MAMA RAMA WAY: 1984 ON

Mama Ramadhani

A young man on a bicycle wobbled to a stop under the giant acacia tree. He jumped off, propped his bike against the trunk, and immediately started talking to Njovu, the farm manager. I stood on the porch, trying to remember where I'd seen him. A thin lad, his brown-skinned legs stuck out of floppy shorts. His stick-like arms protruded from his faded t-shirt. Ah yes, I remembered, he was one of Mama Ramadhani's people.

Mama Rama was what we called her. And everyone called her place Gorofani Junction because it sat astride the main road from the highlands to Mangola. She welcomed many people at her compound. They came to eat at her little café, sitting in huts or outside in the dusty yard with chickens and donkeys. Visitors from outside Mangola used her guest houses for overnight stays. Locals often just hung about being sociable or waiting for transport.

Mama Rama's place was a social node. She was one of those strong, warm women integral to a community; she knew everyone and everything that was going on. The village chairman had introduced us to her soon after we'd come to Mangola. Seeing her handsome face and kind, amused eyes, I'd had an intuitive feeling she would be a worthwhile and vital person to get to know.

She was an Iraqw woman, her distant ancestors migrating from the horn of Africa southwards through the Great Rift Valley over hundreds of years. They settled on the Mbulu Plateau, south of Mangola. Most of her tribe still lived there in the highlands between Lake Eyasi and Lake Manyara.

Mama Rama was middle-aged, single, with no children of her own. Yet she seemed the titular mom for a wide array of relatives. A diverse lot of people came and went from her compound, making it a busy, noisy, and delightful place. Children ran around singing and playing, chickens strutted in and out of houses, clucking and fleeing from pursuers. There were ducks quacking, goats nibbling, and donkeys heehawing while trucks on the road roared by covering all with filmy clouds of dust.

When I got to know her, Mama Rama told me about her husband, who'd long ago gone "walkabout." She spoke with no regret. She did well on her own, supporting herself and her entourage by renting out sleeping space, serving meals, and keeping livestock. I liked her style, her sway, her smile.

Now I looked at the bicycle boy. Although I remembered he was from Mama Rama's clan, I couldn't remember his name. We were still new to Mangola, peripheral to the village community. I wasn't familiar with faces, let alone names. People's names here seemed drawn out of some grab bag of words derived from family, clan, tribe, the Quran, the Bible, places, days of the week, and historical events. To my surprise, this man's name popped into my muddled mind: Issa. Mama Rama's clan were Muslims and had Arabic names. Issa was one of the few names I'd looked up: it meant salvation or protection. What might Issa be saving or protecting?

I turned to go inside, hoping to get out of sight. Issa noticed. He called out to me in Swahili, "Mama Simba, ngoja, Mama Ramadhani amekupelekea kitu." *Mama Simba, wait, Mama Ramadhani has sent something for you.* He held out a soiled cloth bag. Inside were eight lovely eggs, brown and white, large and small. I smiled, thanked him, and told him to wait while I tried to find some money to pay. But Issa shook his head. With a genuinely friendly smile, he said, "Zawadi kutoka Mama Rama." *A gift from Mama Rama*. It was a gift I knew I could not refuse.

Issa brings eggs

And so, Mama Rama gave me my first lesson in trade and balances. On another day, Issa brought a bottle of fresh milk. Neither David nor I drank local milk because of the dangers of brucellosis. David had contracted that disease twice from drinking unpasteurized milk. We were also both somewhat lactose intolerant. So, whenever fresh milk was offered, I tried to refuse it or give it away. Cash, in return for any item given, was never accepted.

Over the early years of knowing Mama Rama, I learned reciprocity. Each time she sent something I'd try to give something that might be of equal value. She sent eggs; I sent back a bag of sugar, or maize meal, or packets of tea. Mama Rama might send me a roasted chicken or little lumps of fried dough called *mandazi*. I answered with popcorn, chocolates, and sweets for the children. I'd receive a bunch of bananas and send back a ripe melon. Once I bought some big laying hens for her. She gave me their eggs.

In addition to the goods, I offered services, like rides to Karatu town. She countered with solace and refreshments. "Mama Simba, you must be tired having to go to town. Here, sit, have tea, and some of these mandazi." I responded by mending small hurts of the ever-present kids in her household. I donated bandages, gave kids shoes, brought corn for the chickens.

After four years of knowing Mama Rama while living on Mangola Plantation, David and I applied to the village for a piece of farmland of our own. The village council gave us a half-hectare of land for growing vegetables, but it was far away from our house. Mama Rama offered to exchange our plot for hers, conveniently located on the other side of the river from our homestead.

I made a promise to her to clear and fertilize the overused plot, and to employ Issa. We agreed he would work on the plot weeding, planting, and chasing away the monkeys. Another role he would play would be the essential link between us and Mama Rama.

The garden arrangement went well. I made sure to send Issa home with some of the produce—especially the cooking bananas and papayas, okra, and tomatoes. Mama Rama would send back fried and baked goods, as well as eggs. The balance of trade continued. One day, when her old mother was very ill and needed urgently to get to Karatu hospital, Mama Rama sent over an empty jerry can.

That was an invitation to fill it up with the fuel she knew we had. I gladly gave it. Later, when the old woman died, a burial ceremony was planned. I sent over a big bag of sugar and several new mats so her many guests could have a place to sit and drink sweet tea. I kept trying to hold up my end of our continuing see-saw of give and take. It seemed almost a game, an ongoing competition of favors, both frustrating and fun. I was relearning something that must have been part of human society for centuries longer than our current cash economy.

Mama Rama was unpretentious, putting on no airs for visitors at any social level, be they local farmers, politicians, researchers, foreigners, students, tourists, rich or poor. We fitted into her relaxed social nexus about as well as any of the others; she always made us feel welcome. We'd sit on a stool in the shade of one of her huts and have simple, friendly conversations with local people who would never have come to rest at our compound.

Sitting at Mama Rama's among locals gave us a sense of place, of being part of the broader social scene. Perhaps being there gave local people a way of seeing us, too. Most villagers still did not understand why we chose to live in this out-of-the way place with no obvious way of making money out of our situation.

We certainly were not living in Mangola to get rich, a fact we hoped became more evident over time. David and I were attempting to survive at a level where we could provide much of our food and earn a living from our little publishing, artwork, and guiding business. We tried not to be pretentious or presumptuous: we owned no fancy equipment, no TV, no big stereo system, no generator, no expensive car. The fact that we were foreigners made us stand out enough, and we didn't want to be even more visible and seen as privileged.

The lessons that Mama Rama taught us about the local trade economy were valuable, and she taught us about balancing relationships as well.

On occasion, Mama Rama would come to our place, especially once we had moved to the far side of the village by the Chemchem Stream. She'd usually come alone, calling out the greeting we all used, "Hodi, hodi," an announcement of approach. We would return, "Karibu, karibu," the welcome invitation. She would appear, swaying from side to side as she waddled slowly along the path into our compound.

She might be tracking down a goat or coming to bring yet another gift of dried fish or eggs. Whatever the reason for her arrival, I ignored the inconvenience of having my task interrupted to sit down with her. We drank tea and ate cookies while talking about the village, the people she sheltered, or what her resident researchers there were doing. I always felt good about such encounters, a chance to give her back a little of the pleasure I got in sharing time, tea, news, and stories at her place.

One especially delightful researcher story she told me was about an anthropologist named Monique who came to study the livestock keeping Datoga tribe. She usually stayed at Mama Rama's place, where she could glean local information. But staying at Mama Rama's had its risks—security was relatively lax. Monique's camera disappeared one day. Mama Rama was furious that anyone would take anything from one of her guests.

"I was angry, very angry," she told me, speaking in the simple Swahili we shared. "But I knew who had probably taken the camera. There was a man who lived with maybe-wife up the hill behind me. I went there. I put my panga (machete) under my kanga and went up to his house. I told him he had better give me the camera."

She smiled then chuckled, adding, "He looked so scared. I thought he would run away. But he went into his hut and came back with the stolen camera."

Mama Rama had a reputation for fairness and firmness and was loved by many. Even so, I worried whether her minions looked after her as well as she did them. After a donkey kicked her hard in the leg, an abscess developed from the tear in her skin. I checked on her frequently, urging her to get treatment, but she refused to go to a hospital or even a local clinic. The wound was slow to heal, and she limped. There followed a long spell when Mama Rama was having what she called "fevers." "My blood is not good," she told me.

I was concerned she had blood poisoning or infection from the donkey wound. She looked haggard but brushed off my attempts to get her checked by anyone medical. I had luck one day at the mnada, the region's monthly livestock and supply market. On that day, the Flying Medical Service also arrived. When I spied Mama Rama starting to limp home in the dust and heat, I conned her into my car. Instead of taking her home, I took her to the thatched clinic by the airstrip, where she relented and let the doctor examine her.

His conclusion? Menopause. Mama Rama laughed when the doctor explained what she was going through. I did too. We held each other and shook with mirth. She happily accepted normal wear and tear over the years and the final departure of monthly problems. She brightened considerably afterward and put on more weight.

Our teeter-totter relationship of giving and receiving included some bumps. Mama Rama and I had one meaningful conflict over the shamba (farm plot) she loaned us. Early on, as I was organizing the planting on the plot, I decided to cut back the thicket of cooking banana trees straggling around the boundary. I wanted more room for the sweet banana as well as rows of vegetables.

Mama Rama came herself to complain: "Mama Simba, you remember, the shamba is mine. I have loaned it to you. You have caused a problem. I planted banana trees. The fruit is mine. You have planted different bananas. Those are yours." I apologized profusely and tried to mollify her by giving her the papayas and sweet bananas I'd grown as well as other produce.

Some months after the banana tree incident, I heard Mama Rama calling out from across the stream. "Mama Simba, Mama Simba, I am here!" At first, it was hard to locate the booming voice. I peered through the dense screen of papyrus and saw her standing on the opposite side of the stream. I was happy to see her but worried she'd come with a complaint about something I had or had not done on the shamba. I sighed inwardly and shouted back, "I am coming to get you."

"How?" she shouted back.

"In our boat," I called.

"No!" she yelled. "I am afraid of boats. I am afraid of water. I cannot swim."

"Just wait there," I called, already in the boat. I paddled through the papyrus tunnel to the landing on the other side. Mama Rama stood there like a flowering tree, covered in bright red and orange kangas, a flowered blue and white shirt with a pink paisley scarf on her head. Her hands rested on her big hips, her face with a grim smile combining fear, determination, and amusement. As I pulled up, she hoisted her skirts and kangas and, without a word, stepped into the boat.

That she would trust me enough to be paddled through the papyrus and across to our dock under the fig tree made me feel proud. She grabbed the sides of the boat and tried to steady herself as she put one foot on the wooden platform. I didn't dare try to help her because I knew this trip was a challenge, a personal test of her courage. She bravely got out of the boat, stood tall, and glided to the kitchen area where she sat down on the bench with palpable relief.

She looked at me sternly, reached into her voluminous clothing, pulling out a sack of mandazi. "I have come to see you. I was looking at the shamba. It is very

Jeannette and Mama Rama in boat

healthy, very clean, full of good things. Please send Issa with some of your sweet bananas when they are ripe."

I was enormously relieved, as well as pleased. I made tea, and we chatted about local events, the price of onions, the girl bitten by the rabid dog, perfidious local politicians, and the bootleggers still operating in the swamp. Before she headed home, I offered to take her back to the other side with our boat.

She nodded with tight lips then said, "Mama Simba, the boat ride. Yes, I liked the boat ride. But I do not want another boat ride. I will walk home from this side."

It was her way of telling me one courageous act was enough for one day.

On a day months later, I realized it was her birthday. I wanted to give her something special. Even though we seldom exposed our pains, problems, or gravest concerns, we were—in my opinion—good friends. We were able to give each other respect, understanding, and love without a lot of spoken words.

I chose a visual expression of these feelings, painting her real name, Hawa, on a ceramic teapot. I padded it in little sacks of tea and sugar, wrapped it up, and took it to her. Her wide smile and moist eyes as she held the pot told me she was delighted. I was too; I'd seldom seen her look so happy. She turned the teapot slowly in her big rough hands, admiring her name and the colorful flowers I'd painted. In her gruff voice, she said, "Asante Mama Simba. Asante sana. Asante sana, sana." I glowed from her repeated thanks.

Through the first months of our time living near the Gorofani village, I had tried to keep our trades and gifts with Mama Rama as equal as possible. But as the months passed into years, I eventually abandoned the account sheet of giving and receiving. Having Mama Rama as a friend was like taking turns pushing one another on a swing, gently or hard, up and down, back and forth. She was there for me and I for her, despite our differences. Her presence and our interactions significantly eased any feeling of loneliness I might have had. I deeply valued our dynamic, balancing bond of friendship.

CHAPTER 8
THREE BOYS
ABANDONED BROTHERS, THEIR FATHER, LESSONS IN PARENTING: 1984–2003

Sam, Gillie, and Lenard

Who were these scruffy kids? Why were they hanging about our place? I caught glimpses of them shuffling barefoot along the dusty road, sitting under a shade tree or vanishing into the sunflower patch. One midday, they were lurking by the spiny euphorbia hedge behind our house. Trying to look friendly, I greeted them with the usual Swahili plural greeting, "Hamjambo?" They replied, a little awkwardly, with the expected "Hatujambo," looking down at the ground either out of shyness or respect.

I asked the three bowed heads, "Mnaitwaje?" *How are you called?* The tallest boy responded: "Lenard," scrunching his lips as if he was sorry the word had slipped out. Lenard was thin but looked strong, maybe about 9 or 10 years old? It was hard for me to guess the ages of these underfed children. I turned to look at the other two. They were about the same height, both dressed in rags. One was fuller in the face; the face frowned at me. Maybe he was 8? The other one was thinner, ganglier, but as tall as the round-faced boy. Somehow, he seemed younger. He fidgeted and kept his eyes down. Possibly he was 6 or 7.

The smaller two didn't say anything at first, but Lenard nudged the round-faced one, who muttered, "Samwel." Another wait. I looked at the third boy, the narrow-faced one. "Gilbert," he said, and sent me a glance as swift as a hawk passing. His grim face focused again on his dirty, bare feet. I wondered whether what I had seen was a scowl of anger, fear, or yearning. I looked them over.

Lenard was obviously the oldest, taking responsibility for the other two. Samwel seemed to wear a permanent pout but was the heartiest looking of the three. Gilbert seemed especially pathetic, with sad, tired eyes. I remembered a line from a song, "Even his feet look sad."

Len offered the information, "Sisi ni ndugu." *We are brothers.* The Swahili word "brother" could refer to a close as well as a distant relative or even just good friend. All three boys looked so unlike I wondered if they had different mothers or fathers. So where were their parents? Why were they roaming around the farm and not going to school?

I beckoned them to follow me to our porch. All three followed silently. They stood at the bottom of the steps while I went in to get some bread. I spread the slices with peanut butter and honey then offered the boys the sandwiches. They accepted them politely, suddenly turning to vanish quickly along the back pathway.

Later the same day, Njovu, our farm manager, came by.

"Those three boys hanging around, who are they?" I asked.

"They're the sons of Mzee Lenard," Njovu explained. "He lives near you, by the river, in the tin hut. He's recently been released from prison. Lenard is from my tribe, the Ngoni. We take care of each other, so I give him some work and some money."

I looked across to the copse of acacia trees where the tin hut hunkered in the shadows. The "rondavel" was made of panels of metal that could be bolted together to form a small building. It was hardly better than a stick-built shack and did not keep out the cold, heat, or scorpions. I'd seen the bent, old-looking man Njovu was talking about. He passed along the road between our house and the tin hut, but I'd not seen the boys with him. Njovu was still explaining, so I turned my attention back to him.

"The mother of the boys, Lenard's wife, brought the boys here and just left them. I am helping both him and his boys. But it is difficult. Mzee Lenard spends his money on piwa. He is not always good to his boys."

Piwa is a distilled liquor made illegally from molasses, not at all like the local beers brewed from bananas or maize. Piwa could include "flavorings" such as fertilizers and contaminants such as lead because the moonshiners put the distillate through car radiators to cool it. Piwa was not a good thing, yet our village seemed to be the leading supplier for the Mangola region.

Njovu noticed I was thinking, not listening. He waited until I looked him in the face, then he said, "Mzee Lenard is so drunk most of the time he doesn't think of the boys. He doesn't feed them properly. My wife makes them some food almost every day."

Hmm, I thought, was that a hint, a warning, an explanation, or an excuse? I wasn't pleased to know we had an ex-convict, a drunken and negligent father, as well as three neglected boys as our neighbors. Njovu said Lenard had been jailed for stealing a truck he'd been hired to drive. His real skills, though, seemed to be building and thatching. But with his present reputation, hardly anyone would give him work except Njovu and the bootleggers in the Chemchem swamp. I found him lying on the road more than once, too drunk to walk.

Boys and young trees

I joined the Njovu family in providing some extra food for the boys in exchange for their doing a few easy chores fetching wood and pulling weeds. They even worked with me to plant a forest of baby trees on a bare patch of ground. I would see those trees grow along with the boys who helped plant them.

One day David found the trio with a dead bird—a beautiful red-and-yellow barbet. Sam had killed it with a homemade catapult. "What a pity, to kill such a lovely bird," David told them in Swahili. The boys looked at their feet, accepting the reprimand. Even a small bird could be a meal for a hungry boy. I exchanged the dead bird for stew and bread, explaining that I wanted them to keep things alive, not kill them. They never again killed anything except fish for food.

With familiarity, we came to call the boys by the names they used for one another: Len, Sam, and Gillie. I modified their names, of course. One day Big Len and Sour Sam brought Gillie to me, burning with fever. His narrow face was flushed, his skin chalky. I took his temperature and asked Big Len, "When did the fever start? Does Gillie get fevers often?" The two questions took a while to sink in. I should have asked one at a time.

Len told me they all got fevers. The fever usually started in the afternoon. He said, "I think it is malaria. We think Gillie is having an attack." From David's and my own experiences, I knew malaria was most often the cause of a quick onset of a high fever.

Gillie stood shivering, hugging himself, even though his skin was hot to the touch. I settled him on the porch and quickly brought wet cloths for his forehead. He numbly drank the rehydration drink I made for him, then swallowed the camoquin tablets I gave him. I was taking a risk giving him the medicine at all. But I felt it was the best choice since we used it for our own malaria attacks. The drug didn't seem to have many adverse side effects and didn't need a prescription.

After a few days in our spare bedroom, Gillie recovered. I escorted him to the tin shack, wanting to see where they and their father lived. The interior of the hut was mostly bare. Some mats covered the cement floor, but there were no blankets nor mosquito nets. I gave them bedding, and we hung nets. I hoped the father would approve but I didn't see him for many days.

The boys and I settled into a routine. In the mornings I would find Len, Sam, and Gillie hanging around our place. They waited for me to hand out jobs along with attention and food. In the afternoons, they usually disappeared, possibly to the village or to play games in the dry bed.

Over time, David and I started taking on more and more responsibility for the care and welfare of the three. The weight of responsibility was mostly my own. David didn't really like the boys hanging around. He knew he would be away often, leaving the boys and me together with double the mischief that could ensue. I assured him that I would handle what came up. I also had Athumani to help me. I need only draw in David if necessary. I knew his typical good nature and tolerance meant he would adapt to the foster father role.

Looking after the boys was a relatively light cloak at first, hardly noticed. Later it became a heavier garment, binding my movements, weighing me down. Even so,

I never made much of an effort to free myself. Why? Because basically, I liked the kids. Also, I enjoyed seeing what they did and how they behaved. They were alternative windows into our social world.

Another fostering factor was that I wanted the experience. After college, I'd worked as a probation counselor for Los Angeles County in California. The shelter where I worked handled abused and abandoned children. There were plenty of destitute children, and they all needed help. Foster parents were all too few. At the time, I made a private vow not to produce my own children but to adopt or foster some when the time came. Now here were three abandoned boys ready to be nurtured. They were in a lot better shape than some of those I'd worked with in L.A. County. There we dealt with children left in cardboard boxes on the freeways, kids beaten by parents, molested by strangers, their minds as scarred as their bodies.

I was curious about the father and his relationship with the boys. He was seldom around. I suspected he might be actively avoiding us. Sometime after Gillie's recovery from malaria, I talked to Njovu about the boys and their father:

"Shouldn't they be in school?" I asked.

"Most certainly," he replied. I waited for more information. He did not offer any.

"Well," I posed the obvious question, "why aren't they in school?"

Njovu pursed his lips, trying to find the right words. "Their father hasn't put them in school."

"Well, tell me please, why he hasn't put them in school?"

Njovu just shrugged, saying noncommittally, "Shauri ya Mzee." *Business of the elder.* That meant it was the father's problem, not his.

The boys hung about our place so much I reckoned it was my business as well. They went barefoot, were always hungry, wore dirty clothes, and had no jackets. And they didn't bathe, they had a stink like rotted watermelons and onions. I wondered why the father allowed the boys to wander around aimlessly. They needed to go to school to learn, mix with the local kids, and get established.

Not knowing fully what I might be letting myself in for, I asked Njovu for help. We needed to convince the father to put the boys in school. I naively believed that the father would respond to the nudge. I imagined seeing the boys in the afternoons and weekends after school. I had pleasant images of clean, well-fed boys in school uniforms, helping me water trees. I now laugh at the notion.

I invited Mzee Lenard over to discuss the issue. He refused to come. He rejected my invitation the second time, too. Finally, Njovu managed to persuade Lenard to meet with me. I will never forget the short man who came that day. Mzee Lenard arrived with a defiant stance, head up, walking purposefully to the bottom of the porch steps. He wore shabby trousers and his cleanest dirty shirt. He waited, straight-backed, enduring my greetings.

He squared his shoulders, like a soldier, then lowered his head slightly and nodded. Was that a sign of submission or a return greeting? I beckoned him to come onto the porch. He cautiously approached; I gestured to him to sit. Athumani brought tea and cookies. Mzee Lenard eyed the cookies as though they'd hop off the plate and bite him. He carefully removed one and held it in his hand.

We talked in Swahili, I've forgotten about what, probably the farm, his work. I'm not good at small talk with strangers; I felt awkward. I wanted to get to the point, so I launched my main concern:

"Your boys need to go to the village school."

"Sina kipingamizi," he said, *I have no objections*, a wonderfully vague and non-committal Swahili phrase, like answering "OK," to "How are you?" To me, it meant neither yes nor no and seemed entirely too cautious. I tried harder to get a more supportive response.

"If they go to school, you will have to sign them in at the village with the head-teacher," I said.

"Yes," he said, looking down at his full teacup. I offered him another cookie.

"So, will you take them at the start of term?" I asked.

"No."

I sighed, a sigh of non-understanding. I waited, not knowing how to proceed.

Pursing his lips as though begrudging his answer, he said, "I cannot afford to buy them the school uniforms. I cannot buy notebooks. I cannot pay their school fees."

I sighed again, but this time with relief.

"This is not a problem, Mzee Lenard," I said. "We will supply them with what-ever they need for school."

I paused and tried to catch his aimlessly wandering gaze. I intuited he was a proud person and would detest being indebted to us. So I added firmly, "You can pay us when you can."

It was his turn to glance at me and make a soft sigh of relief. He rose, deftly tucked his cookies in his pocket, and left.

And so, the boys started school. Mzee Lenard settled back into doing farm chores and supplying fuelwood to the illicit booze factories hidden in the swamp. I started providing Big Len, Sour Sam, and Gillie with clothes, food, medicines, and things for school, including notebooks and soccer balls. In addition to material things, we tried to be attentive to their needs, took care of them when sick, rewarded good behavior, and gave them hugs. Those gifts were usually accepted with some embarrassment, stiffly, stoically.

Parenting wasn't totally a trap, and it wasn't entirely an act of generosity or kindness on my part. By fostering the boys, we were also promoting a relationship with our new community. That included not only the school but also an unknown network of tribes and neighbors. We two foreigners were also being fostered.

The boys would teach us much about growing up in a rural village in East Africa. In the villagers' minds, no one should be without children. Fate had provided us with three ready-made boys to become a part of our lives, and to some degree, also their father, and much later, their mother. And so, we became foster parents.

It was relatively easy to supply the boys with clothes, food, and work to do. A more enjoyable parental function was to introduce the boys to the wonders of the local world. We took them on trips to the wildlife parks, towns, and other exciting places. But, as all parents know, and we still had to learn, the real work of parenting is teaching life's valuable lessons. Good parenting means instilling good habits, manners, healthy practices, honesty, responsibility, and consideration for others— in short, personal and social skills.

Parenting seemed to involve many different lessons at once. This is illustrated by what I called, The Lesson of the Lamps. The boys still slept in the barren metal rondavel. We did not want to take them away from their father but did want to improve their conditions. We gave them mattresses to go with the sheets, pillows, mosquito nets, plus lamps to eat and read by. Teaching them to care for these few things was one of my first tasks. Although they learned how to wash themselves, their bedding, and clothes, I had to push them to do it regularly. Then there were those hurricane lamps.

Teaching the boys required many sessions. Len and Sam learned quickly, but

Gillie reading

Gillie took a lot of reminding. I was teaching the boys to read, and Gillie was the one who took most avidly to books. Hence, it was he who needed light the longest at night. By default, it became Gillie's task to look after the lamps. I'd find him on the porch or outside his tin hut reading next to a wavering flame with soot-covered glass. His clothes often smelled like the kerosene he'd spilled on himself.

"Gillie," I'd say, "I'll have to take the lamps away if you three can't learn to take care of them properly." Gillie would look at me with his guileless expression as though he was a newborn innocent.

I'd catch myself giving a lecture: "You must wash the glass and trim the wick before you use the lamp. You need to go outside to fill the bowl, in case you spill the kerosene." I'd pause and stare into Gillie's face, trying hard to emphasize the warning. "Spilled kerosene is dangerous; it can start fires. You could get badly burned."

Gillie would blink at me, saying nothing. "Do you understand what I am saying, Gillie? Don't blame Len or Sam if the lamps are blackened, broken, or the wicks don't burn. Taking care of the lamps is your responsibility."

At this point, I would know I was wasting my breath. The word "responsibility" didn't carry much meaning or weight by itself. I had to follow through with praise, admonishments, and constant checks. The lamps were just one example; there were so many others, such as helping with chores, getting to school on time, returning tools, doing homework.

Athumani looked after the boys when we were away, adding to his many other duties. Njovu, Kaunda, and others also helped guide the three. Slowly, Len, Sam, and Gillie seemed to learn how to care for themselves as well as things. It took all our combined efforts to instill what we could.

We began learning our own lessons about parenting when we first came to Mangola and have not yet ended. We've found amusement, consternation, and problems as well as some of the joy and sorrow every parent knows. Parenting was a two-way education for all of us, including Mzee Lenard and the Missing Mother.

And one early lesson that I learned? Don't try too hard to teach young boys to clean lamps to your standards; you'll just get frustrated.

CHAPTER 9
WHAT NEXT? AN INTERLUDE AT FLYCATCHER FARM

LEAVING MANGOLA, EXPLORING ALTERNATIVES: 1987–1989

Tree senecios on Kilimanjaro

Leoni broke the news. "Sorry, but we've finally found a new overseer for Mangola Plantation. He'll need the house. I'm afraid you'll have to leave." We thanked her, but beneath the waves of appreciation cruised dark sharks of apprehension. We'd lived on the farm from May 1984 through April 1987. We'd enjoyed three relatively calm years hiding out, exploring, getting to know people, learning, creating. We'd become enmeshed in a lively, challenging society and we loved the wild landscapes. We didn't want to go. Living in Mangola had not been easy, but what now?

We imagined scenarios of our future with so many alternatives; freedom of choice can be a burden. Yes, we did realize we were privileged to be able to consider different prospects. We had each other, good health, education, with some ability to tolerate ambiguity and risk. We set ourselves to our customary decision-making process; we discussed options, agonized over them, got bored talking about them. We made lists, weighing pros and cons until specific options dropped to the bottom. A few facts and ideas floated out of the mess, and we grappled with them like swimmers caught in tidal debris.

We had a short wheelbase Land Rover, clothes, books, and tools. For our income, we had the saleable items we produced. We'd started a series of activity books for children, written some guidebooks and articles, made displays, maps, and cards. Those items we created gave us just enough money to support us modestly. David had painted enough pictures for a one-man show in Nairobi. The event was a success, but it didn't make much money. Tour leading didn't either.

If we were to survive financially, we'd have to live very cheaply and boost our business somehow. Or—gasp—we'd have to move somewhere where we had to compete for jobs. Neither of us wanted to move back to Europe or America or some other Western-style country. We didn't fancy going to another African country, either. We didn't fully realize yet how connected to Mangola we had become, held by an emotional bungee cord. Instead of complete freedom to decide, one end was attached while only the other end was free and flexible. How far could we stretch it?

When you don't know what to do, travel! Thus, our decision was a diversion. We set out to explore Tanzania. We happily put off the big decision and tackled the small. We moved our things into temporary storage at Gibb's Farm, thanks to our tolerant and supportive friends Margaret and Per Kullander. We said goodbye to dear Athumani and family as well as Njovu, Kaunda, and villagers like Mama Rama and Saidi Kimaka. Len, Sam, and Gillie were left in the care of Njovu, and possibly their father.

We had to leave Mangola during the rainy season, the worst time of year to travel. It was going to be a challenge, but a good time for the country to reveal its true nature. We would listen to what Tanzania told us as we roamed the country.

Herbert, our Land Rover, was a jaunty craft with a roof rack and front-mounted jerry-cans for extra fuel. Our first destination loomed, literally: Mt. Kilimanjaro, the highest and most inspiring spot in all of Tanzania. At the time, I was writing a guidebook to the mountain for Tanzania National Parks, and David was doing the maps and illustrations. We aimed to visit Kili's western slopes—the Shira plateau—to survey the terrain, explore the trails and huts, sketch, and photograph plants. From

Kilimanjaro, we wanted to head to the coast then make a long loop west into the interior before heading back north to face the cliff of indecision.

We took along a pungent reminder of Mangola, a load of garlic.

"Mama Simba, please take this big sack of my best garlic. I know you'll get a good price for me if you sell it in town," said Petro, a neighbor who was recovering from a long illness. I agreed, reluctantly. I paid him an inflated price and told him I'd bring back more money if the garlic sold well.

We set out at the end of March when there was to be a striking solar eclipse. What sort of portent was that? The weather warnings didn't eclipse our enthusiasm as we made our way to Arusha, then across the vast plain between Meru and Kilimanjaro mountains. The time of year is etched in my memory by the sight of the Big Dipper when it emerged from the clouds: upside down, right over Kilimanjaro. The dipper's bright bowl of stars was arrayed like a crown over the flat-topped Kibo dome.

Big Dipper over Kilimanjaro

We ground slowly up a rutted track through farms and forests. At 10,000 feet, we pitched our tent among giant lobelias and senecios. The first night the sky was clear. Stars sprinkled across the sky twinkled brightly as we walked on the high plateau. The next day it rained, wrapping us in fog and drizzle. We moved our camp into a cave. The damp settled on our load of garlic like a poison.

After some days of hiking, camping, and photographing, we left Kilimanjaro's slopes and headed east. The smelly sacks of garlic went along with glee. When we stopped to camp in the remote Mkomazi Reserve, I laid the garlic out to dry; the bulbs spread their putrid aroma unto the heavens.

Everywhere we went, if it wasn't raining, we'd let the garlic out of the car to foul the surrounding air. I'd sit and pick out the rotting and moldy bits each day, just to keep us from being asphyxiated by the smell. It also reminded me daily of Mangola. I asked myself again why I'd accepted a load of vegetable matter destined to reek of decay. Daily, David endured with only the gentlest of puns poked at me: "I know we are the pesto friends, but you could use a little less garlic in the mix."

Eventually, we made it to the coast, and I tried selling the driest, firmest heads of garlic. Not much reward there. Next, I tried braiding the long leaves together into attractive hanks to sell and give away. Garlic proved a popular gift, but we'd lost and thrown away at least half the load on our journey. Sales didn't bring nearly the price I'd paid.

At last, we could really start to enjoy our trip. There were friends all along our route, lovely coastal beaches, remnant forests with surprising birds, crowded towns, mountains covered with trees and plants new to us. It was a wondrous adventure, a whole book full of delights, disasters, and road problems. Inspiring encounters with Tanzanians enriched many experiences, such as the time we were mired in mud, stuck for hours behind a line of trucks, buses, and cars. Our turn came to be pushed through the muck. I had the terrifying role of driver. Policemen, military men, locals, and David were the muscle behind the Land Rover. I laughed and cried as the mob cheered, slithering through the gooey ruts until I bounced onto drier ground.

Our conclusion after this remarkable journey was that we loved Tanzania more at the end of the trip than we did at the beginning. And we still liked garlic—at least in food, if not in the car. The safari led to our first major decision: we would stay in Tanzania until pushed or pulled away. In the meantime, we urgently needed to pin down where we could live next. Our little publishing and artwork business demanded a stable base if it was to survive financially. Luckily, our friends at Gibb's Farm let us stay while we sought our next abode.

We looked at places from the coast to Lake Victoria. There were not many to choose from, not only because we were fussy, but because there were few opportunities for living and working in the beautiful places we preferred. We'd had experience managing both Ndutu Lodge in the Serengeti and Gibb's Farm for our friends, so when offered a job as managers for a small tourist lodge, we accepted. We would work without pay because we wanted to be free to move on when we needed to. No contracts, no long-term commitment.

The owners of Flycatcher Lodge were happy to have us be temporary managers at their modified farmhouse. The small lodge crouched on the slopes of Mt. Oldeani among deep green rows of coffee bushes. Flycatcher Lodge was several kilometers away from an eroded, declining village, also named Oldeani, halfway between distant Mangola and burgeoning Karatu town. In short, the coffee farm-turned-tourist lodge was in a forlorn spot, the embodiment of neither here nor there.

It looked especially unwelcoming on the day we arrived, slipping and sliding up the last of several steep slopes in the rain. Access would be a problem. The main farmhouse held gloom around it like a cloak, and the gardens sulked like neglected children.

Flycatcher Farmhouse, Oldeani

We parked among dripping silky oak trees that bordered the drive. At the front door of the main building, a young, pretty woman stood smiling on the steps. "Karibu," *Welcome*, she said. Felista made a small curtsey, stuffing her dust cloth into the pocket of her apron. She introduced herself as the housekeeper for Flycatcher Lodge. Behind Felista stood a large middle-aged man with an impassive face. That was Dominic, the dependable butler.

Tseama, the cook, joined the introductions. He was shriveled and grim, the oldest member of staff, once upon a time a safari cook for the European settlers. We met a night watchman and other helpers who cleaned, did laundry, or collected and chopped wood. Two taciturn young men did carpentry jobs at the lodge

Such was our staff during our tenure as lodge managers for Flycatcher Safaris. Why had the company chosen the name "Flycatcher"? The word brought to my mind a childhood image of noxious yellow coils hung from a ceiling fixture to catch houseflies. It also reminded me of those horrifying machines that zap insects and leave a burnt smell. Flycatchers were not pleasant images.

On the safari circuit, the word had an even worse meaning. In Arusha, "flycatch-ers" referred to the touts who stood on street corners and hassled tourists with offers of cheap tours to the parks. A "flycatcher safari" implied 10 young backpack-ers crammed into a clapped-out Land Rover.

What the Flycatcher owners had in mind was an entirely different image, namely the paradise flycatcher. This is a colorful, stylish bird, a beautiful mascot for a safari company. Flycatcher Safaris was a growing business at the time we became involved. Three owner-operators handled various responsibilities: the initiators were antique dealers from Switzerland who put in money and clients. A local Iraqw man from Mbulu named Tido was an experienced safari driver and guide; he handled the clients on safari. An Indian family based in Arusha town provided logistical support and vehicles.

This may have been a unique combination, but it illustrated the multi-racial society of Tanzania. The three operators had developed a business specializing in

Paradise flycatcher

safaris for Swiss clients. Being a specialist outfit, they wanted to have a small, exclusive accom-modation for their guests. They leased the old farmhouse. It became Flycatcher Lodge, a private, cheap, and manage-able base. The lodge had much more charm than the large, impersonal lodges within the famous wildlife areas of the Ngorongoro Conservation Area and Serengeti National Park.

The solidly built main house had an appealing entry, a dining area, two guest bedrooms, and a back room where we stayed. There were two more guest rooms in a separate house nearby. The furnishings were sparse but comfy, the bedrooms set up Swiss-style, with duvets folded onto the neatly sheeted beds. Guests were already using the place when we came to look after the lodge.

The rest of the place looked rundown, the main building and grounds begging for renovation and maintenance. The kitchen had no shelves for storage. Food was spread out on sacks on the concrete floor. Tseama, the cook, used *jikos*—metal char-coal stoves—set on the floor. Charcoal dust and smoke settled all around, exuding an unappetizing odor. Water was not reliable, let alone hot. We heated the water by burning wood under metal drums. The wood had to be laboriously collected from the surrounding coffee farms.

Organizing cars and helpers was a constant challenge. The roads were terrible, full of ruts and potholes, slick and muddy in the rain, dusty soon after the sun struck them. The silky-oak trees lining the dirt roads had been planted for timber as well as shade for the coffee bushes. Fine, except their limbs broke off during every storm, and their flowers caused me, and many guests, to sneeze violently.

David took on the challenges with a mix of reluctance and the zeal he always devoted to necessary tasks. I took on managing staff and looking after supplies and tourists. I also tried to bring the gardens and lawn back to life. The flowerbeds were plentiful and planted with some bulbs and exotic plants. Most were overgrown weed patches.

Finding supplies was demanding because there was little in the way of produce, eggs, or milk in the vicinity. We tried to cope. In the beginning, we were happy to have a place to stay while we decided what to do. As the weeks passed, we found the work increasingly daunting. Securing supplies, organizing repairs, coddling the guests, and overseeing the staff kept us busy and exhausted.

The cook was steady but uninspired, the food rather bland. He tolerated us and did not add spice to our lives. Felista was more fun, flouncing around, talking a lot, even singing. I developed a bond with her. I also developed some rapport with Dominic after he was stung in the vegetable garden by a bee. He went into shock. I had to find coffee pickers to help haul him inside, where I nursed him for hours. He recovered. I bought him an epinephrine injection device he kept in his jacket pocket ever after.

We didn't feel comfortable on the slopes of the mountain among the tight lines of coffee bushes. The mountainside environment was totally different from the wild, arid Mangola we had come to love. We longed for the myriad sounds and sights of the bushland. On Oldeani, the coffee monoculture was not inviting to wildlife. The air felt fuzzy, moist, laden with pollen, and toxic from the constant spraying of the coffee and bean crops.

With binoculars, I could see distant farmhouses on other coffee plantations and a remote, mysterious monastery. Far below our farmhouse, clusters of workers' huts huddled in the folds of the slopes. Dirt tracks crisscrossed through the coffee, some leading up into the wild forests of Oldeani Mountain bordering the farm not far above us. We had little time to explore. The lodge demanded all our time and attention.

The activities of two people, in particular, became part of a domestic drama at Flycatcher Lodge. The stars were Felista and Tido. Felista was a Chagga from the Kilimanjaro region. A slim, comely woman, she was taller than most of the local people and moved with grace. She dressed well with a sense of style.

Felista wasn't married. She told me, "I really want a career in tourism. I want to earn good money rather than being tied down to a man. I don't want to be burdened with children." I smiled to myself. I'd heard this from many young women in many places; I waited for the time when a man would change her mind.

Tido was thin with the sharp features of many of the Iraqw people. He looked older than his age, wrinkled and bony, but he had a most warming smile that lit up his stern face. Unfortunately, his face usually had a burning cigarette in it. Tido was the head driver of Flycatcher Safaris and an excellent guide. He could fix cars as well as find elusive leopards. He got along well with guests and the lodge team alike. We looked forward to his arrivals because he always listened to the gripes, complaints, and the personal stories of all the lodge workers. They would stand in the kitchen, Tido wreathed in smoke, talking and laughing together.

I suspected Felista and Tido were developing a relationship when I saw how hard they tried to be impartial in each other's company. They were careful not to gaze at or talk to each other for too long. Felista was in charge of the guest rooms but often disappeared to her own room when Tido was around.

One day, she and I were straightening the lounge area in the lodge. She stood by the couch with a dust cloth in her hands. She twisted it and looked down as she asked me, "Nowadays, we women with careers don't want to get pregnant. But it isn't easy to know what to use or where to get help. Do you know about these things?"

She knew I did because we had conscripted one of our friends to give the staff a little talk about how to prevent Human Immunodeficiency Virus or HIV. He demonstrated with condoms and bananas, which made his audience both uncomfortable and amused.

I answered Felista as best I could, telling her about local clinics, IUDs, condoms, and pills useful for preventing pregnancy. We both agreed that sexual abstinence or coitus interruptus were not realistic forms of birth control. Some other sort of prevention was needed. I concluded with warnings about unprotected intercourse because of sexually transmitted diseases, especially HIV, as risky as having a child.

Felista made little swipes at surfaces of tables with her dust cloth as we talked about men and relationships. She looked a bit grim, but I took the chance to ask her, "Is there a man you find interesting or you really like?" She twisted the cloth and looked away.

"Well...I still want a career and enough money to buy what I want. I also want enough money to help my parents. They are getting old now. I don't want a husband yet."

I took note of the "yet."

During this busy time, it became apparent Tido and Felista were lovers. In fact, Felista admitted to me she was pregnant. A baby boy was born, a real darling. The Swiss owners encouraged Tido and Felista to get married. A large wedding was planned to include many family members and local people as well as other guests, including us.

The reception was to be a particular delight; we dressed up for it. Since Tido was an Iraqw, as were most of the people living around Flycatcher Farm, there was a throng of these Ethiopian-looking people at the reception. The women, all clad in their best dresses and kangas, sat in long rows on chairs set on the front lawn. Many more were in the kitchen, stirring beans, making salads, cooking rice, and roasting corn.

The Chagga contingent representing Felista's side of the union was there too, mostly dressed in fancy polyester outfits. Two separate bands and choirs provided loud, competing, and dissonant music.

Tido and Felista

Felista and Tido were ushered to their brightly decorated table on the short green lawn. They sat facing the crowd like royalty while guests sat in colorful ranks in their tribal zones. Fringe people like ourselves had tables further away. We settled in our places while waves of murmurs and chuckles lapped at us.

Out came the FOOD. Women and youngsters emerged carrying plates of fragrant pilau rice, stiff ugali topped with hearty dollops of stew containing greasy chunks of beef, sheep, or goat.

We ate outdoors, starting out seated in neat rows. The rows rapidly became disordered. They twisted and turned as people moved about, abandoned chairs, pulled the tablecloths off to sit on them, or just sat on the grass. Although they impeded movement, I was delighted with the flowerbeds I'd replanted. Soon trampled by the throngs, they were still full of showy arrays of pink lilies, blue iris, golden marigolds, and stunning red and yellow zinnias.

The wedding guests came one by one from around and between flowerbeds to place cash on platters set in front of the wedded pair. Felista and Tido began to look as weary as if they'd climbed to the top of the mountain that formed a backdrop to the event. They forced smiles and mumbled thanks while the pile of notes heaped up. There were also more tangible gifts: goats, chickens, clothes, bags of maize, sugar, and rice, all placed carefully in the house or put into cages or tied to trees outside.

It was a memorable day, the setting splendid, the weather perfect, the music lively. All the guests were extravagantly happy for the couple.

Some months later, Tido and Felista and their baby moved to Arusha. When we met in town, we noted Felista and the baby looked fine, but Tido looked increasingly ill. He still smoked, and his skin was thin and wrinkled as if he was drying out—like a plum turning to a prune.

It wasn't many months before Tido was confined to bed. I saw Felista and asked her, "Is it cancer or HIV?" She nodded sadly, "HIV." After expressing my sympathy, I could not avoid asking her about herself.

"Have you been checked for the virus?"

"Yes," she said. "They tell me I'm OK."

"And how about the baby?" I asked.

Felista looked down and mumbled, "The baby is OK, too."

I wondered.

Tido wasted away, as all HIV victims did during the decades before effective treatment. The Flycatcher Safari people helped support the family during these stressful times, giving them a TV and video player and many movies to help Tido enjoy the last of his life.

David and I went to see them in their little house at the edge of town. Tido was still the quiet stern looking fellow he'd always been.

He no longer smoked. Felista looked worn out and thinner than ever as she tended Tido carefully. Her head seemed shrunken, and the tiny rows of her hair, carefully plaited, reminded me of the rows of coffee bushes at Flycatcher Farm.

We were sad to see Tido so emaciated. His bony hand felt hot when we said goodbye, but he still had his charming smile. All too soon after Tido's death, Felista also died of the same disease. The young son died, too.

With the family dead, something died in me as well. Their passing took away most of the remaining good feelings about our time on Oldeani Mountain and Flycatcher Lodge. I placed a mental and emotional gravestone in the lodge gardens. I would take my memories and affection back to Mangola and plant them there.

CHAPTER 10
PLOT BY THE RIVER
HOMESTEADING AT CHEMCHEM: 1987–1990

Saidi Kimaka and his bike

A surprise came riding a bright yellow bicycle on a dull day at Flycatcher Lodge. Saidi Kimaka, our former village chairman, rode up to the farmhouse where David and I were hauling a cupboard to one of the guest rooms. He came on the bicycle I'd given the village. That was quite a stint because the road to the lodge was uphill for many kilometers. David asked in a teasing voice, "Did you come from Mangola on that old bike?"

Taking David's absurd question literally, Saidi said, "No, but after I got a lift to Oldeani village, I rode up from there."

We gave him tea and banana bread while he caught us up on village news. Finally, he leaned back in his chair and spoke sternly, "You don't belong up here on the mountain. We want you to come back to Gorofani. The village council will welcome your request to get a plot of your own."

What an invitation! It went straight to the heart of our growing dissatisfaction with our life at the lodge, but was it realistic? I looked at Saidi, trying to formulate a question. "Saidi, do you think the village council would approve our application for a lease?

"Certainly," he said, with a little frown, as though we shouldn't doubt him. He added, "Don't think about it too long, or we might forget you, or someone might grab the land you'd like to build on." We promised him we'd let him know soon. He smiled, said goodbye, retrieved the bike, and rolled away down the mountain slope.

David and I revived the idea of moving back to Mangola. We talked it over with our friends at Karatu, at Ndutu, and in Arusha. We got advice, most not very encouraging. Our friend Margaret, who had lived in the Karatu and Oldeani area for most of her life, gave us the wisest advice: "Besides all the toil, expense, energy, and time of building, you would be taking on the village. If you live under the eye of the village, you will also be committing to days of hassle, requests, and interruptions. Are you ready for such involvement?"

We mulled it over. What was there about Mangola that attracted us so strongly? Why would we seriously consider going through all the trouble to build there? Yes, we wanted to experience again the unique happiness we'd enjoyed. We remembered vividly waking up to each day with its promise of mini-adventures and challenges. We loved the mornings with bird song, the evening walks in the cool sand of the dry riverbed, the explorations into the hills along the vast Eyasi lakeshore. The longing for daily surprises from encounters with colorful and fascinating people also motivated us to return.

The peace to pursue our projects, to learn more about the environment and people, to have a real home to welcome visitors, were compelling factors, especially for me. For David, going back to Mangola had the attraction of learning to build, making something unique, challenging his varied skills.

Although our rational minds fought the decision, down deep inside, we had already committed ourselves emotionally. To get a rein on those decision beasts swimming in our brain stems, we made a contract with one another: if the village accepted us, we'd select and build on a suitable site. For a decade, we would give in to our desire to live longer in Mangola. Ten years for a lease if we got it, and then, well, more agonizing decisions later.

But we did make an exit plan right at the start: we firmly promised each other that before 10 years had passed—definitely—we would make clear plans to depart. We didn't want to remain in the hinterlands of Tanzania for the rest of our lives; we knew we would be better off somewhere less demanding as we aged. Also, living in a remote pioneer village was not predictable; borders and bureaucrats might mean having to leave at any time. If we did indeed build a home, we knew we'd have to give it away or sell it when we left. If the village or no one wanted our place, we would demolish it. That was our ultimate bottom line.

Decisions made, we applied to the village for a lease. Our application would be considered at closed meetings. That way, the villagers could discuss frankly whether or not they wanted these two outsiders. While we waited for a verdict, we carried on with the problems of managing the lodge on the dreary slopes of Oldeani mountain. David built a storeroom, repaired buildings, put a window in our dark back bedroom, and struggled to get enough wood.

We fought the gloom and cold with fires of coffee logs to heat rooms and water. David spent days wrestling with our Herbert car and helpers to get trailer-loads of firewood up steep muddy tracks from the plantation. Then he had to saw the logs up by hand.

I took care of people, fires, and gardens. Bright bouquets of cut flowers and fresh vegetables helped cheer us. Time spent gardening was my therapy while I coped with morose staff, obtaining supplies, and turning the bleak surroundings into a welcoming place for the lodge guests.

David with a load of coffee logs

We sometimes escaped to Mangola to see people, dry out, get warm again, and show visitors around. Such visits reminded Gorofani people we were still waiting.

Nothing happened for months. We waited. A year passed. Sometimes our Mangola friends came to see us. Saidi Kimaka returned on the yellow bike. He came to tell us our application had not died or disappeared. "Pole, pole," said Saidi. *Slowly, slowly*, the same phrase used by all Kilimanjaro mountain hiking guides. "Be patient," he said. Things were proceeding slowly, maybe surely?

Weeks later, when David was away on safari, a message came from the current village chairman. Julius Meruss sent a letter telling us to arrive at the village office in Gorofani on a specific day. No reasons were offered. I sighed. Was this to be a goych of our expectations, a scorpion sting? Did we need to pay another fee? Do more paperwork? Would we get a formal rejection of our application?

I had too many questions; answers were waiting at Gorofani village headquarters.

I looked around Flycatcher Lodge to see who could travel with me down the Horrid Road. We had no guests at the lodge, so I invited the washerwoman, her little boy, and Dominic, the lodge butler. On the Horrid Road, it was always wise to take helpers along. If needed, they could push, dig, find rocks, or, if all else failed, go for help. I didn't know how long the meeting would take, but at least some of the Flycatcher staff would have a day out.

The midday sun was somewhere up above, trying to penetrate the mist as we left the lodge. We wound our way down and around the mountain slopes, joining the main road just past the silent hulk of the Tanganyika Farmers' Association barn. Its bright blue doors were open to reveal piles of farm tools, hessian bags, fertilizers, and poison sprays. I found someone to fill our fuel tank, and once on the road to Mangola, I began to feel better. My companions were in the relax-and-let Mama-Simba-worry-about-it mode. They chatted amiably among themselves as we descended.

We arrived at Gorofani village office without breakdowns.

Entering the main office, we squeezed our way through the many chairs that crowded the space. Chairman Julius Meruss greeted us with a solemn face. He said, "Karibuni, tafadhali kaeni, subiri kidogo." Welcome, please take a seat and wait a while.

We all sat. We waited. More people arrived and greeted us. They sat and waited, too. Although everyone in the office was being friendly, I was anxious. I don't like ambiguity. I didn't know why we'd been summoned. We waited politely, but I began to get edgy and impatient. I knew I'd lose points, but in my frustration, I finally asked the chairman, "Tunasubiri nini?" *What we are waiting for?*

He answered, "Chakula." *Food.*

I raised my eyebrows. Meruss saw the question on my face and responded: "The food is coming soon. I have sent people to get things. Mama Rama is cooking some of the food, and there are others in the village. It is taking some time, but it will arrive. Would you all like a soda while you wait?"

Sunrise shone into my mind. We were waiting for a party to begin! Was it to be our welcome-to-build celebration? I was excited enough to ask another direct question. "Have we received permission?"

"Yes, the village council has approved your application." I grinned with relief and shook his hand.

After two hours of waiting, the food came: big pots of beef or goat stew (hard to tell which), rice, vegetables, and platters heaped with Mama Rama's freshly made chapattis (flatbreads). By then, many more people from the village had joined us. Everyone sat around in the hot afternoon inside the village office eating, smiling, chatting about the road, the price of onions, the weather. It was an excellent effort. I only wished I had known it was coming. I could have anticipated the event with delight rather than dread.

Beans for the celebration

I felt a bubble of excitement on our drive back up the Horrid Road to Oldeani. When I saw the isolated Flycatcher Farmhouse, I smiled. I felt relieved to think we'd be leaving the gloomy abode. David was happy, too, when I told him the good news. We knew building a home at Mangola was now in our future. We were eager to get started.

Our most urgent task was to find a place to build. We wanted to live somewhere along the wild west side of the Chemchem Stream, opposite Gorofani village. We could easily imagine what being on the village side would bring: moochers, sick people, opportunists, beggars, the curious, thieves, and the politicos. Our friends in the village disapproved of our desire to live away from other residents. "The other side of Chemchem is too far," they told us. "It is not safe. The place is full of wanderers, prospectors, bandits, bad men, wild animals, and convicts from the nearby prison." Their admonishments did not deter us.

Up and down the Horrid Road, we went, exploring Chemchem and returning to Flycatcher Farm to run the lodge. We persevered, spending stolen days exploring along the Chemchem streamside. We put up our tent in the shade and listened to the sounds of wind in the branches and papyrus. The rumble of hippos, the barks of baboons, and birds chirping and singing filled us with joy. The delightful smells of water and blossoms filled the clean air.

We watched cattle, goats, and local people drift by our campsites. We walked along the stream past fishermen and onion dealers hauling sacks across on fragile papyrus bridges. Our friends came to camp with us. Weeks passed. At last, we were sure of the best of all possible sites. It was beautiful; it spoke gently and firmly to us: "Stay here."

The land we wanted lay alongside the Chemchem Stream. The stream flowed through a tunnel of tall papyrus. Openings in the screen of papyrus allowed access to spots where we could swim, boat, and collect water. Huge fig and fever trees hovered over small patches of grass and bushes. Further away from the stream were clearings where sturdy tamarind and acacia trees provided shade and shelter.

Further upslope, a strip of bush acted like a buffer between the attractive riverine vegetation and the open, scraggly, near-desert. The plants growing there were the hardy survival strategists like spiny sisal and pokey aloes fighting for space among thorny commiphora trees. The final ridge was a natural boundary. On the other side, the land stretched down through dramatic bushland where isolated baobab trees marched to the distant shores of Lake Eyasi.

In choosing this spot, we traded a vista for the sheltered feeling among the trees near the stream. It was peaceful, welcoming, and smelled wonderful. The trees were the best part. We especially liked the tamarind trees with their solid trunks and limbs, feathery leaves, and orchid-like flowers. Their tangy fruit pods could be soaked to make marinades and a delicious, refresh-ing juice.

Another prime asset of our chosen spot was a small spring emerging alongside the river. That source of water was free of contamination from upstream bathers, campers, baboons, vervet monkeys, and

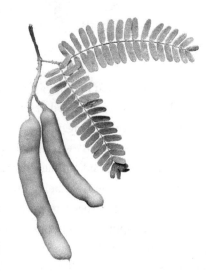

Tamarindus indica, *fruit and leaves*

hippos. We worried about our precious spring and the river, afraid that building on the site might pollute it. We consulted with planners, builders, and doctors. They reassured us that if we built long drop toilets far from the stream and proper septic tanks a good 50 yards away, that we would not taint the water.

The next steps had to be taken by the village council members and elders. We needed their approval for our chosen site. On one auspicious day, we all met at the village headquarters. The group included our former village chairman, our current chairman, the district representative, Mama Rama, our doctor friend, the current headteacher, the local Lutheran pastor, the local Muslim leader, and assorted businesspeople and council members.

This throng set out from the village to walk to Chemchem. The midday sun pounded us as we passed through the open grassy meadow and around the springs. It seemed a lot further than a half-mile to the start of what we envisioned would be our plot. We paced out the strip of roughly 10 acres along the stream. We stood under our favorite tamarind tree to discuss access and building sites. David and I wandered off to give our village council a chance to talk in private. We looked at them as they conferred, anxious about their decision. Their beaming faces told us the answer as they beckoned us to them.

Cheery faces, genial handshakes, and nods came with the announcement: "We have general agreement. This site is acceptable." David and I held hands as we followed our leaders back to the village, feeling like happy parents who'd just learned they were to have a baby. Our baby already had a name. Our future home would be "Mikwajuni" (mee-kwa-ju-nee). It translated to "among the tamarind trees." Raising our baby houses among those trees was going to take some learning and doing.

Since we were going to build a "permanent" house, we were required to get our plot officially surveyed. That involved a lot of driving to get the district surveyor. He walked the boundaries and made measurements. He pounded rebar stakes at the corners of our parcel. The surveyor demanded that we encase the posts in cement. Within a few weeks, locals had pulled them all up. That was because everyone knew that concrete markers meant treasure was buried under them.

Whenever we could get away from Fly Farm, we camped on our plot and planned out where and how we would build. We made lists of what we needed. First, a place to store supplies and tools and a well-sited long-drop toilet that would not foul the stream. We'd also need a place for helpers to sleep.

Finding workers was not as easy as we had hoped. There was not much of a surplus labor pool in Mangola. We recruited a couple of hefty but rough guys from Oldeani. Kind friends at Tarangire Safari Lodge loaned us a rondavel, an old prefab hut made of sections of galvanized steel that bolted together. Dismantled, it just fit in our Land Rover for the journey from baobab-studded Tarangire National Park to the tamarinds of Mikwajuni.

We set up the rondavel in our future kitchen area. Now we had a storeroom. We borrowed several old but sturdy canvas tents to house additional people. That included a cook we hired from Oldeani village. We got a more massive tent for our three boys. They just showed up one day happy to rejoin us.

David and the men set about digging a toilet pit and stockpiling what we needed for our first building. Rocks for foundations sprouted in abundance on our plot. We collected them in wheelbarrows. Gravel and sand were near at hand in the beds of seasonal streams, easy to shovel into the Land Rover.

We found a man in Oldeani village with a plantation of young eucalyptus trees and brought long poles down on every trip. Cement bags, wooden boards, and beams came from further afield. We contracted with farmers on the shores of Lake Eyasi for bundles of palm fronds for thatching.

As we assembled all these parts of the puzzle, the vision became a reality. We started to build, an effort that consumed our energy for fascinating, joyful, heart-rending years.

Getting thatch at Kisimangeda

CHAPTER 11
BUILDING MIKWAJUNI
A DAY BUILDING AMONG THE TAMARIND TREES: 1989

Building, 1988

Imagine a reasonably typical building day. Wake to the sound of whistling. Is that a bird? No, it's the sound of Pili, coming to pour water on the cement blocks. Sigh and think, here we go again. Another day building at Mikwajuni.

The day I'll describe is a composite of building days. And yes, I did wake to a whistle. I peered up through the fine mesh that formed the roof of our tent. The rising sun flickered through the fern-like leaves of the tamarind tree above. It was cold; I pulled the blankets up around my cheeks and rolled over. David's side of the mattress was empty. I remembered, he'd gone yesterday to cloud-bound Oldeani and Flycatcher Lodge for supplies of cement and wood. I expected him back midmorning.

Hadada ibis

Whistler carried his early morning tune towards the kitchen area. I dozed. Suddenly a loud *HAAAA HAAAAA HAAAAAA!* jolted me wide awake. That was the evil laughter of a hadada ibis flying away from its roost nearby. Whistler had scared the bird away.

I sat up and fumbled for my small travel clock. It said 2 a.m. I shook it hard until it started ticking again then reset it. I guessed reality was around 6 a.m. The bird-alarm told me it was time to get up. I pulled a shift over my head, murmuring *ha-ha-haaa* to myself, imitating the bird's laugh to help me get going.

I have a motto, "Be prepared for the worst, and it's bound to be better." Preparation meant getting myself into a good mood, too. Breathing deeply, I pulled on the zipper to open the door of the tent. The teeth jammed together like a kid refusing to let the dentist into his mouth. I gritted my own teeth and jiggled the zip carefully. Here was my chance to practice the patience I needed to get through the day.

Finally, the zipper slid up, and I stepped outside. It was cold enough to wear two kangas, so I wrapped one like a skirt and the other around my shoulders for a shawl. The soft cotton cloth felt good, comforting. I implored the tent zipper to close, encouraging it by rubbing a candle stub along its teeth. We needed to keep out monkeys, squirrels, mice, ants, and creepy crawlies. Finally, the zipper shut its mouth without complaint. I smiled as I patted the tent top.

My first chore was getting water for making and curing cement blocks. I drove Herbert the Land Rover to the edge of the stream. Backing it up to a break in the thick stand of papyrus, I could feel the tires settle on soft earth, warning me not to go closer. I opened the tailgate and set up two empty 55-gallon drums, then the hoses, then the pump. Water started flowing. Later, I'd take the full drums up to the block-making site.

I scanned around and spied Whistler Man already taking up his position among the concrete blocks and waved a hello. Pili, his real name, meant "two," a common name for a second-born. Pili was a short, stocky fellow prone to sores and scorpion stings while handling blocks. I was pleased to see he wore work gloves as he took damp concrete blocks from their frames and stacked them.

Our building plan involved lots of blocks. We were building small circular houses. Each structure required blocks for the outside and any interior walls. We'd started our first building in an area carefully chosen for its centrality. The *baraza*, or meeting point, was our kitchen area, also our eating and greeting place. There we already had tables, benches and the metal-paneled rondavel we used as a temporary storeroom.

The kitchen house was to be a block-built all-purpose store and workroom. The next house planned was David's den, his workspace, and our temporary bedroom until we built the next house. That was to be a guest house with a proper indoor bathroom. We'd live in the guest house until we made our own house.

An essential building in our planning was a typical village house with a large porch, for staff and our boys. That would be in a separate compound. An adjacent site was destined for a rondavel. Researchers who often came to stay with us could store things and come and go as they liked. That added up to four round houses, one rectangular house, and two metal rondavels.

Our ultimate dream was to build a two-story studio for ourselves if we had the energy and money left.

David and I were trying to build wisely. We followed the adage, "You build your life a day at a time and have to live in the house you build." I made a special effort every day to find some pleasure in the hard work of building Mikwajuni, despite sticky zippers and workers who forgot to wear gloves.

I went to my second chore, determined to see the humor in guiding our temporary cook through breakfast. Reaching the kitchen area, I greeted Kefti, our head builder. He was easy to get along with, a steady sure fellow with an even temper. When we went to Karatu to find him, I asked, "Do you think you could bear to live and work in Mangola with us?"

David had joked: "Mama Simba is a tough boss." Kefti looked at David, then at me, obviously trying to understand what David meant. I also stared at David; was he teasing me or hinting to Kefti that I was in charge of work details? David didn't like telling people what to do, but he would have to help orient and guide our builders. He just looked off sideways with a bland expression, so I turned my attention back to Kefti. He blinked, pulled his shoulders back, and said, "Yes, I'll come to Mangola."

We were relieved, because we desperately needed a reliable and competent builder. We felt lucky to get Kefti; not only was he a skilled mason, he could handle floors, roofs, and framing. He proved to be indispensable, as well as likable.

Kefti came to us with his sidekick Pius. On this day, they were mixing mortar for the blocks on the inside wall of the kitchen house. Like most of our other buildings, the circular house would have a diameter of six meters. The kitchen house would be divided down the middle by a wall. One side was for storage of fresh and dry supplies, pots, pans, and a backup propane stove. The other half would be a secure, lockable room for medicines, camping gear, lamps, and business items. We were eager to get the kitchen house finished.

Kefti

Already the kitchen area was a busy place, with people milling around. We'd chosen the spot because of the flat-topped acacia tree that dominated the area. With its contorted limbs and sharp white thorns, it looked like a curmudgeon offended we would intrude on its living space. In truth, it was a very friendly tree. Vines dangled from its limbs, forming a windbreak and spreading welcome shade over the big sturdy table and benches where we had meals, conversations, and games.

We cooked meals at a campfire confined by a ring of stones. The smell of wood smoke meant breakfast was underway. I walked faster. I could smell pancakes burning. Ama, our temporary cook, was an odd fellow, an old Iraqw man from Oldeani village. Friends recommended him to us because he supposedly had experience as a camp cook. He had a huge family and was desperate for the job, so we hired him.

Ama's skills immediately came into question. For instance, when I first asked him to make banana pancakes, he wrung his hands. With a worried frown, he said, "Pancakes? Bananas in pancakes? Well, I suppose so if you show me how."

I missed the self-directed and competent Athumani. I wanted him to return to us and had gone to his house to beg him to come. "Sorry, Mama Simba, I don't want to cook for a building crew. I'm here now, in the village. Mama Furaha and I are trying to build our house and grow crops on our shamba. I can't come to work for you now."

I sighed and wished them well. Secretly I hoped Athumani might be tempted to return later on. I held out a lure: a house built at Mikwajuni, especially for him and his expanding family. Plus, a higher salary.

Our earnings from our business and leading safaris allowed us to hire a cook and some helpers. But we needed to draw from capital to pay for the workers, building materials, and another old car. We knew we would probably never earn enough while in Mangola to pay back what we were taking out. We tried our best to use our money wisely. I considered paying Athumani well a wise thing to do, not only for my mental health but for our social well-being too. I readily admitted to myself I was a better person in Athumani's company. He didn't tell me no to the house and job offer, but he didn't say yes, either. He wanted time to think about it. Meanwhile, we had the nervous, well-meaning, but incompetent Ama.

"Good morning Ama," I said, "Please, after breakfast, let's sit together and decide about the main meal of the day." He nodded,

"Yes, Mama Simba," he said, nodding his head repeatedly, then adding, "Well, there is the problem of the meat."

What meat, I wondered. We had no meat, until David returned. I sat down with Len, Sam, and Gillie, who were dutifully eating the burnt pancakes that oozed uncooked goo from their middles.

We went through our morning routine of greetings in English and simple questions about their schoolwork. We then switched to Swahili to talk about home duties. Today when they came home from school, they'd help plant posts along the boundaries. We were using commiphora sticks that would take root and form a living fence.

After breakfast, the three boys set out on their half-hour walk around Chemchem Springs to the primary school in the village. I watched them leave with mixed feelings. The boys had asked to come to live with us as soon as we started building at Mikwajuni. They seemed glad to come home to their foster parents, even though "home" was only a flapping tent. I was pleased they wanted to be with us, happy for their help, but wary of their dependence.

Ama continued making pancakes, piling them on a platter at the edge of the fire. We had not only ourselves but a crew to feed. The primary builders, Kefti and Pius, were from Karatu. They were strong, competent, and responsible. They never drank alcohol, never complained about sleeping in a tent, and usually stayed in the compound at night. They were sociable too, playing cards or reading books with the boys.

I watched as Kefti and Pius tackled the problem of lifting blocks to set on another level. I had to laugh when Kefti hoisted up a block, one foot on the wall and another on Pius' shoulder, using him as a ladder. They were marvelously inventive.

Our two workers from Oldeani were not up yet. They were less skilled and motivated. I watched them emerge from their tent, looking tired and unkempt. Their job for the day was to dig holes for the fence posts and clear another building site. They headed for the small shower and toilet area upslope away from the kitchen. I sighed as I saw their tent flap unzipped, an open invitation to the monkeys and baboons. I went to close the zip.

The air in their tent was foul with the smell of unwashed, sweat-soaked clothes, and sour fermented brew. In the gloom, under their cots, were jugs, probably empty now. They bought it from the bootleggers in the swamp. Not wanting to let on I'd noticed anything, I just zipped up the flap. As a white woman, I was not supposed to address men about their behavior. David needed to talk to them about their lateness and drinking, though he too was reluctant to do such a task. I frowned at the thought that we might have a firing and hiring chore to do. Yuk. I tried mumbling the ibis refrain of *ha-da-da-ha-da-da* to redirect my mind.

Tossing aside future personnel problems, I turned to greet our expert block maker, Ibrahim. He and Pili, his helper, seated themselves at the table. Ibrahim was a tireless and amiable worker. Our dear friend Aadje, the owner/manager of Ndutu Lodge in Serengeti, had "loaned" Ibrahim to us. Ibrahim was eager to come and brought along Ndutu's block-making machine to do the work.

Ibrahim and blocks

Back at Flycatcher Farm, we had hired two carpenters to make doors and frames. On this building day, one of David's chores was to see them and collect the window frames and Land Rover storage boxes he'd commissioned. David planned to bring one carpenter, Pascal, back with him. Pascal would be yet another addition to our crew. He'd stay with us and help install windows and door frames.

David made each supply trip as efficient as possible. While he was out doing the heavy lifting, collecting supplies, and fixing the car, I stayed to run the show at the building site. Between us, we kept up a constant flow of staff and supplies.

I went to check on the watering situation. The drums were full. I drove to the block-making area. The stacks of drying blocks needed dampening. I watered them myself, not wanting to call the block makers from breakfast. When I got back to the big outdoor table, the crew were finishing off the pile of pancakes and swigging down cups of sugary tea. They left one by one, turning to their chores. I told Ama to sit down and eat while we had a moment's peace. He reluctantly did so. I strained ants from the syrup while Ama spooned sugar over his pancakes.

We were eating when David arrived, a plume of dust following him down our entry road. He was driving "Blue Car," an old long-wheelbase Land Rover we'd bought off a friend. We needed a car that could carry larger loads than Herbert could manage. In addition to his wooden boxes, he'd brought fresh fruit, rice, beans, meat, poles, fuel, and mail. He also brought Pascal, the carpenter.

David and Pascal sat for a well-earned breakfast while I drove Herbert back down to the river for another load of water. The shade felt so good, making me realize the sun was high, the air already hot. I splashed myself with water and returned to the kitchen area to deal with the supplies David had brought.

I checked what had come against the list I'd sent. I kept the shopping lists Ama prepared because they were little puzzles to solve. For instance, on his list were: achicho, kabechi, chanizi kabechi, letus, lix. You have to say the words out loud to translate this Swahilized English: artichokes, cabbage, Chinese cabbage, lettuce, and leeks.

I smiled then laughed, not at Ama, but at myself, remembering one of my first lessons in this hybrid Kiswinglish language: Years ago, I saw a card on the side of a train we were boarding: "Tikiti fasklas." I was puzzled until David told me to say it out loud: "ticket first class."

I watched as the last tiers of blocks went into the kitchen house wall while I put away the groceries. Now the crew could construct the ring beam. But before they set the frames for the beam, David noted one window was crooked. Without pausing, Kefti and Pius picked up their long knives known as pangas. They hacked at the blocks until the opening was right. Such simple fixes amused me.

David rose from the table to check out a new source for gravel. He rounded up tools and helpers and drove off. I did another water run to the block factory where Ibrahim and Pili were mixing concrete. They stood around a heap of sand, gravel, and cement, pouring water into a crater they made on top, then shoveled the

ingredients together, mixing and mixing. After reaching some mysterious ideal con-
sistency, the men poured the wet slop into the block-making machine. They tamped
it down with the weighted lid, then with a long handle they levered the new block
out on its little wooden pallet and set it aside to cure.

Back at the kitchen, Ama had finished clearing things away. At last, we could
plan the main meal of the day. Ama sat uncomfortably at the table, nervously twist-
ing a rag in his bony hands. I said in in Swahili:

"David has brought some beef. Should we cook it today, or keep it for tomorrow?" I instantly regretted asking an "or" question because it often flummoxed
Ama. It did this time.

"Well, ah, humm," he mumbled. "Maybe it's good to keep it, but if you say we
should use it, I can cook it today. There isn't much room in the cooler. Maybe cook
it in a sauce? But we don't have many tomatoes, but we do have some potatoes."
Ama rose to his feet.

I searched for patience and the *ha-ha-ha* element. Trying hard to keep my voice
soft, I said, "Please sit down, Ama. The meat, Ama. We were deciding on the meat."

I decided I'd save him the trouble of decision making, as I should have done
first instead of giving him options. I
told him, "Cook the meat today, Ama.
Now we can plan the rest of the meal
together." We agreed on chunks of beef
with fresh vegetables and potatoes in a
big stew served with ugali, the standard
maize mush everyone liked but me.
I'd also make a salad of finely chopped
Chinese cabbage with avocadoes
and tomatoes.

Ama, the worried cook

Although we didn't make gourmet
meals, we ate well at Mikwajuni. Our food was fresh, most of it bought or grown
locally. But cooking was hot work, and I knew Ama had little endurance and
strength. I told him, "Rest now, while everyone's away."

He looked worried, his usual dog-eyed expression. He said, "Mama, now I will
do the laundry; there is time." I shrugged and went to find dirty clothes. First, I went
to the boys' tent where I found the deflated globe balloon I'd given them, on the
floor. I blew it up and hung it from the center post. They'd once used the globe as a
football. I got the hint, so I bought them a real soccer ball to use. I pulled off their
sheets, picked up towels and clothes, and took them to Ama.

My next stop was our tent. Carefully opening the zipper, I looked at the alarm clock that claimed it was 10 a.m. The sun and shadows told me it was well past noon. I collected sheets and clothes, then gritted my teeth as I closed the sticky zipper.

Back at the kitchen, I put the laundry in the wash bucket and noticed the crate of precious beer David brought. I took some bottles down to the stream to cool. We had no refrigerator. We cooked fresh each day. All the leftovers got used by the end of the next day. To keep things cool, I put them in the cold river or in a basin of water with a wet cloth draped over it and let the wind do the cooling.

I did another water run to supply the tireless Ibrahim and Pili, who were filling the molds and levering out blocks. I had calculated we needed about 400 blocks for the outside walls of each house and more blocks for inner walls. Each block was 5 inches thick by 9 inches high and 18 inches long. They were an excellent size to exercise your arm and leg muscles when lifting them into wheelbarrows and piling them in stacks that became apartment houses for scorpions. Ah, in this supposedly idyllic lifestyle, I mused, there is always a metaphorical scorpion lurking somewhere.

David and helpers returned with the first load of gravel. They unloaded and went for another run. The day was sun-scorched, the wind cutting—high time for a dip. I went to the streamside and jumped in. Whew! So good. Clambering out, I heard a little *hu-ha* sound. I looked up into the shady canopy of the fig tree and saw a vervet monkey watching me. I had to smile as I noticed the array of fuzzy grey monkeys sitting on the big yellow branches. With their black hands like mittens, they reached for figs and stuffed them into their mouths. Young monkeys were climbing through papyrus stems and wrestling in the grass. Their antics made me laugh out loud. I felt refreshed by the water, shade, and the monkeys, all of it reminding me that Mikwajuni was a magical place, worth much love and labor.

Back at the kitchen area, David was inspecting the work on the ring beam. We discussed how to roof the storeroom. I wanted it secure, impervious to rats, snakes, thieves, and fire. David decided to pour concrete over wire mesh on top of boards for the ceiling, an example of his usual creative approach to a problem.

While the men unloaded the sand, I went to pick tamarind pods for "mkwa-juice." That was my name for a cooling

Vervets in fig tree

drink everyone liked. I had perfected the recipe: fill a big basin with the stiff, brown pods. Remove the outer shell of the pods. Put the sticky fruit and seeds into a bowl. Pour two quarts of boiling water over the pile. Let them soak an hour or more. Pound the mess and squeeze out the juice. Strain through a big sieve or open-mesh cloth. What is left is a brown, pulpy juice. Diluted with water and sweetened sugar or honey, it's one of the most delicious and sustaining of juices, fresh and tart.

I tasted the juice and called the crew to get a break and a drink. Smacking lips and dumping sticky glasses in a big basin, the crew went back to work. Soon it would be time for dinner. We tried to finish chores by late afternoon. Evenings were for resting. The block men pressed out the final blocks and started clearing up.

I dashed to my tent to get my camera and took photos of the men doing their jobs. I planned to make an album so we could remember how Mikwajuni grew. It would remind us of all those trips to get water, sand, gravel, the piles of blocks, the poles and beams. Snap, snap, then I sat with Ama in the shade of the mighty acacia, cutting up potatoes, meat, and vegetables for the stew.

The compound grew quiet as work stopped. Workers disappeared to bathe and change clothes. Ama toiled over the fire as I wiped and set the table. The gang assembled and sat down on the benches around the table.

We were hungry. The stew was substantial, and the salad with tamarind juice dressing a special treat. After clearing up, people dispersed. Whistler asked me for an advance on his pay; Pius asked for his share of soap; the two men from Oldeani went off to the village; Ama finally took a rest. Len, Sam, and Gillie came home from school and ate up the stew with freshly baked bread. Off they went, to do their planting in the prepared holes.

The washed clothes were hanging on the line stretched between two trees, so I collected, folded, put them away, and made beds.

As dusk descended, so did the mosquitoes. The crew and boys mostly just tolerated the buzzing and bites. They sat in the lamplight around the kitchen table playing cards, laughing and teasing, slamming cards down with a thud. Pascal joined in as part of the team, destined to stay with us for years.

David and I were too tired to do anything but creep off to the sticky-zipper tent. We crawled under the clean sheets and listened to the hoots of owls and the murmur of voices from the outdoor kitchen. Peace. Yes, the clock had stopped ticking. I turned it over and decided to trash it. Each day determined its particular pace, bird-by-bird, block-by-block. I didn't need to measure it with a clock.

CHAPTER 12
SPIRITS OF THE SWAMP
AN ADVENTURE IN THE SWAMP WITH OUR THREE BOYS: 1990

Jeannette and boys in swamp

Living and building along Chemchem Stream gave us a daily dose of wonders. We delighted in the sounds and sights of our wild neighbors. Monkeys and birds flickered in and out of the tree canopies, civets and leopards left tracks on the streamside paths, and hippos laughed in the papyrus swamp.

Other, more mysterious sounds came from the swamp: sinister, suspicious clangs, bangs, and bonging. My determination to track the source of those noises rose with each dissonant concert.

One day I let my adventurous spirit, that unruly child of curiosity, go free; the three boys chose to accompany their crazy Mama Simba. We walked along the streamside to the head of the Chemchem oasis. One of the most substantial springs began there. The water surged out from the rocks, forming a rivulet that wandered towards the wind-tossed forest of papyrus.

At the edge, I stepped into the gurgling water. Standing in the shallow stream, I listened carefully. The distant voices of people came from across the meadow from springs on the village side. Nearer came the mutter of the papyrus heads and the chatter of the boys behind me. There were no hippo snorts, no baboons arguing with one another. The loudest sounds were the bonging noises coming from behind the screen of papyrus.

I looked at the boys. Gillie had a silly smirk on his face; the know-it-all look children have when they realize the adult is going to do something stupid. But he followed me anyway, stepping cautiously into the stream. Len stood trying to make up his mind whether or not to enter this dangerous area. I could almost see his thoughts walking across his face, reluctant but determined to fulfill his role as con-scientious Big Brother of Gillie and Protector of Mama Simba. He, too, stepped into the water.

But Sam hung back, his face set in his usual pout. I looked back at him over my shoulder and waved a little goodbye. He seemed timid and reluctant, maybe feeling unwanted, though we beckoned him to come along. We left him there on the grassy bank. I hoped Sam might run for help if he heard us scream.

The three of us sloshed along the stream that led us through a fringe of foliage. The papyrus swamp at Chemchem was vast, spreading out where water from numer-ous small springs chose countless channels to meander among the papyrus stems and tall trees. We carefully selected watery paths through open spaces as we waded towards the mysterious metallic gonging sounds. We kept our heads down, step-ping slowly to avoid tripping on sharp rocks or submerged spiny fever tree limbs.

Warily we felt our way towards the *bong... bong... bong* coming from the interior of the thick stands of papyrus.

I was only slightly worried about the hippos hidden further downstream in their deep pools. I felt confident they would not come anywhere near the noise that attracted our attention. Even so, I stopped often to listen carefully for hippo noises, their soft harrumphs, and deep-throated bellowing like laughter. We didn't want to meet territorial hippos that might attack us if we invaded their watery territory. During our pauses, we reoriented towards the clangs. Hippos didn't clang.

The streams widened and narrowed, intertwining with each other. We looked for booby-traps in the water. It was easier to see when sunlight dropped down through the vegetation, but not at all easy when our feet stirred up mud. Every so often, we glanced up to avoid the drooping branches of the drowned fever trees, their wicked thorns as long as my fingers. We pushed them aside carefully and proceeded.

A piercing scream made our hearts pound. A dark bird lifted off from a limb and flapped away. Even though we knew the hadada ibis well, its screech still jolted us. Three intrepid explorers breathed deeply with relief.

The water deepened as we went further into the swamp. The trees were taller, thicker, and older, with entwined vines hanging like curtains. Gillie let out a cry as he slipped and grabbed for vines, pulling them down on him. Len and I untangled him and waited to see if he felt too frightened to go on. But he nodded and pointed ahead into the channel through a dark green wall of papyrus.

Papyrus stems stood stiff and tall, their mop-like heads about four times as high as Gillie when he stood tall. We entered the channel, unable to see much further than arm's length. Pushing the stems aside, we tried to find a way through.

Gillie and Len stayed right behind me as we forged on, up to our waists in water. Closer now, we heard hissing as well as the ominous thumping. I assumed the sound had to be someone pounding on an empty petrol drum. A 55-gallon metal barrel was called a "pipa" (pronounced pee-pa). I envisioned a Piping Pipa luring us onwards, a drummer on a drum, driving us to doom, *boom-boom-boom*.

I laughed at myself, enjoying this little adventure. I was feeling bold but wondered briefly if the boys were afraid. Too late now, we were almost there.

Pushing our way onward, we came to open water, rimmed with a shorter kind of papyrus. The tall papyrus and trees stood further back, away from the sunlight shimmering on the pool. On the far side of the stretch of open water was an island with a huge tree growing on it. We paused, listening. The gonging had stopped.

All was quiet except for a *bloop-bloop-bloop*, like some living thing gasping and burbling in the shadows. The glare of the bright sunshine on the water made it hard to see into the shadows under the island tree. Gradually I could make out an unexpected sight: a pair of old shoes set neatly on the bank.

The gonging on the metal drum resumed, suddenly louder. Then abruptly, it went spookily quiet again. I got goosebumps. I turned to Gillie and Len to check if they were frightened. They both stood absolutely still, staring back at me, eyes wide, their bodies tense. They were ready to turn and flee. We listened to the gurgle of the water, holding our breaths. Suddenly there was a giggle. The green gloom ahead kaleidoscoped into patterned cloth, flecks of color, and glimpses of bodies.

Moving further into the sun-splashed water, we saw more. There, on the bank, was the curved edge of something red and round. It was a barrel, the pipa! Shuffling closer, we could see a blue drum and another rusted grey one, and two gaily clad, giggling women.

One wore a headscarf and a wet, dirty kanga wrapped over her dress. She beckoned to us with a cupped hand. I was transfixed. So were Gillie and Len. The boys probably suspected what we'd find in the swamp but never dared to investigate. Now they were as amazed as I. We had found the source of the sound.

There were more than bongs and hisses. We inhaled the strong smells of molasses, alcohol, and wood smoke. Coils of plastic tubing hung from the metal barrels surrounded by bottles, buckets, and cups. This place was the core factory for producing illegal booze. The steady, soft *bloop-bloop* sound rose from the tubs of bubbling liquid; the hissing came from the fire under the drum. A plume of smoke filtered upwards through the leaves of the big tree. The distillation process was in full swing. The potent spirit was drawn up through tubing and a car radiator, presumably to cool and add poisonous lead flavoring to the brew.

Headscarf Woman greeted us amiably, coming to the edge of the bank to lean over, offering me a pink plastic cup. I knew it was a sample of her brew, called piwa, *liquor*, the local rum. Gillie and Len recoiled with apprehension as I took the cup, still standing waist-deep in the water.

Having come all this way into Never-never Land, I was undoubtedly going to try the concoction. I sipped, really just putting my tongue in the cup. One taste was enough: burning and strongly alcoholic—battery acid dissolved in lighter fluid. The Swahili word piwa is derived from "pure"—pure spirit—but the stuff they brewed in the swamp had plenty of impurities: lead, rust, dirt, fertilizer. Who knew?

An exceptionally loud *bong-bong-bong* shifted my attention from the cup of brew to a man in the shadows. He had turned an empty drum upside down. Now he beat on it to dislodge some slimy goo. Despite its unpleasant taste and method of production, piwa was widely consumed in Mangola. Piwa rotted the brain and punished the liver. Drinking a full cup could make a person drunk.

I didn't like the piwa industry any more than the taste of it. But I knew that humans would always concoct something to soothe their longings and despair. They'd find something to make them feel better for a while. Besides the spirits brewed in the swamp, there was always fermented maize mush available. On special occasions, men of the Datoga tribe made rather good tasting honey mead.

I returned the cup to Headscarf Woman, who smirked, then drank the rest. She was barefoot. I looked at her muddy feet as she stepped back from the bank into the shadows, staggering a little. I guessed she'd sampled her product. The shadowy men working among their barrels behind the women nodded at me and turned away, probably so I wouldn't get a good look at them.

I made no effort to identify them. The brewing crew recognized me, but seemed to accept the crazy white woman who was here with two of the boys who lived with her. They knew I would do nothing to endanger their operation. We lived too close as neighbors. If I made a fuss, they could easily have their revenge, such as burning down our thatched roofed houses or carting off our possessions. I would not risk alienating them; I wanted their trust.

High-powered liquor of the sort they were brewing was illegal. The brewers did not want to be caught. Even though some villagers welcomed the booze, the village elders had to take the position that distilling wasn't welcome in the Chemchem swamp. If they caught the piwa people, the authorities would have to imprison them somewhere else because Mangola had neither police nor jail. The simplest strategy was to ignore the piwa industry for as long as possible.

Gillie tugged at my kanga and whispered, "Twende." I agreed, "Ndiyo, twende!" *Yes, let's go!* Len looked relieved as we hastened back the way we had come, or so we thought. The maze of streamlets led this way and that. In our haste, we stumbled often, fell a few times, and got stabbed by thorns. Finally, wet and scraped, we escaped from the swamp. It seemed hours since we left Sam. We were glad to find him still sitting on the bank, frowning at us.

"Sam," I said. "Tumeshinda!" *We had success.* We left our fears in the swamp and now felt rather proud of our little adventure. We told Sam we found the gonging sound and the people making piwa. He told me, "I knew they were making piwa. Once, Father took me in there. He drank the stuff. I had to stay there and get teased by those people. It was awful, all the noise and the smell."

To ensure no one in the village would know we had been to the piwa island, I told the three boys to keep quiet about our discovery. I hoped the bootleggers wouldn't take offense at our visit and cause us trouble. And they didn't then, but shortly after, their activities caused a misfortune in our lovely, mysterious Chemchem swamp.

On a hot, muggy afternoon, David and I were by the riverside, cleaning our boat. Suddenly we smelled smoke and soon after, heard a series of loud metallic pings. "That sounded like gunshots," I said.

"It's just the piwa barrels being moved around," David said. "Maybe the piwa people knocked over their fires, and the dead papyrus or woodpile caught." As he spoke, the smoke smell got stronger. Tendrils of smoke filtered through the screen of papyrus on the other side of the stream. I distinctly heard two more bangs in quick succession.

"Those are gunshots," I said firmly. This time David agreed. We headed to the kitchen and collected most of our crew. Armed with knives (mainly for slashing papyrus), we left our compound, followed by Len, Sam, Gillie, handyman Pascal, watchman Gwaruda, and chief chef Athumani. Our little gang went along the path winding alongside the stream.

At the head of the many springs was the village campsite. We emerged from under the giant fig and fever trees and scanned the open grassy field. Ahead we saw some people we knew, setting up tents for a safari group. To our right was a scene of mayhem: smoke and flames and loud crackling issued from the swamp. Fifty or more people were milling about. A friend in the village told us, "The police and army men have come. They are rounding up the illegal brewers hiding in the papyrus swamp. They have guns."

My memory immediately conjured the picture of shadowy piwa people with their barrels of brew and the *bloop-bloop-bloop* sound coming from the island. Were those people being shot along with their barrels of lethal liquid?

Alarmed, we moved closer to the edge of the papyrus forest where flames were shooting up through the dense smoke rising from blackened fronds. Arrayed in front of the fiery scene, we could make out the police and army men. They were dragging and rolling barrels from the swamp. Two valiant vigilantes were shooting other barrels full of holes. They looked smug watching the bootleg brew spill onto the ground while the felons looked on in dismay. As in old cowboy movies, the bootleggers held their hands up to show their lack of weapons or to fend off a physical attack. Their faces were grim. I wondered if they were sadder about losing their precious product or being caught.

Woman putting out fire

Women called to one another. A cacophony of shouts, laments, and cries of distress echoed across the swamp. The posse had kicked over the fires and the dried-out stands of papyrus burned fiercely.

Villagers and passers-by came from the village side of the Chemchem Springs. Some brought buckets to fill with water to contain the fire. They knew it could quickly spread into the maze of papyrus, igniting dead tree limbs that screened the village's bathing, washing, and water-drawing spots, and move to the huts downstream.

The fire brigade was busy filling buckets, passing them along to others who doused the burning papyrus. They soon smothered the central fire, but not before it had blackened most of the plants around the Chemchem meadow, campsite, and the village spring. Feeling rather useless, we took photos, talked to some of the villagers, and started home to Mikwajuni.

On our way, we passed the camp being set up for tourists. They would arrive the next day, after the fire was out and police and bootleggers had left. But the stories and signs of the roundup, the flames, and the mayhem would still be vivid. Would they find this wild west show intimidating or a memorable addition to their safari? Whichever, the charred swamp would not be attractive. The sour, acrid smell of burnt papyrus would taint the air for days.

The papyrus grew back, the bootleggers returned, trade routes and exchanges were re-established. Things went along in this way for some years. As time went by, we felt increasingly apprehensive whenever we got the whiff of molasses or the smell of smoldering fires. Would there be another fire, another raid?

The bong-bong of barrels being cleaned became almost comforting to me. Like the hippos snorting, it kept some unwanted people away from our side of the river. Most local people didn't care for the bootleggers or the hippos. While the hippos were killed one by one, the piwa brewers were chased away, group by group. Religious people, especially the sober Muslims, didn't approve of the business. Wives disliked the available alcohol; it led to the disappearance or death of husbands and drained household cash. Piwa brought illness and abuse.

But brewing piwa wasn't mainly about the product or the drunks; it was about money. People accused the village officers of actually encouraging the distilling business because they were getting a cut, a steady profit from piwa sales.

Our village officials could clear their names by making a show of cleaning out the bootleggers. And they did.

Local and district officers arrived from towns outside Mangola. They came to our place to warn us. The highest-ranking official told us in English, "I have brought the police. They will clear out these despicable ruffians. We'll rid the place of them all."

His policemen nodded eagerly, drinking the tea I gave them in gulps. They were proud they could trash the illegal brewery and round up the shadowy characters. They kept repeating that this operation would make the neighborhood "safe." I realized I felt safer with the "despicable," weaponless brewers than the men who came with guns. The bootleggers and we had maintained a balance of avoidance. Although a mutual menace, we respected each other's privacy.

Suddenly we heard banging and cries, voices shouting from the swamp. The roundup had begun. The heroic posse left to investigate and supervise.

Later, we heard the rest of the story. Issa, who worked for us on our garden plot, had been conscripted to help in the anti-piwa campaign. He gave us the details in Swahili, and in English.

"The posse found 30 barrels of booze. All the barrels got dumped out. It smells foul over there. Chemchem Stream will be polluted for days. The police caught four people brewing piwa deep in the swamp. They dragged them out one by one. One fell in the swamp and almost drowned. Now the police are searching the village for another dozen people whose names they got."

Jeannette, wearing hat, and captured drums

Although I was impressed with the efficiency of the operation, I felt oddly concerned about the miscreants. I was partly glad that law and order had prevailed. Another part of me wanted the lawless, irresponsible bootleggers to have a place in our world too. My little nugget of concern, my sympathy for the piwa producers, wasn't rational. Those people in the swamp made something some people wanted, and others did not. Likewise, the hippos in the swamp were wanted by some, not by others. I could sympathize with both the lovers and the despisers of the untamed and wild.

The boys never went deep into the papyrus forest again. Neither did I. Even so, sometimes I found myself straining my ears for sounds of hippo snorts or the *bloop-bloop-bloop* from the spirits of the swamp. In all our remaining years in Mangola, I listened in vain.

CHAPTER 13
JUMODA
ONE PERSON, MANY PERSONALITIES; CULTURES AND LOCAL JUSTICE: 1988 ON

Jumoda and warrior under fig tree at Chemchem

We first met Jumoda under a giant fig tree at the Chemchem Springs. The handsome youth had been talking with a black-cloaked Datoga warrior who strode away as we approached, his stick over his shoulder.

In contrast, the young man who turned to us was dressed in a Western-style shirt, a brown sports jacket, and pressed khaki trousers with a camera strap over his shoulder.

"Hello, my name is Jumoda," he said. "I live in Gorofani near Mzee Bashki's boma."

We knew of Bashki because he was a respected elder of the resident Datoga livestock keepers. That tribe had been living in the Eyasi Basin for hundreds of years. We were a bit surprised that Jumoda, though a Datoga, was not wearing the traditional black cloak. I looked at his polished shoes, smart attire, and camera. His whole demeanor suggested a young man stepping away from his culture.

"Here," he said, handing us a photo. "I was coming to your place to give you this picture I took of the boys who live with you."

I took the photo he'd taken of Len, Sam, and Gillie. While David and Jumoda chatted, I studied the young man. He had poise and a friendly, outgoing manner. Jumoda was very enthusiastic about many things: his tribe, our village, Tanzania. He seemed to like learning about the world beyond. Our first meeting impressed us. This youth was a charmer; he would make an impact. He profoundly impacted our lives.

Jumoda often came to visit us at Mikwajuni. He struck up relationships not only with us, but also with our three boys, the workers, and with visitors as well.

We saw him even more often after he started working with a friend of ours. He got the job in a roundabout way. A Japanese researcher named Morimichi Tomikawa, a medical doctor, as well as a professor of anthropology, often visited Mangola. He led Japanese research teams and came himself to study the Datoga people.

The Datoga are part of a larger group known as the Barabaig, a Nilotic tribe that migrated south with their cattle from northern Africa centuries ago. They were pushed out of the lush Ngorongoro highlands by much more recent invaders, the Maasai. They gave the Datoga the name Mangati—enemy.

The ousted Mangati moved south. Some stayed and tried to survive in the harsher lands around the Eyasi Basin. Jumoda had been born into a long-established Datoga clan living in the Mangola area.

Tomikawa had a lot of friends, including Jumoda's family. Our anthropologist friend asked us if there was someone in Mangola, a Datoga, who would serve as a useful guide. We asked the professor. He was a quiet, thoughtful man who took his time to answer. "Jumoda," he said finally.

We were curious why he'd nominated Jumoda. We thought of him as friendly and smart, but too immature to work with researchers.

"What about your good friend Bashki, or another elder of the tribe?" I asked. "Wouldn't they be much more experienced and helpful as a guide for a foreign researcher?"

The sage answered enigmatically, "The young man needs development; he will be learning. The old man knows too much."

Our anthropologist friend hired Jumoda. She was happy with his help, though she found him a bit naïve and pushy around her study groups. We awaited Jumoda's "development" as he worked with her and, later, with her student.

Jumoda often came to our place in between his jobs with the researchers. He'd sit at our communal table and chat with anyone. He had a competitive nature in playing cards. He also challenged the boys or workers to stick fights. Sometimes when the matches got too rough, we'd have to ask him to calm down or go away for a while.

Jumoda was very proud of being a Datoga and of his particular clan. He seemed to think of himself as a warrior. He had bigger goals, as well. He wanted to learn to drive, speak English, and earn lots of money. We wondered if his modern ambitions would override his respect for the ways of his ancestors and their devotion to cattle keeping.

Only rarely did Jumoda wear the traditional black Datoga cloak. Instead, he usually wore t-shirts and jeans. I wondered if he even had a cloak of his own or if he borrowed one when he wanted to look like authentic Datoga. This mix of modernity and tradition intrigued me; I empathized with his struggle to find a balance.

I invented a small project with Jumoda that let us spend time together. I wanted to understand him better while probing his balance between ambition and tradition. He probably just wanted to earn some money and an excuse to hang around our place. Our project was The Cloak.

One market day, Jumoda and I were wandering among the piles of goods laid out on the windblown, dusty ground. I asked him if he would make me a *ngorori*, the traditional Datoga cloak. He agreed. I bought the cloth on the spot. Later I bought the decorative buttons and beads.

Jumoda frequently visited over several weeks while he sewed the white buttons onto the black cloth and fringed the edges. It took more buttons and time than I'd expected. He spent an exceptionally long time making the fringe at the bottom of the cloak, putting colored beads on each of the hundreds of fringe strands. We chatted as he worked. The topics ranged widely.

Land: "We must take care of our land. It's the basis for everything."

Charcoal burning: "Trees are important, we need the shade and the wood for beams and poles. Anyway, charcoaling is illegal."

Immigrants: "These people who come in, from all over, they are taking the land, our water, and destroying everything."

Wildlife: "There used to be lions here, elephants, and even rhinos. Newcomers are pushing out the wild animals."

Hunting: "We Datoga don't hunt to get meat, but it is good the Hadza can hunt. Foreigners shouldn't be allowed."

Tribal futures: "We livestock keepers, how can we survive if outsiders bring their cattle here during hard times. Those people use up our dry season resources."

World futures: "If we get so overpopulated, then what? And what about HIV? We need more education."

Jumoda wearing cloak

At last, Jumoda finished the buttoned, fringed and beaded cloak. Sewn into it, for me, were many aspects of Jumoda's personality. My working conclusion was Jumoda was likable, intense, opinionated, and ambitious. He fascinated me. I saw some of myself in him, for better and worse. I observed his interactions with others with interest.

A particular relationship he developed revealed many aspects of Jumoda's character. For a while, a lad lived with us whom we nicknamed "Cowboy." Jumoda called Cowboy *Kobe*, the Swahili word for tortoise— perhaps because he was, like Jumoda, a bit stubborn and hard-shelled. The two young men were a striking pair, white and black, the one from a wealthy family in Texas and the other from a rural livestock-keeping family in Tanzania.

They both were agile, fit, handsome, and keen to test their skills. They were often together, sharing their brawn and thoughts in a mixture of English and Swahili. They worked together on supply trips, such as driving our Land Rover to collect sand from a riverbed. They fought too, verbally and physically, fist to fist and with sticks. Once, Jumoda hurt Cowboy, but they were soon back together. When Cowboy left Mangola, he gave Jumoda a knife.

In 1991, Jumoda stabbed a man. He used Cowboy's knife. We worried that Jumoda might be imprisoned, his life ruined. But he wasn't put in jail. The whole conflict taught us not only about Jumoda but rumors and local justice. Getting the facts was like trying to grab fish by hand from the Chemchem Stream.

The conflict concerned a cow. Jumoda sold a heifer at the mnada—our monthly cattle market. After the sale came the fight. In one version of what followed, Jumoda accused the buyer of shortchanging him. The buyer called him a liar, Jumoda stabbed him then ran off, bloody knife in hand. He ran straight into a nest of booze drinkers who bopped him with their sticks.

Another version held that Jumoda was set upon by thugs and tried to defend himself with the knife. Yet another tale said Jumoda started a fight with the buyer who had the support of buddies who proceeded to beat up Jumoda. Most versions of the event ended with Jumoda sitting in a police car, bleeding. Trying to summon clarity out of the roiling rumors reminded me of waving a handkerchief at a smoky brush fire.

I wanted to hear the story from Jumoda. When he was released, he came to report.

"I knew you'd be worried, that is why I came straight here," he said with a charming smile. He gave me his version of the tale:

"I was with my father's brother. We went early to sell a young cow belonging to this uncle. A guy from Karatu bought the animal. We took the money and gave him the owner's certificate. A couple of hours later, the fellow found us in the crowds and demanded his money back. He said he'd return the cow. We told him, 'No. No trading back.' He argued. We did not back down.

A little while later, he and a friend came up behind us. They held my uncle by his arms, fished in his pocket, pulled out the money, and put in the certificate. We said, 'OK, if you feel that way, take your money and go.' Someone else came and bought the cow. So, we had our money again and went home."

Jumoda paused. I looked at him expectantly, sure that there was more to tell. He continued, "I returned to the mnada early in the afternoon. I was wandering around when the hoodlum came back. He started to tease me. Four or more thugs from Karatu joined in. They told me I was a black mzungu, imitating foreigners, not a real Datoga. They pulled at my t-shirt and started pushing me around. Two of them took sticks and started hitting me. I couldn't let them do that. I pulled out my knife to scare them away. One ran away, but the nasty one who'd started the fight got sliced on the shoulder. It was not a bad wound, barely a scratch, just enough to bleed a lot. The ones who had thick sticks hit me on the head and shoulders."

Jumoda paused to demonstrate his wounds. "All this happened near the main cattle corral. By that time of day, there weren't many people. No one knew I was Datoga. I didn't have time to look for friends. None of the strangers would help me. After slicing the ringleader, I went to the police. They are always around on mnada days. I asked to sit in their car where I'd be protected."

Jumoda looked at me. I kept a straight face. "What happened next?"

"Well, the bloodied man was taken off to Karatu. He got patched up and sent home. Then Boniface, the Mangola Area Officer, came by. He saw me sitting in the police car and asked the police why. The police told him I wounded a fellow with a knife in a fight. Boniface told the police I was well known and a good person. He told them the fight was probably started by the gang of toughs. Then we all went to the police station in Karatu. The District Officer was there. He knows my family and me. He told the police I was an OK sort of fellow who worked for Mama Simba sometimes."

Jumoda paused, looked at me, smiling. But his last statement did not please me. It worried me. Why did working for me give this youth any credence or status? I didn't like that our reputations were linked. I hoped to be seen as an innocuous mzungu, a foreigner, who just happened to live in rural Tanzania. Being known by the authorities was more worrying than reassuring.

I listened to Jumoda with full attention as he continued his tale.

"The police in Karatu knew who the hoodlums were. They often pull this stunt of buying something then demanding their money back. They like to pick fights to show how tough they are. I shouldn't have got involved, but I couldn't just let them annoy me."

The clearing-up of the incident involved getting the families together to decide what to do. No one wanted a court case. Jumoda had to be present for the decision-making. I wished him well at his meeting. Besides sorting it all out, I hoped he would learn not to let himself be provoked. It would be another one of his lessons in personal development.

Several days later, Jumoda came back from his meeting and told us, "It's all fine now." I'd heard the phrase too often and knew it covered hours of negotiations, the trading of promises and goods. I pestered him for a peek under the "fine now."

"Well, I have to pay a heifer or a cow to the fellow's family, he said. "He and I have to exchange a sheep or a goat. We have to supply honey for beer, too."

Justice had been done; we were all relieved. The two youths had followed their traditional customs. Now feelings were soothed; balance restored. It was a harmonious outcome, a "restorative circle."

The case of the stabbing occurred when Jumoda seemed genuinely attached to us. He sometimes did odd jobs at our place, such as sorting our greeting cards into packets, talking all the while. We liked hearing his news of the village and figured he told stories about us, too. We jokingly called him our village spy.

Over months, then into years, we continued to learn from and teach Jumoda. We gave him practice in speaking English. We taught him to drive. When he was reasonably competent, we loaned him our car for short local trips. He took village officials to collect the bags of illegal charcoal and sacks of grains to grind at the village mill.

We took him along on trips to Karatu and Arusha town, to reserves, national parks, and special events. He became like an elder brother to our three boys. He learned better English. As time went on, he established a solid reputation as a local expert and guide.

On trips to Arusha, he made the rounds of tour operators. We introduced him to friends of ours in tour companies. During the more than six years we worked with our village leaders to develop the village campsites at Chemchem Springs, Jumoda became the local star guide. He began earning a good income and wanted more. He got a plot of his own in the village and married. We lent him our car to get building supplies: we donated thatch and poles.

Eventually, Jumoda bought a car and took on tourism big time. As Jumoda "developed" into a leading figure in the local tourism business, he began to attack us in subtle ways. That was an unpleasant time for us. It also revealed an ugly part of Jumoda's character.

Jumoda

Over the years, as we watched him develop, Jumoda's bridge ceased to be a springy one between traditional and modern. He built a solid structure of his own, rigid, with tollbooths on either side. He demanded payment for his help. He wanted rights and privileges beyond what most local youths would dare. He attacked us by manipulating village officials (see The Campsite Saga chapter).

Jumoda was like the round, red Mangola onion, with outer layers of charm and intelligence over inner layers of conceit and cunning. His deepest layers seemed to be self-doubt battling with self-righteousness. And, like the onions, he could make us cry.

Sometimes we loved him, and sometimes we loathed him. I think of him fondly because he taught me much about being careful with judgments and making assumptions about people. Did I ever really know him?

In my mind's eye, Jumoda wears modern, fashionable clothes, and an enigmatic smile. He also has that traditional black Datoga cloak wrapped around him. It covers his many layers and the stings he could give. Jumoda has been my life's favorite social scorpion.

CHAPTER 14
JANDO
RITUALS AND RELATIONSHIPS: 1989

Jumoda and the jando boys

My evening walk through the baobab trees had taken longer than usual. I returned home in the last afterglow of sunset and found Gillie waiting on the couch in the gloom of our porch. He'd grown tall since he and his brothers came to live with us. Gillie was now about 11 or 12 years old, Sam 13, and Len maybe 14 or 15. Gillie's lanky form unfolded as he stood up from the front porch bench. He politely greeted me with "Shikamoo Mama."

From someone I lived with, this greeting was too formal. My mental alarm bells started ringing. Gillie made a sort of bow and stretched out his hand with a folded note pinched in his fingers, as though afraid it would burst into flame. A letter delivered by hand in remote Mangola made me as nervous as a midnight phone call in a more modern world.

I opened the note warily. Gillie's handwriting was unmistakable, but all three boys had signed their full names: Gilbert, Lenard, and Samwel. Yes, this letter contained a serious message, one I had better read carefully.

I went inside to read by lamplight. After formal Swahili words of greeting, came the word *ombi*, meaning request. The word following the request puzzled me. The three boys were requesting a jando. My thoughts flicked through what might be jando. A trip? A radio? A game? Something for school or soccer? I was ignorant of this word.

I went outside to ask Gillie what it meant. He looked at the ground then glanced up at me. "Jando inamaana tahilwa," he muttered in a shy voice. So, I'd learned jando meant *tahilwa*, another word unknown to me.

Mystified, I went to find my Swahili dictionary. Gillie waited patiently on the front porch. It took me some time to decipher that what he pronounced as *tahilwa* was *tahihirwa*. It meant to be circumcised. The word "jando" meant the initiation ceremony or ritual associated with circumcision.

I stood there, my mind whirling. It had never occurred to me that circumcision mattered to the boys. They sometimes went about naked when they were little and swam naked most of the time. Upon reflection, I remembered there'd been signs they'd become increasingly modest. Out of their allowances, they'd been buying themselves fancy shorts at the monthly mnada market. Nowadays they always swam in shorts, too.

Later, I learned it was when swimming publicly, uncircumcised, that village boys teased the threesome. The teasing had finally pushed them to come to me. They'd got up their courage to ask me to help organize a jando.

If the boys thought this was important enough to write a formal letter to me, I reckoned the issue must concern them deeply. I re-read the request, pondering what to do. Gillie sat on the couch, often glancing at his brothers waiting for him down the short path at the outdoor kitchen table. Sitting down opposite Gillie, I looked at his shadowed face and said, "Certainly. I agree with a jando."

I was committed, even though I had no real idea of what a jando would entail. Gillie went off happily to tell the others. I stood and stared after him thinking, Jando! Mama Simba is going to learn something new.

I sat back down to think. Circumcision is common in Western culture, a rather odd tradition when I thought about it. Baby boys—like my husband, brother, and father—were circumcised soon after birth. In college, my studies and questioning gave me some answers about why the deed was done. I'd learned that circumcision was not a worldwide practice. It was the custom in certain cultures, a permanent and public demonstration of a male's status in society. Male circumcision also had implications of cleanliness and health.

In Africa, the cutting of the foreskin is often an important rite. It's a coming of age ceremony, a demonstration of a boy taking his place in his tribe. In the case of these three boys, born outside of their Ngoni culture, what would be the appropriate ceremony? What would be the proper procedure?

The initiation rite was a secret among the men of many tribes. Note the gender: men. Here I was, a woman of the Western world, put in the position of trying to understand and design appropriate preparation for the circumcision of three Ngoni boys. Traditionally, they would receive instruction from their father and the older men of their community: lessons in correct social behavior, customs, and marriage. There was no way I could take on the role of teacher.

David would be in no better position to take on the role of a tribal elder. He had never been as involved with the three boys as I was. David's quiet, private nature made the boys act as though he was unapproachable, a diffident patriarch. Better to ask Mama to organize something so personal as a jando. Thinking of either David or me trying to impart tribal values to the boys before a circumcision ritual made me laugh out loud at the absurdity. It amused me so much that I immediately felt better about the jando.

Once committed, I started to work out how I could organize a proper circumcision ritual. My first thought was I needed help. The whole Mangola region was a mishmash of tribes. New attitudes and practices tangled with tradition. Both the Datoga and Maasai tribes still had ancient circumcision rituals. Cohorts of boys from about 11 to 18 were circumcised in batches. Beforehand they convened for all-male retreats, feasts, and ceremonies. We saw newly circumcised Maasai boys on every safari to Serengeti. White ash masked their faces. They wore headdresses of birds they'd killed and dressed in black cloaks, naked underneath.

The Iraqw and Bantu tribes did not so blatantly celebrate circumcision. And the Hadza did not have a tradition of circumcising boys at all. So, where did these three boys fit? I needed some elders in our community to help decide what to do.

The next morning, an anxious Mama Simba summoned the courage to talk it over with Athumani, our resident elder. Although he was from a Bantu tribe, I hoped he knew about the customs of the other tribes as well. Maybe he and some others could invent a circumcision ceremony more meaningful than merely finding a doctor to cut off the boys' foreskins.

In the morning, after the boys left for school, I asked Athumani if he had time to talk. He nodded and sat down with me at the table. Embarrassed, I hummed and hawed then broached the subject.

"Athumani, the boys have asked for a jando." I waited to see Athumani's reaction. He nodded. I pushed on with, "What exactly is jando? What does tahihirwa mean nowadays?"

Athumani sat, his calm round face composed. He did not reflect my embarrassment, but it took him a while to compose an answer.

"Jando means the ceremony of circumcision. Tahihirwa is the cutting."

"Athumani, I probably can arrange for the doctor in Barazani to do the cutting. But I want the boys to have some ceremony and preparation. As a woman, I can't teach the boys about all the things their elders would."

Athumani nodded slowly in his sage way, saying, "Yes, Mama Simba, you would not be the right person to talk about manly things to the boys."

Who would be the right person? I knew right away who. I smiled. "Athumani, do you think we could get Mzee Lenard involved? He is their father, a Ngoni. Certainly, he needs to teach the boys about their tribal values. Could you see him and ask him?"

Athumani was quiet, his expression troubled. I could almost hear him thinking: Mzee Lenard is a stubborn man. He doesn't look after his three sons. He will be reluctant to get involved.

Athumani hesitated then said, "Well, umm, maybe. Perhaps. I don't know. I will try to find him in the village tomorrow. I can ask him to come to see you about this."

"Thank you, Athumani," I said, with real gratitude.

Days passed. Despite Athumani's invitation, the father did not come to see the boys or me. There was always some excuse: he was too busy or absent on some trip somewhere. I let go trying to find him as I gradually got used to the idea of jando and felt more comfortable talking about it. When David returned from his safari, he was almost as shocked as I about the circumcision request. Then he laughed, "Oh

Mama Simba, you do seem to attract and delight in dilemmas." He encouraged me to do what I could to find local men to help.

I talked over the jando idea with some of the village elders I trusted, including our former and current village chairmen. They agreed that if the father would not take on the instruction of the boys, other men should do so. But what men? Cultural guidance from too many different village men would be in bits and pieces. There would be no intimacy or immersion in tradition. Jumoda, our guide to many local customs and a traditionally circumcised Datoga youth, offered to instruct the boys. He was eager for the job.

Although Jumoda was young, he was like an older brother to the three boys. He could teach them something. But I didn't trust him fully with the education of the boys. I wanted the wisdom and abilities of the older men such as Athumani, and our guard, Gwaruda, a circumcised Datoga elder. They and the village chairmen could cover subjects like morality, sex, marriage, social responsibility, and whatever else pre-circumcised boys learned. I never knew what the boys were taught; I didn't dare to eavesdrop on their conversations nor ask them.

When the boys were out of school for several weeks having sessions with their guides, I thought about the actual circumcision. I rebelled against the thought of traditional razor blades or knives used for the job. As pseudo-parent, I couldn't allow the boys to submit to what could be a very infectious procedure. The boys needed a proper doctor. Our village chairmen gave me advice on who might be qualified and willing. A doctor at the catholic hospital in the village of Barazani agreed.

To mark the event, the boys decided that after they healed, they wanted a celebratory party.

"Can we invite anyone we like?" asked Big Len.

"Sure," I said.

"Can we play our music?" asked Sam. "Real loud?" he added with a sly, challenging look.

"Well, umm, sure," I said.

"And eat popcorn and mandazi and sodas, too?" asked Gillie.

I gave up and turned all the arrangements over to them. We'd planned to give them a new radio as their jando gift. It would be perfect for producing loud music for their friends.

I'd not given up on the boys' father, even though there was no response to any of the messengers or messages. I talked to Athumani. He lifted his eyebrows as though thinking, but not saying, Mama Simba, you still do not understand how hard it is to get Mzee Lenard to come to you. He doesn't want to be involved.

I scanned Athumani's face and sighed. "Please, try once more."

He did, but again Mzee Lenard didn't answer. Days passed. Finally, I sent the "tough boys"—Jumoda and Sam. I told them they had to go to the village to hunt up the father and demand a reply. To my surprise, they brought an answer, but it wasn't what I wanted to hear. I received a verbal message: "I accept whatever you want to do with them."

His answer frustrated me. I gathered the three boys and told them, "Your father's answer is not good enough. He needs to see you; we need his approval, if not his involvement." They frowned, glanced at each other and looked down at their feet. They did not want to deal with him.

My determination to involve the father became a personal challenge. After some more messages back and forth, I contrived to meet with him. We conferred at the edge of the meadow above the Chemchem Springs. It was a quiet private spot where we could talk alone.

Mzee Lenard said, "I am pleased the boys are getting some instruction before the jando. Athumani told me they are learning some important things."

He seemed relieved the boys had other men as teachers. Mzee Lenard looked sideways as he told me, "I know little about my tribe's traditions. What you are doing is good. It is enough."

Despite my pleas, he wouldn't commit to being involved, but I persisted with my requests. He finally agreed to go with the boys to the hospital. Once plans were laid, I stayed in the background. I continued to urge the boys to see their father, though I doubted they made much effort. Before the due date, I sent the boys off with Athumani and Jumoda to Barazani village to meet the doctor and learn what to expect. They came back beaming—the operation was set for a Saturday.

The week before the circumcision, the boys had sessions in our compound. They also went off to the village, intending or pretending to see the father. By the end of the week, the boys acted subdued and distracted. On the night before the cutting, I sent them to the village to remind their father he'd agreed to come on the trip to the doctor.

By nighttime, all three boys looked concerned and unhappy. Gillie said he had a headache. Sam went to bed early. Len felt so cold he slept in the seasonal heat with two blankets in our tiniest guest room, the one I also used as the "quarantine" room. I hoped the boys' moodiness and unease was just from nerves and not malaria.

Saturday morning, on jando day, I found the boys carrying boxes. Handyman Pascal, in his usual uncommunicative fashion, had decided to clear out the kitchen house in advance of whitewashing. He'd conscripted the three boys. I was glad to see the team working together. Having to help clear, clean, and whitewash could help keep their minds off the coming ordeal.

The time approached for departure. Jumoda appeared, ready to transport the victims to the doctor. No father. I told the boys to get ready to go with or without him. Meanwhile, I sent Jumoda off to look for Mzee Lenard. The boys went to bathe, each with a fresh bar of soap. Their short hair was crowned with water droplets as they assembled on our front porch.

I looked at them wistfully and wished I could paint their faces with ash or ochre, as is the tradition of many tribes that circumcise boys. My imaginings evaporated as I looked at these modern lads. They would never paint their faces. Wearing only their new shorts underneath, the boys covered themselves with the new black cloaks I'd bought them. For this event, I'd given Jumoda the traditional black robe he'd made for me to wear. It was a symbol of ancient and modern customs. They were ready.

Jumoda returned without Mzee Lenard. We waited for an additional hour for the father to appear. But finally, I sighed my usual sigh of frustration and disappointment—another goych; another promise unfulfilled. I gave the boys the money to pay the doctor. Jumoda got into the driver's seat of our Land Rover, surprisingly adept in his voluminous cloak. The boys piled in, too.

They were about to set off when their father shuffled in. I welcomed him, grinning in relief. He did not smile back. Off he wobbled to the car and got in. I reckoned he'd been drinking, maybe to get up his courage. The three boys, their dutiful father, and Jumoda, went off to the hospital together. My sigh was deep. I wanted this event to be over.

Time passed slowly. I was anxious and fidgeted. At dusk, I heard the distinctive sound of our car's engine. It rumbled down the road and stopped. Jumoda turned off the lights. It was quiet. Doors opened, and three young men stepped out, looking grim and dark in their black shukas. They greeted me solemnly in response to my "Hongera." Congratulations. They picked up the bowls of meat soup specially made for them. Immediately after eating, they headed for their room.

I turned to Jumoda and asked, "Where is Mzee Lenard?"

"He wanted to be dropped off at Chemchem, to walk back to the village," he responded. "Mzee Lenard came with us but refused to go into the doctor's room with the boys. He sat in the car. I took them in, one by one. Len had to go in twice to be treated by the doctor because of his bleeding."

That worried me. But I was glad to have the boys back, well, almost intact.

All day Sunday, the newly circumcised boys rested by Athumani's house or sat around the kitchen table. I saw little difference in their behavior. They ate happily and listened to their new radio. I watched them to see any signs of trauma. Len seemed fine, and Gillie, too. But Sam said he had problems with the string (why a string?) on his penis and needed to have it retied. I took him back to the doctor, but no one was around. On the way back, Sam insisted he was OK. Len and Gillie supported him, so I didn't make a fuss.

The boys took their time to recover. Athumani and I made special meals for them. We didn't ask them to do any chores until they wanted to. They seemed to enjoy being lazy. We were all looking forward to the end of the healing period marked by their "Popcorn Party."

But on the third day after the cutting, Sam admitted he had swelling "down there." Jumoda took Sam back to the clinic, where the doctor gave him one single shot of penicillin with no plans to provide more. I carried on giving Sam penicillin pills from my stock, following the prescribed schedule from my No Doctor book. Sam got better, resumed his normal pouts, sulks, and frowns. Gillie got himself up and around, assembled some books, and started learning words again. Len took responsibility for some kitchen jobs. The father faded back into whatever village life he had. Life went on.

The boys, who I kept reminding myself were now young adults, seemed proud of their new status. They looked and acted more mature. All three took on their household duties more often without me having to nag them. They thanked us for their allowance money and the gifts we gave them. They more often came to ask me for something they wanted and put things back where they found them.

The celebratory Popcorn Party took place with enthusiasm. David and I tried to close our eyes and ears as the party erupted in the kitchen area. We gave the space entirely to the young men and their guests. Len, Sam, and Gillie and their friends devoured junk food, wriggled and jumped exuberantly to loud music.

David and I withdrew to our porch, feeling relieved and satisfied that we had all survived the modern jando. We had a glass of wine together, listened to the cacophony, then retreated to our bedroom to celebrate life in our way.

CHAPTER 15
MNADA: MANGOLA MARKET DAY

A BUSY MARKET DAY, A LIVESTOCK RAID, AND LESSONS ON SOCIABILITY: 1993

Gourd seller

Our village hosted a monthly outdoor market known as mnada. Primarily a cattle market, herdsmen brought livestock from all over the northern Lake Eyasi region. People and goods also flocked to the market from even further away. Mnada attracted sellers of medicines, booze, clothes, and shoes. Market days were always busy and noisy. They were also full of surprises, demands, and disturbances. Most mnada days followed a predictable pattern, but the one I describe here ended in a twist.

This particular day started with the cry, "Hodi, hodi!" Ho-dee, ho-dee is the *Hello, hello* call when people enter our compound. Visitors already, I thought, as I gathered shopping baskets and made lists. I leaned out the door to see who was calling. Usually, I resented interruptions, but on market days, there was no hope of avoiding them. With David on safari again, I had to deal with all comers. The usual mnada day had taught me to expect a deluge of people and events. My hope for the day was that I could get through it with a reservoir of friendly feeling.

I called "Karibuni!" *Welcome y'all*, the typical response to the hodi-hodi call. Two handsome Datoga men strode into view, carrying spears. They wore their traditional black cloaks decorated with white buttons, fringes, and odd objects like little combs, mirrors, and keys. I didn't recognize them, but today I'd resolved to be sociable, so I came out to greet them.

"Greetings, Mama Simba. Do you remember us?" asked the taller of the two in Swahili. That was a question I dreaded. I had no clue who they were. But it's a good idea to be friendly to men with gleaming spears.

"Of course," I lied, "What can I do for you?"

"Are our pictures ready?" said Tall Datoga. I kept my face blank, trying to think; pictures, what pictures? Luckily Short Datoga said, "You took photos of us last month."

I grimaced as I remembered. Yes, I'd taken photos of these two when they came by dressed up in their market day finery. Alas, the film had been double-exposed; there were no digital cameras back then. How could I explain about film and exposures to these two black-cloaked warriors?

"I'm so sorry! Your pictures didn't come out," I said apologetically. "But do come later in the afternoon, and I'll try again." This tactic only pushed problems further into a busy day. I wished I'd had the courage able to tell them "no" outright, but didn't have the nerve.

Here in outback Mangola, I always felt I must do all I could to secure people's goodwill. We foreigners, I reasoned, needed to be seen as "good guys": helpful, cooperative, and friendly. To fulfill this image was a challenge. Trying to be an extrovert conflicted with my natural introversion. I told myself that even though I didn't welcome photo duty, I was lucky to have two local men comfortable enough with me to ask. My twisted logic didn't ease my regret for taking on the job. But on this day, I'd resolved to go-with-the-flow, put on a smile, and cheer myself into sociability mode.

Rubber tire shoes

I heard water gushing from the outside taps at the kitchen sink and saw Len, Sam, and Gillie washing their cups and plates. They were up early and already had eaten, looking cheerful, eager to go to market. I gave them a mission: their list included two hind legs of goat, two kilos each of oranges and pears, new shirts for themselves, and a set of aluminum cooking pots. I also gave them their monthly bonus, cash to spend at the mnada on whatever they liked. They scampered down the trail out of the compound, keen to join the crowds, and enjoy the festive atmosphere.

Athumani had agreed to stick at Mikwajuni for the day, and I was grateful. He had a stable, calm presence and the ability to deal with most anyone in a gentlemanly way. That meant he could deter unwanted visitors as well as welcome friends. Mangola market day brought people from all over, trying to sell, buy, borrow, or steal things, or to snoop. On market days, we had an open house policy for local people and friends, many of whom came from distant places. So mnada was a day of stress for me.

The Datoga men were just the beginning. Next came a stream of visitors whom I liked, but together they inevitably drained my social reserves.

Stool Man: A grouchy old Isanzu man selling rough-hewn wooden stools. I bought one, so he'd have some money to spend at the market and go away promptly.

Hamisi: A Hadza youth. He came to try to sell me the shirt I'd given him in exchange for his stone smoking pipe. I smiled and shook my head. "Hamisi, no deal.

I'll give you back your pipe, and you can keep the matches and soap I gave you. You can use the soap to wash the shirt and maybe sell it to someone else."

Papaya Man: A withered, likable Somali who grew onions and papayas on a neighboring plot. I bought all four of his papayas.

Precious Stone Man: a shifty-looking Sukuma man offering a dirty bag full of stones. He claimed the rocks were of great value. How was I to know? He also had some old British-made brass coins with holes in them. I bought them for cash with good intentions to make a necklace for a friend (I did, about 25 years later).

Matayo and Mille: Two of my favorite Hadza friends. I hadn't seen them for weeks. They looked great, smiling and healthy. They told me they were back from the other side of the lake. I offered my sympathy for their long hike and gave them tea and cookies. They'd come to say hello instead of selling, and I appreciated their friendship. Matayo told me that on the other side of the lake, there were ever more livestock herders, Maasai as well as Datoga. "There's bound to be trouble between those two tribes one of these days," he said. That was prophetic.

The midday heat and all the activity made me feel like I was being stir-fried. To get out of the wok, I took some fruit and bread to the streamside to eat alone, letting the bird song and shade soothe me. But sounds of voices and laughter from the kitchen area meant I needed to check what was going on. I went to face the crowd. There were three distinct clusters: a group of Hadza, three policemen types, and two tourists.

Tourists: I dealt with the tourist couple first. They'd heard I ran a guesthouse and came to our place to check us out. I disillusioned them. I couldn't get them to reveal who misled them but advised them to camp at the village campsite. Then pointed the way out, glad to see them leave.

Game ranger and police officers: The game guard was a nuisance, often pestering us for money, lifts, or bullets. I usually tried to refuse all his requests. This time it was for a lift. "I cannot take you. You will get a lift at the mnada," I said. We argued a bit, he realized I meant no, and the posse left.

The Hadza family: This was my favorite family: Pandisha, Abeya, and their children Adam and Abande. They lived far away at the north end of Lake Eyasi. On mnada days, they often walked many miles to the market. They brought me mats and baskets as well as amusement and cheer. I gave Abeya her mat money.

Adam, the clown, teased me, saying, "Ah, Mama Simba, you are so cold-hearted. You need to give me money. It was me who carried my mother's mats all the way. Up and down the gullies, I carried the mats. All along the dusty road, I carried the mats." He tried to look wilted and weary. "So far, it is. So far. I am so tired."

I tried to look nonplussed, but couldn't hold back my laughter. They all joined in. Chuckling, all four left with the mat money to buy things at the mnada, leaving me feeling better, too.

Our boys came back and put away the supplies they'd bought. I gave them the job of defenders of the home front, together with Athumani. Now I could take time for my foray to the mnada. I wrapped my drabbest kangas around me, one for a skirt over my shift and another one as a shawl. I took one extra to wear over my hat and hide me as much as possible from sun, dust, and strangers. I slipped out along the fresh-smelling, shady, streamside path, emerging on the open main road.

The mnada site occupied a large, open area with easy access off the main Mangola road. Plenty of room to park trucks and cars, donkeys and carts. In addition to cattle, people brought goats, sheep, donkeys, and chickens. Corrals new and old held the livestock, while salespeople spread their goods over the bare ground. Most used mats, tarps, or tables while others had shaded stands and booths.

Each place sold a specialty such as new rubber tire shoes, used shoes, old clothes, new clothes, traditional medicines, dubious modern ones, cloth, hats, pots, pans, tools, meat skewered over fires, stews, and sweet things. Alcohol was illegal, but secret, well-known spots could be found here and there.

The glaring sun beat down on everyone milling at the site. Swirls of dust scoured the barren ground, covering me with grit. I paused at the empty cattle corrals; empty meant the main auctions were over. Trucks full of meat on the hoof were leaving, the animals packed together so they couldn't move.

I skirted around the edges of the marketplace until I came to the mitumba section. Mitumba is the name for bales and usually means big bales of items cast-off by people in wealthier countries. Each bale contains specific types of things: children's clothes, women's clothes, jackets, shoes, bedding, curtains, or towels

Visitors from abroad were often appalled to learn their donated wares were sold at public markets. David and I tried to explain the wisdom of the practice: you give your old clothes to a charity. They take the best things and sell them in their home country. The items that don't sell are bought from a charity by a trader who sorts and bales them for export. Another trader buys these bales then sells the individual items for a small profit. Local people get to choose what they want for a price they can afford. Critics complain that the mitumba system might discourage local enterprises. But we see that local cloth and t-shirt making businesses, for instance, are flourishing, so for now, the system works, and everyone benefits—recycling at its best.

Woman selling clothes

The mnada seemed especially lively and colorful with more tinsel and glitter than usual. The used-clothes merchants were wearing headbands stuffed with bright bits—feathers, leaves, and scraps of cloth. They called out their wares: "Beautiful trousers today," "Shoes, new shoes, sports shoes," "Hats, best hats, caps, best caps." Covering myself with my kangas and tying my hat on tight, I forged into the melee.

Man roasting meat, "nyama choma"

My quest on this hot, dusty afternoon was to find clothes: a jacket for the old disabled man who made unique baskets for me; pretty dresses for Athumani's girl children; t-shirts for our boys. I bargained for new kangas for Abeya, Athumani's wife, and myself. I waited in the partial shade of a rack of cloth, enduring stares and greetings from strangers while the itinerant tailor hemmed the kangas. The smell of grilling meat drifted by on a wave of hot air; I realized I was hungry. I looked longingly at a man cooking chunks over a fire but couldn't face trying to eat meat with any dignity at the crowded market.

Feeling a surge of weariness wash over me, I wanted desperately to leave. I tucked the hemmed kangas into my basket and walked briskly through the throngs of people. My head down, I bumped into Saidi Kimaka, our former village chairman. He grabbed my hand, greeting me warmly. I summoned a smile and assured him we would be soon coming over to his café in the village. As I turned to go, I felt my smile collapse. I didn't want to see anyone else, even a friend. There wasn't a drop of sociability left in me.

Hiding beneath my hat and scarf, I beat a retreat out of the mnada labyrinth. In my hurry, I tripped on the corner of a vendor's mat and knocked aside his little bottles of medicine. There on his mat were vials full of bright colors: red, green, blue, and yellow. I wondered what was in them. Maybe he had some potion to restore a good mood? I mumbled a greeting and an apology.

Medicine man

He looked up and answered some of my latent questions: "This red bottle has medicine to strengthen the blood, the blue is to ease pain, the green is to lower fever, the yellow gives pep and energy." At least, I think that is what he told me in his low, gravelly voice. I certainly needed what was in the yellow bottle. But I merely apologized and gave a respectful bow. He seemed surprised by the gesture and smiled broadly. I felt a trickle of friendliness seep back into my emotional desert.

On I went, but my hopes for reaching the peace of our homestead evaporated when I spied the two Datoga men at the kitchen waiting for their photographer. I stopped next to a fig tree, actually hid briefly, and crept along another path into our house. Putting my purchases down, I went to search for my camera. I almost wept when I found it wouldn't work. The men took my excuses and apologies with good grace, happy that I'd promised to take their pictures another time. Once again, I'd burdened myself with a future obligation.

I sat down and rested my head in my hands, trying to understand why I didn't dare to say no. It was getting dark. I was so tired I thought I'd collapse on the spot. Athumani had gone home, and the three boys were eating rice and beans, which didn't appeal to me in the least. Instead of eating, I crawled into bed and fell asleep immediately.

I was in one of those deep troughs of immobility when someone pounded on my door. I thrashed my way to consciousness. My first thought was it was an emergency: the boys in the throes of food poisoning, a knifing at the mnada, a bullet shot from the ranger's rifle, an overturned truck, David in an accident. But it was none of these terrible events.

I dressed and went to the porch. Standing there was our alleged friend Jumoda with some other Datoga tribesmen. "Jumoda, can't it wait till tomorrow?" I groaned. "It's late; I was asleep."

"No, it can't wait, it's important. You have to help us," Jumoda demanded. "The Maasai have stolen four groups of cattle. Over 300 are gone!" He was extremely excited and repeatedly gestured in the direction of Oldeani Mountain. "They drove them away towards the rift. You must drive us to Ngorongoro and Karatu. There we can get rangers and police officers. They will help find the thieves and return our cattle."

Ah, hot-blooded youth! I thought. I did not want, desperately did not wish to drive anywhere in the night. I summoned all my resolve and said firmly, "No, I will not go up the Horrid Road at night. Even if we did drive all that way, no one at the

Ngorongoro gate would do anything tonight." Jumoda tried another tack. "Well, you can take us to Endamagha. From there, we can join the others."

"What others?" I asked. Jumoda waved his arms again towards the mountain. He paused, alert. I heard it too, the war cries of youths rushing off to chase the rustlers.

I think my sighs of frustration must haunt Mangola to this day. Most ardently, I did not want to jounce across countless arroyos, canyons, and ditches on a long drive in the dark to chase after rescuers, rustlers, or cattle. I didn't want to be Jumoda's pawn. There were other cars and rescuers in the village, why pick on me? But a no without explanation would mean more badgering. I tried a diversion. Gritting my teeth, I told Jumoda, "David is away with our car. There is only the researchers' car. It is not my car, and I don't like using it. I've no idea if it works or has enough fuel. Is this trip essential? Please think about it."

I hoped the vigilantes at the kitchen would think of a plan not involving me. I went off, pretending to check the researchers' car. I looked at the fuel level and tires and started the motor; alas, it rumbled to life. It was after midnight when I went to sit at the kitchen table to await the decision of the Datoga men. They were milling around, gesturing and arguing with one another. I was so tired, I put my head on my arms and fell into a doze. Jumoda jiggled my shoulder and told me their decision: "Take us to Ngorongoro in the morning."

I was too tired to argue so merely nodded. I went back to bed and tossed and turned with apprehension. I did not want to go, let alone in a car not belonging to me, to a place where I'd have to cope with inevitable drama.

My punishment for lack of social courage was awaiting me with the glow of dawn. Jumoda arrived to ensure I was going. I had a bit of satisfaction in that I was already up, dressed, and in the driver's seat. He got in, and we drove over to the village office at sunup. I waited in the car while Jumoda went into the gloomy build-ing to get news. I put my head on the steering wheel, hoping the little gods of the universe had worked some magic, and I would not have to drive up and down the Horrid Road.

Ah, joy! The village secretary was there with good news.

"The cows have been found and rounded up. They are on their way back." Jumoda looked very smug at the news, saying, "The Maasai must have fled when the Datoga chased after them. Those cowards know we Datoga are strong. We would pursue them relentlessly until we got our cattle back."

I doubted that very much. Cattle rustling was a dangerous game between the Maasai and the Datoga. At least this time, no players were killed or wounded. I was so relieved that I agreed to give the village secretary, Jumoda, and two others a ride to Endamagha for news.

I didn't even have to drive far. After only a stomach bouncing half hour, we met some of the warriors coming back from the rescue. They were elated, crowing about getting the cattle back. With a nod to me, six of them piled into the car bringing in an overpowering smell of woodsmoke, sweat, and road dust. They squeezed together, careful to put their spears, sticks, and clubs on the floor. I was glad to be merely their driver as they jostled one another, talking and laughing about their heroic deeds and the cowardly Maasai. We bumped our way back to our village, where they could sing their praises to one another and the villagers.

After unloading the men, I stopped by Mama Rama's to say hello. She waddled up to me with both hands extended, greeted me warmly, sat me down on her best chair, then disappeared briefly. She returned with a flask of tea and a plate with her doughnut-like mandazi. She asked me if I heard about the cattle rustling.

"I sure did," I said wearily.

She tilted her head, looked at me with concern, and changed the subject. I listened to her rattle on about the price of sugar, cloth, onions, and the bad state of the roads. Chickens pecked at our feet; children ran in and out laughing. Our conversation was simple, just soothing social grooming. I was so grateful. Here was one person who wasn't asking for anything from me, and I felt my reservoir of goodwill starting to fill as she filled my cup with tea.

CHAPTER 16
VILLAGE CAMPSITE SAGA
A FIVE-ACT DRAMA ABOUT A VILLAGE, PEOPLE, WATER, AND LAND: 1984–2003

Chemchem campsite

ACT ONE: CHEMCHEM CAMPSITES–EARLY DAYS

In 1984 when we were newly settled at Mangola Plantation I felt restless. I wanted to visit the Chemchem oasis. I needed to see the bright birds and monkeys in the papyrus swamp and smell freshwater and flowering trees. Having no car, I set out on foot. Wrapping myself in kangas like a Bedouin in the desert, I picked my way over wind and sun-blasted fields with their rattling dry maize stalks.

Halfway across the barren ground, I made a detour to a tree-lined irrigation ditch full of water. Jumping over small channels plugged with wood and mud, I paused to watch a farmer opening a channel into his onion field. Further downstream, a pump started up, stuttering and coughing. I'd learned that a few wealthy farmers had installed pumps and pipelines to bring the water to higher fields. Everyone else relied on gravity flow from the springs.

Only gradually had I begun to understand the complex water system of Mangola. To keep the main irrigation canals open and water flowing to farms demanded cooperation. At a later time, the village council asked me to photograph a work crew. My photo shows some of the many plot holders who worked together to maintain the irrigation system.

Villagers working on irrigation ditch

Continuing along the irrigation ditch, I hurried towards Chemchem Springs and entered the oasis. It looked like a stage set: open grassy spaces with a fringe of papyrus and a background of shady tamarind and acacia trees. I was still on the village side, where I passed through clearings grazed down by livestock. The smells of dung mingled with the scent of water and vegetation. A brisk breeze stroked and refreshed me. I paused by the nearest stream, splashed water onto my dusty face, and gazed around.

Nearby, women chattered as they filled their buckets or bathed at the female section of the springs. They waved; I waved back. I moved onwards, keeping my face averted as I passed the hidden bathing spot for men. Ahead on the path was a large pond the villagers made by piling earth and rocks to dam one of the major Chemchem streams. The biggest irrigation ditch emerged from one side of the dam to continue towards the farm plots.

People surrounded the pond. Women dressed in colorful kangas balanced plastic buckets full of water on their heads; boys rode bicycles with containers strapped behind their seats, and men poured water into leather panniers on the backs of donkeys. Whole families milled around, filling bottles, jars, and plastic buckets. They carried them or loaded them into carts pulled by hand, donkeys, or oxen. The place was busy, noisy, obviously central to village life.

Trying to keep out of sight and in the shade, I hopped on rocks across the shallow streamlets. Along the way, I saw a mysterious concrete foundation and large citrus trees before coming to the edge of a grassy space. I gazed over the meadow, the traditional campsite area near the springs. Now several tents bloomed like grey-green bushes in the clearing. A plume of smoke drifted up from a fire near the dining tent. I smiled at the peaceful scene.

Standing there, appreciating the view and cool breeze, I listened to the swish of the blossoming acacia branches overhead. The hum of insects made me think of bees. Slightly alarmed, I looked up to the flowers, then down. The buzzing came not from bees, but flies. Pretty, iridescent green flies were circling my legs. Then I caught the smell. Shit. My right sandal was in a pile of it!

Gritting my teeth, I stumbled backward into a streamlet. I sat on a rock to wash my shoes, thinking about what I stepped in. I looked at the campsite carefully. Where were the toilet tents? I didn't see any. Was the "poopetrator" a local or a tourist? I didn't see any soiled toilet paper, but then, the person could have stuck it under a rock or used their hand. Ugh.

A boy herded his goats across the clearing and stopped at the camp. The cook chased him away. I was glad the area was still wide open to both residents and herders, not fenced off for the sake of tourists. But did local herders or fishermen "do their business" here? I didn't think so. Most likely, the culprit was a camper.

Disgruntled at the mess in this precious spot, I mused about keeping the Chemchem area clean. The camping area and springs were used by locals as well as tourists. I'd not heard of any rules for bathers, launderers, wood collecting, fires, or where to drive and park vehicles. Such management issues were not high on the list of concerns for our village officials.

The shitty campsite problem bothered me to the point that I became a player in the Chemchem campsite drama. First, I went to our village chairman's house to ask Saidi Kimaka what, if any, policies were in place to keep the springs safe from pollution. His wife told me he was away for several days, but he'd come by when he returned.

Meanwhile, David and I went to Karatu to get supplies and visit our friends Per and Margaret at Gibb's Farm. They were personally familiar with the Chemchem camping area and also sent visitors to camp at the lovely spot. They would know about the history and use of the site. Over tea and cakes, we asked questions.

I described my recent stepping into human excrement. "I'm concerned about the Chemchem Springs and campsites," I told them. "It's such a perfect place to camp and becoming increasingly popular. Has it ever been officially protected?"

Margaret told us, "I don't know about protection. As long as I've gone there, it's been considered a public spot. For us, it was our private escape spot. We'd drive down that horrid rocky track, through thick bush and sisal thickets. We constantly worried about the rhinos that could explode from the bush. And the elephants! They could appear silently out of nowhere."

"Sounds exciting," David said.

"We usually camped at the springs," she said, with a distant look. "Ah, it was a little haven of peace and tranquility."

Per continued, "Oh yes, Chemchem is a wonderful campsite. We've had many good times there. We'd laze around, fish, sleep, and barbecue any meat that hunters brought in. Yes, in those days, there were lots of hunters: British, Germans, Greeks, and South Africans. I never hunted, but by the 1950s, Mangola had become a popular hunting ground."

Per paused to sip his tea. I looked at him and prompted, "Was the village very big then?"

"No, no village then, just a scatter of huts. Most people lived on their little farms. It wasn't until after Tanzanian independence that 'Ujamaa'—Nyerere's villagization project—got underway. Then the people were forced to build houses in a village."

David slipped in a question, "Were there any Europeans living in the area at that time"

"Yes," said Per, "A German named Goldenfahn lived at the Chemchem Springs in the '50s. He loved to go shooting. He grew papayas and hot peppers and harvested wild sisal that he shredded with a particular machine. Maybe you saw the cement platform at the springs?"

"Oh yes," I said, "it's still there, and the big orange tree, too."

Per continued, saying, "People called Goldenfahn 'Gorofan,' and you know, that got changed to Gorofani, the nickname of the village now."

Margaret took up the tale, "Goldenfahn left in the 1960s. Other local people were regular visitors at Chemchem. Most called the place "Kambi ya Joji" after a Greek named George. He and his wife ran a garage in Oldeani and came every weekend to camp at Chemchem. Mama Rama was a young woman then and grew vegetables for them. George brought other settlers and farmers to Mangola to hunt and fish. One of them was Hans Schmeling, who liked the place so much he started Mangola Plantation where you live now. Oh yes, and it was George's wife who planted the calla lilies at the campsite."

"Those calla lilies!" I exclaimed. "I've always wondered why they grew at the springs."

Knowing now who planted the lilies at Chemchem, we made a special trip on the way home to see if they were still there. It pleased me to see the white chalices with yellow candles surviving at the low margins of the springs. They became a symbol of transience over the following years as I watched them dwindle and vanish, just like George and his wife, the wildlife, and most of the European settlers.

Calla lillies

ACT TWO: CAMPSITE CONCERNS

Eventually, our village chairman Saidi came to see us with Joseph, the village secretary. After chatting about onions, roads, and schools, we asked if Chemchem had any official protection.

Saidi told us, "I think there is a law against any building, farming, or cutting trees within 30 meters of the Chemchem Stream. But the law isn't followed. People cut everything to farm or graze livestock along the stream."

Joseph added, "It's good, though, that people don't cut down the big old fig trees. It's because we believe that the spirits of the water intertwine with the tree roots. And pythons live there, the guardians of the springs."

That was a nice bit of local lore, I thought. I turned to Saidi, who said, "Our population is growing too fast. We can't look after everything. We have to trust people will look after the springs because we are all dependent on them."

"What about the campers?" David asked.

"Oh, they're no problem. Tourists come. Tourists go," said Saidi.

"Most only stay a night or two," said Joseph. "They camp at Chemchem because it's free, a nice place, close to the main road. Sometimes they come just for a picnic. Sometimes they camp overnight, and sometimes they invite us over for food. Sometimes they even donate a little to the village. Most are good people."

And sometimes, I thought, campers aren't good people. Even though both saw the value of Chemchem, as village leaders, they didn't seem to see the potential dangers of tourism. As tour leaders ourselves, we could see the attraction of the place. We knew that more tourists would come as the news leaked out to Tanzania's hungry tour industry. How could they resist a beautiful, free camping area with spectacular scenery and colorful, fascinating tribes?

Cultural tourism was already increasing along the usual tourist routes. As the trickle of tourists to Mangola became a flood, the inevitable problems would rise on the tide: vehicle tracks, cutting firewood, clearing brush, uncontrolled campfires, toilets, trash, and theft.

We had witnessed the environmental and social damage caused by unregulated tourism in Tanzania National Parks and unprepared villages. All we could do at the time was to gently raise the issues, which we did over the next four years. By then, we'd moved from the village side of the stream to the wilder side. After the village gave us a lease to build our home downstream from Chemchem, we became more concerned and more directly involved with the village campsites.

The predictable problems piled up, as did the heaps of half-burnt tins, garbage, and toilet paper whipped by the ever-present wind across the meadows, festooning the trees and bushes. We switched from gentle reminders to occasional prodding, inviting our village officers to our place to discuss the campsites.

Two leaders emerged on the Chemchem stage: our successive village chairmen, Saidi Kimaka and Julius Meruss. They understood the problems and tried to make plans for guards, trash pits, and toilets. The village council was the supporting cast, offering solutions that were often contradictory or not solutions at all. For example, one day, we startled a troop of vervet monkeys in an open trash-pit, decorating the campsite with a mess of plastic bottles, cans, fruit rinds, and garbage. We learned that the council had decided the campsites needed trash pits but hadn't thought to cover them. We groaned and kept quiet.

One evening Chairman Julius came by for his favorite drink, "Chai ya mzee," *old man's tea*—that is, a beer. As he drank it, I said, "The trash pits at Chemchem are worrying us. We've seen monkeys, dogs, goats, and even children in the pits. Trash and garbage get thrown about."

David added, "Water is seeping into the holes to mix with the debris. We worry that the polluted water provides mosquitoes with breeding ponds."

Julius thought about this and said, "Maybe we should fill them in. But what do we do about all that trash?"

We agreed to talk with tour operators about the trash problem. Since we knew many safari companies, we encouraged them to take out their trash when they left. The good guys took care of their trash, cleaned up other messy sites, and left trash bags for others to use. Gradually the trash problem diminished. But the issue of the toilets remained.

Responsible companies brought chemical toilets with them; other companies dug a shallow pit over which they placed a tent, and the dodgy ones let their tourists do as they pleased. We suggested to our village leaders that they build proper long-drop toilets. They agreed. We donated money and supplies while they hired builders and workers. Although the toilets got constructed and used, neglect and termites consumed them in the end.

By the mid-1990s, Chemchem campsites received a constant flow of tourists, researchers, and students, competing for space. Tour companies fought over who got to camp where. Everyone realized that the area needed a booking system. With bookings came the idea of fees. Why shouldn't the village profit from the visitors? The income could be used for village projects, hiring camp guards, monitoring, and maintaining the sites.

Our village leaders loved the idea of earning fees from the Chemchem campsites. I found myself in an unwelcome spotlight: the village council asked me to collect the fees. They trusted me, which was flattering, but I accepted with grave misgivings. Once money was changing hands, local people would want to know how much was coming in and where it was going. I bought notebooks, a receipt book, carbon paper, and a lockable cash box. The village leaders appointed guards to monitor camps and collect fees. They turned the cash over to me and got a signed receipt. The village chairman or secretary had to sign for all withdrawals. The village leaders frequently visited me to confer and check the books. This system worked— for a while.

Over the next year or so, money flowing in from the campsites attracted attention from all sorts of people. Locals began to start their own campsites. They argued over land, access, and water. Leaders of nearby villages became jealous of the money going to Gorofani village, and officials began haggling over village boundaries and visitor fees. It was apparent that tourism, in general, needed more control. One way to provide that was to appoint village-approved guides. And so, our friend Jumoda became the contact man for Gorofani village.

ACT THREE: THE TOURISTS FLOW

With an imagined trumpet blast, Jumoda stepped into the spotlight. He performed his role with energy and flair, gathering bookings for the village campsites on his many visits to Arusha. An important task was helping sort out the overlapping campers and use of sites. Jumoda gained skills in handling the safari drivers. He greeted tourist groups at the campsites and took them to Hadza camps and Datoga compounds. All the while, he was improving his English, as well as his singular status as a local guide. We were proud of him.

Jumoda profited as he got more experience and more customers. While he was growing in stature and wealth, I was still acting as the campsite banker and money was pouring into the village coffers. Eventually, I resigned and handed the records over to the village council. As I left that council meeting, I felt profound relief, a significant burden lifted; I'd escaped.

After I stepped aside, David and I tried hard to keep a low profile. Jumoda and the council were doing just fine, we thought. We wanted to distance ourselves physically and socially from the campsite saga. We increased our living wood fence all around our home and put a brush gate on the path leading to Chemchem. Village leaders and Jumoda came to our place from time to time to talk about campsite concerns. Together we developed a brochure in English and Swahili. A bright blue kingfisher bird with a red beak perched on a papyrus stem became a symbol of the Chemchem oasis.

More and more tourists came, so the campsites were heavily used. However, the sites were poorly maintained, and bookings got mixed up. Accounts became muddled. Conflicts arose between the campsite guards, guides, and tourists. Most local people, even officials, didn't dare to defend Chemchem rules. They found it hard to say a definite "No!" to outsiders who washed their clothes or cars at the springs, cut wood, or built fires in inappropriate places.

The income from tourism caused problems, too. Funds helped village projects and boosted local business, but there were adverse effects on the Hadza and Datoga, the two tribes most often visited. The egalitarian Hadza were the most affected because all the tourists wanted to see these "wild" hunters. Visitors then pitied their poverty and gave them money or other goodies. Cash caused conflicts and drunkenness.

The Datoga were also a favorite for cultural visits. The hierarchical social structure of the Datoga buffered them somewhat. Also, unlike the Hadza, they had a ready use for extra cash: they could buy more livestock.

Malachite kingfisher

Jumoda and other local guides became rich from fees and tips from tourists and drivers. Enemies arose, alliances formed. We tried to stay out of it all, but visitors continued to come to our compound, asking us for help with everything from illnesses, cars stuck in mud, flat tires, runaway fires, and identifying birds. It wasn't easy to keep our distance. Like the unwanted trash, campsite problems littered our lives.

A particularly thorny problem arose when some birder guests stayed at our place. They and I were doing a bird count, planning to go in convoy with two cars along the south side of Lake Eyasi. David and a Tanzanian teacher friend were already gone, driving around the north end of the lake. Before setting out on our southern safari, I had lots of chores to do, so contrived a morning walk for my visitors while I got organized.

I told my guests, "We've seen seven different species of kingfishers along this river. Lots of other birds, too. We'll be interested in finding out what you see." As I led them to our streamside gate, I told them firmly, "Go along this path towards the Chemchem Springs, but stop before you get to the campsites. Please, completely avoid that area." My two guests looked at me as though I was warning them to avoid a plague zone.

Alas, the birders strayed too near the campsites, lured close by a pygmy kingfisher. Two campers came over to see what they were doing. They were newlyweds, also interested in birds. The bird experts naively invited them back to Mikwajuni to meet Mama Simba, their knowledgeable resident.

I was not pleased to have two visitors from the campsite as an added diversion but offered them some of my homemade mkwajuice to drink. After the toasts to their marriage, the conversation turned to their trip. "We went to see the Hadza," they told us. I nodded absently, my thoughts on preparations for the bird expedition. "Our driver charged us $150 for a visit! We were shocked."

"Hmm," I said, raising my eyebrows at the amount charged but kept quiet. The bride asked, "Wasn't that a lot for such a short visit?" I tried to deflect the inquiry by saying, "Well, I don't know what they charge these days." I looked at the bird experts and tried to change the subject back to birds.

"Hey, Liz, which kingfishers did you see?"

Liz chirped with pride, "Five species: malachite, woodland, striped, greyheaded, and pied..."

But the honeymooners interrupted to grumble about their guide. They tried to get me to tell them local customs, rules, and payments. I didn't want to be put on the spot and tried to close the conversation. "I honestly don't know prices for visits. The guides are making the rules. Personally, I think the Hadza should get food, equipment, useful things, or contributions to the health fund at the local clinics, rather than cash."

I was relieved to see the couple leave. Regrettably, the newlyweds returned to their camp and told their driver all Mama Simba had said and more. His anger flamed; the stage was set for a fight. The driver-guide drove into our compound. He parked in front of our cars as we were loading the last of the gear. Striding into the kitchen area, he yelled at Athumani.

"How dare Mama Simba talk to my guests!" I emerged from the kitchen house, glanced around, and noticed Jumoda just walking in from the open streamside gate. The angry driver swiveled, focused on me, and continued his rant.

"You have no right to talk to my clients. You have no right to talk to campers at Chemchem. You think you know everything. You've interfered with my work. I will see the authorities, Mama Simba. I will cause you trouble, for sure."

I stood staring as he shouted at me; it was so unusual. Most Tanzanians are very polite, avoiding confrontations. We were grateful when Jumoda interceded and persuaded the driver to leave. But he scowled at me, and the angry man shouted, "This isn't the end!"

ACT FOUR: RETALIATION, RETREAT, AND INTRIGUE

The confrontation with the driver ended act four of the saga but the repercussions flowed into the next act. After my bird safari, David returned, too, having been stuck in the lakeshore mud for two nights and a day. He was not in the best of moods when I told him the story of the hotheaded driver. Typically slow to anger, David was tired of problems seeping from the Chemchem campsites. He was so upset about the behavior of the driver that he wrote to the manager of the tour company. We never received a reply.

We retreated even more from campsite affairs. We continued to give occasional talks to select groups, either at the campsites or our place, and also lead tours outside Mangola, a business that dragged us back into the local Chemchem drama. We had friends in Karatu and Arusha, who owned safari companies. One, in particular, specialized in walking safaris. They asked me to help plan a walking safari route, from Ngorongoro down the Wild West side of Oldeani Mountain to Lake Eyasi's shore.

The tour leader for this new safari would be their best Tanzanian mountain guide. They also planned to involve Maasai, Datoga, and Hadza guides as well. I was to accompany the group as a local expert and educator. The hike would end with three nights at the Chemchem village campsite. Our friends were excited about this safari. I was, too; it was the kind of adventure I loved.

Unfortunately, the safari company deliberately left Jumoda out of the plans. We were surprised because we had introduced him to the company, and he had worked on some of their safaris. "Jumoda," they told us, "has become unreliable. He is too busy with his tours. He often fails to honor arrangements. He quarrels with staff, with other guides, and is generally arrogant and bossy." They essentially told Jumoda to get lost.

We only learned of this when we tried to help make bookings for the village campsites on behalf of the company. The village office refused the booking. We knew what happened: Jumoda persuaded the village secretary to write a nasty letter to the company. The letter spelled out that the company was not to deal with Mama Simba; Jumoda was the only official village guide. The radio operator read the letter to us. He said, laughing, "Amazing how Jumoda is now such a powerful scoundrel. He seems to be able to manipulate your village leaders!"

We didn't laugh. We felt stung and tried to figure out why Jumoda was so vindictive. When had I ever interfered with his tour guiding? Possibly Jumoda thought he was not asked to be a guide on the walking safari because we'd objected. Also, there was that nasty driver-guide, a friend of Jumoda's, who got fired.

Our primary concern, though, was how Jumoda had managed to get our village secretary to write such a hostile letter. Jumoda himself also delivered another message, directly to us. The letter stated that Mama Simba and David Bygott were trying to destroy Jumoda's honest tourist business.

Julius

Wow! When had our buddy and protégé become such a monster? Letters flew to and fro like angry bees. Meetings were arranged and mostly unattended. People seemed rather apathetic about the issue, except for Jumoda and us. The tour company was caught in the crossfire.

We continued to puzzle over why Jumoda was acting like a vengeful villain instead of a local hero. Illumination came from one of our trusted village elders, Adam Chorah. We called him "the man of mystery" because he seemed to know what was going on among all levels of the village. He maneuvered adroitly, a behind-the-scenes man with power. Chorah sent word he was coming to see us and duly arrived at our place like a secret agent, under cover of darkness. I spread out dried fruits, crackers, nuts, and cups for tea. After polite conversation, he shared his views about the tourism drama.

"I think we might have a little conspiracy going here," he told us. "I am sure Jumoda is in league with some village officials, most particularly the Diwani." The Diwani was like a mayor. Our advisor continued, saying, "The executive officer is also involved." Another bureaucrat.

Chorah made us understand that these men intended to take over the village campsite as a profit-making enterprise. They also wanted to get hold of our place.

David and I reached the obvious conclusion as he said it out loud, "But you are in the way. They are using Jumoda as a tool to get you out."

This new dimension of village intrigue amazed us. Jumoda was one thing, but a pack of village sharks circling us was far more worrisome. It seemed that the "sharks" were also circling the present village chairman, trying to oust him and gain more power. If so, they could quickly get control of the land.

"What do you advise us to do?"

"Carry on as normal. Most of us value your presence here, and we trust the situation will get resolved, Inshallah, God willing."

Giving the situation over to God or Fate didn't ease our anxiety. We kept our heads down and watched the politicians strut and posture, trying to see the humor in this show. Chairman Julius was fired, then reinstated as chairman; the toothy sharks swam in circles then retreated. Like an octopus, Jumoda kept his tentacles on the campsite bookings, guiding visitors, controlling the safari drivers and manipulating village officials. Nothing happened to erase the effects of the nasty letters.

During this tense period, the Hadza came on stage. They became activists. They wanted to be tour guides themselves. They also wanted control over visiting fees and prices for their artifacts. Assembling at our table in our kitchen area, they complained about the tour guides' arrogance and what they thought of as theft. They spent time learning English. They devised strategies, determined to thwart Jumoda in particular. They demanded to meet with village leaders. We stayed away from all these meetings, merely offering a conference table at our baraza. Nothing seemed to get resolved.

Near the time of the walking safari, the safari company responded to the letter telling them they could only deal with Jumoda. They wrote to the village saying that Jumoda had severely let them down in the past. "We will not work with him again under any circumstances. We do not want to see him when we come to the village campsite. We have appointed guides, including Mama Simba. If she isn't allowed to be involved, we will go somewhere else."

This strong supportive letter buoyed our spirits. But we were dismayed by the copy of the message our wobbly village secretary sent back. "Welcome to the Gorofani Village campsite. Your Coordinator will be Jumoda."

We suspected Jumoda had written the letter himself.

To avoid war at the village campsite, we wasted a whole day trying to find an alternative place. We returned to find our village chairman Julius sitting at the table in our compound. He looked jaunty as we offered him his accustomed old man's tea, a beer. Taking a deep drink, and with an expressionless face, he handed me a sheet of paper. Keeping my hand steady, I read it, expecting yet another sting. Instead, it was a draft of the letter we had been begging for.

I let out a whoop of surprise! The letter said accusations against Mama Simba were false; there was no problem with her being with groups at the village campsite. The walking safari group did not have to have Jumoda as a guide.

I typed copies for each of us; he signed them. We reread the letter with deep relief and laughed heartily. Our reinstated village chairman-maybe-friend accepted another beer, smiled, and exited stage right. But our light hearts were soon weighed down again. In the late afternoon, our mystery man arrived, wrapped in his usual cloak of intrigue. "I am sadly convinced our chairman cannot distance himself from what we are calling the Jumoda faction," he told us. "Julius is his relative, but his clan is not as big or as powerful as Jumoda's. We must take care of Jumoda and his cronies." We wondered what that meant.

ACT FIVE: THE SHOWDOWN

I am away with the walking safari group at the start of the campsite drama's last act. The camp crew came to Mangola to set up the tents at the Chemchem campsite. They later told me that Jumoda had stormed in, furious, saying, "I am the appointed campsite coordinator. You have no permission to camp here!"

The camp staff stared him down. "We do have permission from the village chairman himself."

Jumoda frowned and tried a different tack. "All sites are already booked. You have to find another camp." He sneered, "Go to Mama Simba's place."

The camp manager was puzzled and came to Mikwajuni to enlist David's help. David drove over to the village to look for the chairman and get some support, but without luck. However, he did find Jumoda.

"He was riding his bike towards me on the main street," David told me later, laughing. "He parked his bike, blocking the road in front of the Land Rover and stormed up to my window. I said, 'Hello, what's up?' He started ranting and raving about how I had no right to be stealing his business. He was jumping up and down, almost foaming at the mouth. All the time, I was itching to pop the clutch and drive over the silly bugger's bicycle. But for sure, I'd have ended up paying for a new one."

Instead of just ignoring Jumoda, David and the camp crew decided to clear a camp spot on our plot just in case. In the evening, some village leaders arrived at the Chemchem campsite and apologized for the confusion about camping. While they tried to mollify the tired camp manager, Jumoda appeared. Like an old-time villain, he strutted back onstage full of anger and shouted at everyone. "Mzee David and Mama Simba are interfering with my business. I am the only appointed guide here. Only I can tell people where they can camp!"

Everyone stood astonished and embarrassed. Then one of the village leaders spoke firmly. "No, we do not agree that you are the only guide. These visitors don't want you. We are the village council. These visitors are our guests at our village campsite." Amazingly, Jumoda turned and stomped off, muttering threats.

I arrived late afternoon the next day with the tour group. Relief flooded me like a refreshing shower after the exhausting four-day trek. The tents set under the tall fever trees at the village campsite were a welcome sight. Windblown and footsore hikers settled gratefully into their tents. Jumoda did not appear. It was quiet.

David came to reassure me all was well. But it wasn't. A new sub-plot appeared in the form of Musa, a Hadza friend from a nearby camp. He beckoned us into the shade of a fig tree. "You need to know about Jumoda," he said. "He came to our camp. He's angry with you. He thinks you will bring your guests to our camp tomorrow. He wants to ruin your visit. He told us to tell you only he can bring visitors to the camp. He even offered us a bribe."

We shook our heads, incredulous at how hard Jumoda was working to sabotage the trip. At this point in the drama, we finally could see the humor in it all. Musa shook his head and added, "We all laughed when Jumoda left. He can't push us around." He picked up his bow and arrows and said with a big smile, "See you and your group tomorrow at camp!" He left, chuckling.

Well, of course, we had to visit his camp! Our Hadza friends came to collect us from the village campsite. The tourists thoroughly enjoyed visiting the Hadza, shooting arrows, inspecting huts, and taking photos. The Hadza at the camp were glad to have the guests and happily received the gifts we brought. The walking group had such a good time they not only paid the campsite fees, but they also contributed to the village development fund. Everyone was pleased, except, of course, Jumoda. We all knew he was probably seething.

After the showdown, Jumoda tried a few more tricks to maintain his control. Eventually, he switched tactics and got land further downstream from Chemchem. His campsite and guide business prospered. The sharks circling our plot swam away, for a while. The campsites overflowed with tourists.

Tourism became better managed as more leaders took on active roles. Jumoda started to share the spotlight and made gestures of reconciliation to us. Life went on. Onions continued to grow; water continued to flow. End Village Campsite Saga.

Boat at Chemchem Stream

CHAPTER 17
MAINTENANCE MAN

WHAT IT TOOK TO SUSTAIN OUR RURAL TANZANIAN LIFESTYLE: 1990

David driving the Horrid Road to Karatu

Our life in the bush was made possible, even comfortable, by David. He was often absent from home, away on supply trips, selling our books and cards, taking people on safari, or all of these tasks at once. And he David coped with home chores, too. In Mangola, we were 115 miles from the nearest urban health care, piped water supply, sewage, electricity, and phone system. Everyone lived entirely off the grid. We had to supply all utilities in our remote bush home. David was the maintenance man.

Our past lives had prepared both of us for this adventure. Before we first met, I had worked four summers as part of a gold-dredging crew in a remote California canyon. We hauled all our supplies in and out via a steep trail and lived without any amenities. David had also experienced life in a wild place as part of the team of chimp researchers at Gombe National Park in Tanzania, a long boat trip away from a small town.

After meeting and marrying in England, we spent four years studying lions at the Serengeti Research Institute. There, our "Lion House" looked a little like a suburban Texas home, but most utilities were unreliable or absent. Our Serengeti base was nearly 200 miles from any source of supplies. We collected rainwater in buckets, lit kerosene lamps, and learned to buy fuel, dry goods like rice, and fresh foods like bananas, in bulk. Coping with such demanding environments gave us a sense of what was necessary, how to fix it, and what we could live without.

By the time we settled at Mikwajuni to build our round houses, we were adept at making use of what was at hand. Also, we'd developed some skill in searching out what we needed or wanted. David enjoyed figuring and inventing ways to make our lives easier.

Take water, for example. That precious liquid was our most accessible utility because we purposely built our home near a permanent spring and river. If all else failed, we could haul buckets from the river to boil or filter for drinking. But David did better. He created a plumbing system through ingenuity, networking, and travel.

In the late 1980s, there was little hardware available. David went to what some called the sweaty armpit of Tanzania—the crowded city of Dar es Salaam—to oversee the printing of one of our books and took that opportunity to scout for supplies. He told me the story when he returned.

He'd stayed with Birdman (our nickname for a friend) and told him about needing a water system at our place. "He pointed me to a lot of galvanized steel pipe left over from a water project. He also knew someone in Arusha who was getting one of those big German-built MAN trucks from Dar to use for his camping safaris. We put the pipes in the MAN, and I rode back to Arusha in the truck with my 20-foot lengths of pipe."

From that beginning, David managed to ferry a few pipes each time he came back from Arusha. Persevering, he found a pump and a header tank, thus establishing a functioning water system. A significant addition to the basic water system was a storage tank. David found a place in Arusha town that fabricated sturdy galvanized tanks. He ordered one that held a thousand liters and brought it back on the Land Rover's roof-rack. We were building our main house at the time and had included a reinforced concrete ceiling to support the tank. I watched in awe as David erected wooden ramps and pulled wire ropes over a sturdy acacia branch. With that in place, he was able to winch the heavy tank from the car to the roof space.

Now, we needed to pump water uphill to fill the tank so it could flow downhill into our kitchen, toilets, baths, showers, and hoses. To do that, David walled in one of our little groundwater springs. I'd tested the water to confirm it was free of dangerous pathogens. We wanted to keep it that way, covering the artesian well with screening to deter monkeys, baboons, birds, and any other wildlife.

We bought an electric pump but found we couldn't generate enough power for it reliably to push the water up to the tank. Instead of buying a bigger, more expensive pump, we got an old-fashioned hand pump. That only required manpower. We had plenty. Our young lads didn't seem to mind the work and it kept them fit. They would pump in pairs, listening to the radio or gabbing, spelling each other at the task. We sometimes took our turns, too; enjoying the exercise and cool peace by the stream.

Len and Pascal pumping

David was a water wizard, and the next task he tackled with aplomb was sanitation. We had to deal with a lot of people's excreta. That meant long drops and septic tanks. Digging toilets was relatively easy. We could build little huts, thatch them, hide them, and put water for washing right in or outside the hut. Septic systems required more work and planning. During this phase, we looked for outside help. A missionary architect who built schools gave us a blueprint for concrete septic tanks. Our builder, Kefti, was skeptical, but he and sidekick Pius followed the instructions faithfully. "Tunajenga vyumba ya mavi," laughed Pius. *We're building houses for shit.* The two they made under David's keen eye turned out very well.

Keeping us and our environment clean tended to involve helpful people from other places. For example, when our friends at Gibb's Farm in Karatu were remodeling some rooms at the lodge, they gave us a large, old, cast-iron tub for our private outdoor bathroom. And our friends in Dar es Salaam who helped with the water pipes miraculously found us an insulated hot-water tank. They sent it to us with some hapless visitor in a pick-up truck.

Solar collectors for heating water were becoming available but were beyond our budget. However, just as I used *Where There Is No Doctor* to heal bodies, David had a survival manual for building called *The Wilderness Guardian* by Tim Corfield. The book aimed to help unskilled wildlife managers setting up remote ranger posts and park HQs; it was a gold mine of practical ideas.

David followed the book's instructions to make a solar water heater from roofing metal. He put together a zigzag assembly of metal pipes and painted them matt black. Next, he enclosed the tubes in a wooden box with a glass top, then hooked it and the insulated tank into our plumbing system. The unit worked wonderfully for many years.

Sometimes we'd notice the water wasn't so hot, so we'd go out and hack away the jungle that shaded the collector. Once David had to replace a broken glass pane that the monkeys had broken while bouncing and screaming threats at the black mamba hiding under the panel. Yes, maintenance brought unexpected trials.

Cooking outdoors with wood was a challenge. Both David and I struggled to deal with the demand. We scavenged dead wood wherever we could, usually in unpopulated areas where we wouldn't compete with neighbors. We tried various forms of solar cookers but having to monitor them in the midday heat didn't suit our work schedules. Putting big pots in grass- and leaf-lined pits for slow cooking was hotter and heavier work than Athumani and I wanted to do. I tried out the metal cookstoves with special ceramic linings but scrapped them as being too small. Also, we hated using charcoal.

Finally, we found a simple metal stove that we stationed at our outdoor kitchen, complete with stovepipe rising away from any tree or thatched rooftop. It burned short pieces of wood efficiently. Our night guard gleefully hacked the branches we brought home into manageable sections. For rainy days or quick cooking, we had an indoor propane gas ring.

Refrigeration wasn't a necessity. Most of what we could buy in a market or pluck from our vegetable garden could last several days unrefrigerated, including eggs and the fruits from the trees I planted. We bought fish and meat fresh and ate them the same day. Our home team usually devoured all the leftovers, so we didn't need a fridge for that. During my gold mining days, we had used a simple kind of cool box wrapped in hessian that we kept wet. Similarly, at Mangola, we often put bottles or bowls in a shallow basin of water and covered them with wet cloths. With the constant wind, the rudimentary evaporative cooler worked well.

Simple life and basic amenities weren't enough to challenge David's endless ingenuity. He felt we needed a better supply of electricity. Most people in the village lived fine without it. At night, they used kerosene lamps. Tanzanian-made batteries powered their torches and radios. We learned from them how to get extra use from our batteries by putting them in the sun for a day or two. That kept them going a few more days, but we needed more power than that. We wanted good lights for reading and working at night, and we needed to charge batteries and eventually run pumps, power tools, and a communications radio for our business.

We'd lived with diesel generators at Mangola Plantation, Gibb's Farm, and Flycatcher Lodge. They were noisy, smelly, and unpleasant to maintain. We were willing to sacrifice the power of a generator for the silence of solar energy. While living at the plantation, we'd started using solar panels to run our lights. At the time, we couldn't buy panels in Tanzania, so when visitors asked what they could bring from abroad, we told them to put one or two laminated photovoltaic panels in a suitcase. David put the panels on a roof, bought a charge controller, a deep-cycle truck battery, some 12-volt fluorescent lamps, and—presto—our houses and night-life lit up!

As we built Mikwajuni, David added to our solar array. The direct current from our batteries didn't travel very far along cables, requiring that each of our scattered houses have its own independent power supply. Panels became available in Kenya, and from time to time, we bought some and smuggled them back to Tanzania. Tanzanian customs officials were always on the lookout for duti-able products, and solar panels were not exempt. Besides the bribe money, there was always the hassle of declaring anything of value when crossing the border.

David performed an adroit maneuver on a tourist guiding trip to Kenya. After saying goodbye to the group in Nairobi, he bought a splendid glazed PV panel. It was in a metal frame about as big as a large coffee table. There was no way he could bring the thing back on the bus un-noticed by customs.

His solution was ingenious. He told me the details at home after handing me a large parcel. I unwrapped the gift to discover a garish painting of a stereotyped Maasai warrior with a spear. Smiling, he asked, "Do you like it?"

"Well, my dearest, it's certainly one of a kind! How much?"

"75 watts!"

"75, what?"

David broke into a grin as he ran a paint-scraper across the painting to reveal a broad swath of blue silicon photovoltaic crystals beneath.

He explained, "I spent a few shillings on yellow, red, and black acrylic paint and a brush." In his hotel room, he painted on the glass front of the panel this ghastly "airport art" painting of a Maasai warrior, complete with acacia tree against a lurid sunset. For the four-hour ride to Arusha, he wrapped the pseudo-painting in cardboard to protect as well as hide it. "At the border post, we all got off the bus to declare our contraband," he said. "The customs official pointed at my parcel.

'What is that?'

'It's a picture.' I said, 'A painting.'

'Open it,' he demanded.'"

David unwrapped the hideous object and gabbled in his best dumb-tourist imitation that he'd seen it in a gallery in Nairobi, loved the Maasai and colors, and ended with "Just look at that sunset!" David chuckled as he recounted his performance.

I asked him, "What then? What did the officer do?"

"Oh, he just rolled his eyes at the stupidity and bad taste of the white tribe. Luckily a woman with lots of luggage was pushing me on."

The customs man let him go and turned his attention to the woman's bulging bags.

And so, our electrical system grew, panel by panel. For the times when we needed more power than the sun could provide, David used a hefty inverter. When connected to our Land Rover's battery, it delivered 220 volts A.C. There always seemed to be a carpentry project going on that needed an electric planer. Power tools speeded up the work. I used the inverter for my electric sewing machine, too. We soon learned to keep the Land Rover engine running while draining power from the inverter. Push-starting a heavy diesel vehicle with a flat battery is no fun at all.

All this happened before the era of cell phones, computers, and the internet. For years we had no communication with the outside world except the proverbial jungle drums and cleft sticks. Finally, though, we got a two-way radio. Our friend Pat, the priest-doctor-pilot who ran the Flying Medical Service, obtained the set for us. He came to install it, even climbing our trees to suspend the aerial: a hundred-foot span of two parallel wires. We were surreptitious about having a radio at first because, in Tanzania's paranoid past, some shadowy "authorities" had accused us of espionage. Also, we didn't want to become a communication center for the whole village, though we would use it in emergencies. Eventually, and at great expense, we added bush email to the radio system.

The most vital tool for living in Mangola was a vehicle. And car maintenance was nearly a full-time job for David. He'd bought a plucky little Renault 4 while living and teaching in Dar es Salaam. Though valiant, the Roho, or "Spirit of the Bush," could not cope with the Horrid Road to Mangola. We graduated to an old Land Rover, then finally treated ourselves to a new one. Our Land Rover carried most of our building materials: cement bags, sand, gravel, rebar, beams, planks, glass, and fixtures. It brought home food supplies and boxes of our books or cards we'd printed in town, and it delivered them to the gift shops where we sold them. It transported visitors and neighbors and took sick people to hospital or dead people to their final rest. It carried all the firewood we collected for cooking. Oh, and it also allowed us to explore the very rugged country of the Eyasi Basin, as well as much further afield.

None of this could happen if the car didn't run. Our village had no mechanic we trusted, so David was stuck with all the repairs and cares. I overheard a visitor ask David whether he had training as a mechanic.

With a voice full of resignation, he said, "Fortunately, or not, I learned some basic skills in my penniless student years. I fixed my unreliable motorcycles with inadequate tools under bridges in the English rain." I nodded, both of us remembering our courtship years with that motorcycle breaking down and needing repairs in wet, cold places.

David raised his wrench in salute to the Land Rover and told our visitor, "In our Serengeti years, especially after the mechanics left the research institute, I learnt a lot about keeping these tough old beasts alive in the bush."

To keep our Land Rovers healthy, David had got our builder Kefti to dig a car-pit. It was just outside what we called David's den or hovel. David usually parked the car over the pit so he could quickly check it before a trip.

Kamili, Bashiri, and Yasini working on Blue Car

He told our visitor, "Down in that pit, I can fix tires, brakes, wheel bearings, driveshafts, suspension, and basic electrics. For anything more complicated, we sometimes ask our favorite mechanic, Kamili, to come out here from Arusha."

I added, "We hope that some of our lads will learn about mechanics. It's a valuable job out here. David has managed to get our handy man Pascal trained, and he is already a useful assistant."

We planned every supply run meticulously. For days beforehand, we wrote letters to be mailed; compiled lists of bulk food, drink, and hardware to buy; and accumulated broken things for mending in town. We radioed or emailed friends we hoped to visit, and of course, serviced the car, or at least kicked its tires. We never went anywhere without a high-lift jack, and almost as essential were two spare tires, and a 50-pound steel box full of tools and critical spares. In the wet season or for backcountry driving, we added a shovel, a hoe, a pair of mud-ladders, a bow saw, an ax, and a hand-winch.

For town trips, David made a set of stackable plywood boxes that fit together in the rear of the car. We took sacks and baskets for market shopping, plus fuel cans and propane cylinders to fill. A Land Rover is one of the world's easiest cars to break into, so David installed safety features. For town trips, the rear compartment of our station wagon was isolated from the front by a stout wire screen. He also put plywood shutters inside all the rear windows, a heavy padlock on the back door, and locknuts on all the wheels.

David often preferred to do the town runs alone. He'd wend his way across bumps, over potholes, and corrugations, composing silly songs. He not only endured the terrible roads and breakdowns, but managed to reward himself in little ways, such as having a tasty meal in a dive-y place or visiting friends in their luxurious abodes.

I'd often ask him to tell me more about these long lone trips. Usually, his answer was a brief, "I drive, I do the chores, I come home." Luckily, our visitors could extract more details.

"Well, first comes preparation, checking, loading. Then I hit the Horrid Road. You've seen it—a two-hour slog through rocks and gullies, mud, or dust to Karatu. Before Karatu developed into a town, I had to do the serious shopping in Arusha."

Having come through Arusha and Karatu, our visitors knew those roads and how demanding they could be.

"From Karatu down into the Rift Valley past Mto wa Mbu, the 'mosquito village' is another two hours of corrugated dirt road until the turn at Makuyuni. There I meet tarmac for the last 50 miles into Arusha. But often, especially in the 1980s, it was paved with deep potholes. Crazy drivers would lurch all over the road dodging the holes."

He rocked back and forth, illustrating how he, too, had to coax the car around the holes, inevitably crashing into one.

"Almost always," he said, "there is a car upside-down, a truck, tractor or bus lying on its side—the perils of that road. Other hazards are closer to town, mainly the traffic cops who might stop me, looking for faults and bribes, but usually finding neither." Then comes the mayhem of Arusha traffic: bullying trucks, jostling mini-buses with touts clinging to their sides. The challenge is to carefully weave among the ragged men straining at handcarts loaded with cement or grain, the Maasai on their wobbly bicycles, and the kanga-clad women swaying to and fro with baskets or banana stems on their heads.

I interrupt to offer our visitor and David a glass of precious wine. David pauses to open the bottle and pour. He continues his tale. "In town, I sometimes stay with friends, but often I choose a small hotel. My favorite is one with tasty Ethiopian food and a guarded car park. I have a celebratory dinner and a deep sleep. That gets me ready for the next day, when I start the round of chores."

He pauses, sips his wine, and looks earnestly at our visitor. "Do you really want to hear all this drivel about what I do in town?"

Pete, Abdul, Nancy, Bess, or Ralph, whoever is there, says "Sure, carry on."

David does. "Well, I stumble into the breakfast room, grab some instant coffee, eat an *omeleti* with *tosti*, then head to the bank to draw out cash. Nowhere that I go accepts credit cards or checks. Then from bank to government offices where inevitably I need to apply for some license or permit. I dread being told 'come back tomorrow' or 'come next week.' I won't bribe them, so I often sit down with a thick book and make it clear that I am prepared to outwait them.

"After the officials, I go to our smirking accountant who tells me, 'Sign here and here and leave me an arm and a leg to pay this quarter's tax.' Lunch is a welcome break; then, it's over to Sameer Auto Parts for shock absorbers or brake linings. I don't mind that because of the smart women behind the counter who always under-stand what I want and where to find it."

David grins at me. I raise an eyebrow and gesture for him to get on with his story.

"Well, next is my main chore: I have to go around all the shops that buy and retail our Kibuyu Partners books. All the while, the touts on the street corners are still selling pirated copies of our stuff. Besides having to chase debtors, I see the printer. By evening as shops close, I collapse."

The next day, before leaving town David usually goes to Ikhwan Traders for groceries. I smile thinking of that small Muslim store smelling of spices and detergent. David describes his visit, "I fill boxes with cooking oil, soap, candles, toilet paper, paper towels, plastic cups, a bucket, and batteries. Across the road is the den under the sports stadium where I can buy boxed South African wine."

He pauses, looks into his wine glass. While I refill it, he says, "By then, I've had a near-lethal dose of Arusha. My last stop in town is to fill the car and jerry cans with diesel and to pump up the back tire that has a slow leak. On the way back I stop at the mosquito village below the Manyara rift wall. That's our favorite place to buy fruits and vegetables. The market women usually welcome me with cries of "Karibu, Mzee Simba! Leo vitunguu?" *Welcome, Mr. Lion, Today, onions?* They are teasing me, so I say, 'No thanks, I live in Mangola, the onion capital of Tanzania!'"

Fruit and vegetables at Mto wa Mbu market

I, and our audience, laugh then listen as David describes buying fat avocados, green tomatoes just flushing pink, wrinkled passion fruits, thorny green soursops, and mangos. He continues with, "My favorite task is getting stems of small sweet bananas just starting to ripen and citrus fruit. Then I have to distribute all these things in the back of the Land Rover, while fighting off the mob trying to sell me t-shirts and necklaces."

A side conversation disrupts the flow while we talk about the products available on this route, and the variety of different tribes there in Mto wa Mbu. Like Mangola, it is one of the most ethnically mixed and diverse places in Africa.

David continues his tale with a description of the next to last stint before home. He sighs and lifts his hands, saying, "Up I go, following the steep rift road with its giant baobabs and panorama of Lake Manyara. On the plateau above, I drive through rolling hills with little farms and eucalyptus groves. I reach Karatu. Here I go directly to the open marketplace to buy maize, red beans, wheat, and potatoes. Plump Jane greets me. She's a short, round woman with a cheerful smile and huge...er...watermelons!

"My last stop is the Tanganyika Farmer's Association, where I top up my fuel tanks. I buy some heavy-duty sisal twine, empty sacks, and a wheelbarrow. That has to go on the roof rack, tied with my new rope. Across the dirt road is the post office with three weeks' worth of mail.

"Now it's a push to get home before dark. Back at the car stands a hopeful family. They look vaguely familiar—Mangola people."

I can easily imagine the scene. We learned early on about the impropriety of refusing lifts. It is customary to give rides to people from one's own village whether you know them or not. Besides, we reckoned that extra ballast always helps on the rocky road, and maybe they'll help push if needed.

David describes the final part of the journey, "The husband sits in front with me, gazing ahead while his wife pushes a heavy sack across the rear seat. She lifts her four-year-old daughter into the car and slides in with a big sigh. I check that I have a gallon jug of water handy—you never know. Off we go.

"About five miles out, the little girl vomits all over the floor. I ask them to step outside while I sluice down the metal floor with most of the water. Then I notice that the tire with the slow leak is almost flat. I pull out my jack and wheel-wrench, chock the wheels with rocks, and get to work. In five minutes, I'm done. I wash off the dust with the last cupful of water."

David squints as he tells us how he descends the long slopes of Oldeani mountain with the sun in his eyes. He drives in and out of the gullies, through the charcoal village, over the last ridge, then, at last, arrives at Gorofani village. His passengers get out at Mama Rama's. David doesn't stop for her usual offering of tea and doughnuts. He tells us, "I wave and carry on, turning left at the baobab, honking the horn as I approach home. Athumani and the boys are there in the dusk, ready to unload everything. I'm home at last."

David looks at me with a smile saying, "Yep, and you are there to grab me and hug me. You always seem surprised that I made it back alive. And I'm always glad that I did!"

David in car-pit

CHAPTER 18
PARENTING
FAMILY, BEDBUGS, LEN AND THE HUT: 1990-2003

Mama Lenard and girls

In 1990, David and I left Mangola for England. Our main aim was to buy a new Land Rover and make the arrangements to ship it to Tanzania. There were also family members to see and other duties, like overeating and reacquainting ourselves with telephones and superhighways.

We traded one culture shock for another when we returned to Mikwajuni, trailing our usual clouds of dust. Athumani greeted us with the announcement, "The boys' mother has come."

I blinked, stunned into silence. The mother appearing in Mangola was a situation I had imagined and dreaded. The father had been hard enough to deal with; now, here was the mother. Whatever would I do and say to her?

"I've let her have the room in the staff house," Athumani added a bit nervously. I was relieved he had arranged something, so just murmured my thanks. I looked at David. His face said that he would be there for support, but it was my show. While he unloaded the car, I put on my mental armor, clutched my courage, and went to greet The Mother.

Finally, she'd come, I thought, as I walked over to Athumani's compound. Here she is, the mother who had brought her three sons to live with their drunken father after he was released from prison. That was over six years ago. I tried to compose my face into a welcoming smile. But the long journey abroad then home made me weary. It was not my best time to be sociable. I was nervous too, worried about how we would communicate, whether we would understand one another.

Several females sat on the wide porch of the staff house. Athumani's wife perched on her usual stool, smiling and talking to a jolly neighbor woman I knew. I looked at the rest of the women and girls. A stranger stood up, a short, round, older woman wearing a colorful baggy dress with a kanga tied over it. She nodded at me. So, this was Mama. I nodded back. Mama introduced the others: her youngest daughter of around 12, her grown-up daughter in her twenties, and her big daughter's little daughter of about four years.

"Hamjambo," said I. "Karibuni Mikwajuni." *Welcome all, to the place of the tamarind trees.* I introduced myself by my local name, Mama Simba, and asked the mother her name. She tilted her head as though she had to think, then gave the name: Mama Lenard.

I doubted she was called Mama Lenard at home. A woman is usually named after her first-born. Lenard was not her oldest child. I smiled, understanding her emphasis on being the mother of Lenard and shook Mama Lenard's plump, moist hand. Next came a hand to each of the daughters, but the granddaughter pulled away and quickly hid behind her mother.

"Do join us at our baraza for a meal," I said. "It will be good to see you and the boys together." I offered this more as an announcement than an invitation. Back at the kitchen, I helped unload the car, then jumped in the river to cool and calm myself. I thought about the implications of this visit as I paddled upstream to float in a pool hidden from view by walls of papyrus. My mind whirled with questions: What would I do with these guests? How long were they going to stay? What did she want?

The fluffy fronds at the tops of the papyrus stems bowed and murmured their answers—go with the flow they told me—lighten up, worrywart. I floated back downstream, reminding myself, que sera, sera, whatever will be will be.

Back at the baraza, my support system, Athumani, had left for the day. I was the chef now. I started preparing food: the rice, beans, and the fresh vegetables we had brought home. The three boys came back from school, and I sent them to collect their family members from the upper compound.

David and I both felt uncomfortable, waiting for our guests to arrive. Mama waddled in, clothed in multicolored kangas, her entourage in various polyester outfits that looked prickly and hot. They sat. Len and I served the food.

Mama Lenard took a plate and commented in Swahili, "You have a nice place here. I heard my boys are living with you. You are taking good care of them."

I smiled, relieved that the reports she'd got were positive. I noted she'd used the possessive "my boys." She continued, "Such a long journey to come to see my boys. We rode a bus from Arusha to Karatu, then had to beg for lifts to Gorofani. When we arrived, we were so tired." She looked around at our kitchen area and smiled, repeating her comment, "Very nice here, yes."

"So, where do you live in Arusha?" I asked.

"We are near Njiro," said the big daughter, "my husband works at the Sengo garage there."

"That's great," said David. "We know the owner; he's a friend." The mutual knowledge seemed a tiny thread to link us. The girls giggled and ate while we tried to keep the conversation going. Gradually the tension eased, and we were quietly content with the situation for the moment. Abruptly, Mama pushed her plate away.

"The boys should come to Arusha. They can stay with us. Let them come for a visit."

Her comment sounded odd to me. Was she asking for our permission to let them come? She was their mother; she could take them with her now. Did she want them just for a visit? Len must have sensed the nuances too, because he said, "We like living here. We still have school, but we will come to visit you soon."

Mama nodded and pushed herself up from the bench. Like an elephant matriarch, she marched back up the path to her room, followed by Big Daughter, Little

Daughter, and Big Daughter's Little Daughter, then Sam and Gillie. Len stood to follow.

"Len, please stay a moment," I said, and he sat down again.

"Tell me more about your mother. When did she get here?" I asked.

"They arrived four days ago."

"Do you want to go to visit your family in town?"

"Yes," he said, compressing his lips, looking sideways, clutching his plate. What were the emotions prompting these gestures?

"Would you like to move to Arusha to live with your mother?"

Len looked at his plate; he looked at David, who was leaving the table, getting back to the unpacking and sorting. When Len finally glanced at me, I tried to read his face. He looked anxious, unsure, glancing sideways, away from my gaze. I waited.

"I want to finish school here," he said, a response not clarifying anything.

"We'll talk later," I said. "For now, I expect all three of you to look after your mother."

They did, taking mom and sisters over to the village in the evening. We went to bed before they returned, so I didn't have a chance to ask Mama Lenard any of the intimate or detailed questions swirling in my head.

In the morning, Mama said they were leaving for Arusha. Over a quick breakfast, we found out exactly where they lived in town. We agreed we could write in care of the garage where the son-in-law worked. With farewells all around, Big Len, Sam, and Gillie escorted Mama, Big Daughter, Little Daughter, and Big Daughter's Little Daughter off to the village.

We arranged to take the boys with us on our next shopping trip to Arusha. We were relieved to find Mama Lenard in residence when we arrived to drop off the boys. They stayed for a couple of days while we shopped and did town chores. When we collected them to go back with us, I looked at them keenly. They clambered into the car, seeming eager to get out of town.

Len told us, "We helped our mother, and we walked to shops too. It's not like Mangola. You can buy anything in Arusha." There was a pause.

The voice from the back was Sam's: "If you have money."

They'd used all the gift money we'd given them. I was glad to learn they'd spent it on clothes and the jaunty caps they were wearing, not frivolous things. Later, over a meal at Mikwajuni, they told us more about their time in Arusha: learning their way about, shopping, and helping their mother in her house. Their most vivid recollection was a story told they heard. It was about a man who was stabbed by robbers. He was left for dead on the floor while the thieves stole the mattress from his bed.

Gillie said, "Arusha is a dangerous place." Len and Sam nodded vigorously in agreement.

I said, "Mangola can sometimes be dangerous too. Gorofani village isn't nearly as busy or fun as Arusha town. Would you all prefer to live in Arusha with your mother or stay here in Mangola?"

"I want to stay here," Len said in an uncertain tone. Sam glanced at Len, looked at the ground, raised his face with its usual frown, and nodded. What did that mean? Sam was always hard to read.

Gillie pursed his lips while gazing at each of his older brothers. He lifted his head, looked me in the eye, and said, "I want to go live with mother in Arusha."

I sighed. I wanted to hug the boys, make them feel wanted, not talk. But I felt distanced, standing outside the corral of their inner brotherhood. Hugs were an awkward part of their repertoire.

There wasn't any doubt we had a deep unspoken affection for one another. But we showed our feelings with respect and concern, not hugs. I sighed and turned my thoughts to the practicalities of exporting Gillie to his mother in town.

After the school term ended, I made preparations to take Gillie with me to Karatu. We would spend the night at Gibb's Farm. Early in the morning I'd put Gillie on the bus to Arusha. We had a quiet night. I was up by 5:30 ready to have breakfast and a talk with Gillie. I went to find him and was surprised to find his room was empty. A gardener told me Gillie had left, on foot, towards town. I was upset and set off in the car, picking him up along the road.

We descended to town in silence, me trying to invent a question that wouldn't intimidate him. We waited in the car for the bus to appear as I tried gently to get Gillie to tell me why he'd left without breakfast or seeing me. He told me he didn't want to bother me so early, an unsatisfactory answer. Breathing deeply to calm myself, I went to buy some mandazi at a nearby stand. We munched in silence until the bus came. I caught the bus driver as he got off and paid for Gillie's ticket.

Gillie stood by the car, looking haggard, shuffling his feet in the roadside dirt. Hoping to cheer him up, I retrieved the gifts I'd assembled, handing him a bag with a new shirt, cap, comb, soap, notebooks, and pens. He took the bag then just stood, looking at his sad feet.

I took his hand and put an envelope in it. "Here is some money for you. Use some of it in town but do keep some for the bus just in case you want to come back." He nodded. The roar of the bus engine revving up drowned any more exchange of words. Passengers climbed on board. Gillie and I shared a quick hug. "Safari njema,"

I said. *Have a good trip*. Gillie and the dirty vehicle chugged off, trailing a black tail of fumes.

Gillie was back within a week. We all welcomed him, but he just stood there with his little bundle and a hangdog expression, every bit a loser. I made him a peanut butter and honey sandwich. He gobbled the bread as if starved for days. Silence extended like a sagging wet sheet between us. Finally, Gillie raised his face, fished out a piece of paper, and handed it to me. It was a letter from Mama Lenard.

I unfolded it carefully, looking at the neat, schoolgirl writing, probably written by Big Sister. In essence, the Swahili message said, "Oh, woe is me. I am alone and poor. I cannot provide for this son. Gilbert is better to stay with you."

Gillie was very depressed; so was I. To be rejected twice by his mother had to hurt. I told Gillie to take his things up to the boys' room, wondering how he would absorb this personal defeat. He went head down, dragging his feet.

We carried on with life as usual. Gillie resumed school in Gorofani. He seldom seemed truly happy, avoided responsibilities, and "lost" items too often. We had to trust matters would resolve themselves over time.

Months passed. The three boys continued to live with us and go to the village school. We supplemented their education by taking them with us to town, on safaris to national parks, and other places. We let worries subside. Daily activities eclipsed worry. We had to get the boys off to school, teach them English and math. We went to the village school to watch their soccer games; urged them to do their homework and chores, to be polite, honest, and clean. These were the things most parents try to teach their children—lessons of life.

Sometimes the lessons made me laugh.

One day, Athumani came to me with his regretful Jeeves expression that often heralded unpleasant news.

"Mama Simba, did the boys tell you about the bedbugs?"

"Oh no, bedbugs! No, they didn't."

"Len only told me this morning. I think the bugs came with the driver who stayed in the boys' room one night, more than a week ago," Athumani revealed.

"How terrible! If true, the bugs have had time to multiply for days!"

Athumani and I went to check the boys' room, next to Athumani's quarters in the staff house. I pulled back the covers on the boy's beds. To my disgust, I found egg cases and bugs. Even so, it was fascinating to see the little beasts. I took some bugs to examine under the microscope. Neither Athumani nor I had ever seen a bedbug close up and were intrigued by their flat, round shape.

Bedbug

We discussed what to do. It wasn't the boys' fault that the bugs were in their room. Even so, I was annoyed they hadn't told me or done anything about them. Typical boys, I thought, they'd lived with the creepy crawlies for nearly two weeks without a word. Typical me, I thought, I hadn't noticed they were scratching bites.

When Len, Sam, and Gillie came home, I put on a frown as I confronted them, trying to hide my amusement. "Didn't you notice you had bedbugs? Why didn't you tell Athumani or me? Haven't you washed your bedding in two weeks?"

They answered with vague excuses, blaming each other, and the visiting driver. I rolled my eyes. "Follow me!" I growled. We marched over to their room. "Well, guys, we have to clear everything out. We are at war with the bedbugs, and you are the warriors!"

We carried out the bunk beds, board by board, then the mattresses and bedding, the cupboards, and mats. Sam and Gillie dunked, soaped, and rinsed. While they worked, Len and I sprayed and scrutinized the room. It occurred to me that bedbugs can crawl around, so we went to look over the adjacent rooms of Athumani's family. In the gloom, we peered into every crack and cranny, examining everything with a strong flashlight. We were relieved to find no more bugs or eggs.

We teased the boys about the bedbugs now and then when they scratched themselves. They learned to laugh a little. We hoped the bedbug event taught the boys about dealing with problems as they arise, not letting them settle in to breed.

We did what we could to instill such lessons, but it wasn't easy. Both David and I had to go away often. Athumani and the others in our compound took responsibility for many lessons. The boys seemed happy with the arrangement, but we wondered what they wanted to do next.

The boys had grown into teenagers. They didn't seem to think much about what to do after finishing primary school. Their futures came into urgent focus when Big Sister paid us a surprise visit. She and her husband arrived midmorning with a dozen village kids escorting them into our compound. Big Sister and Husband were weary and travel stained. I welcomed them. Athumani served them tea, bananas, and fresh bread, giving me time to round up the boys. It was a Saturday, so the three had built a papyrus raft and were fishing in the river. It took me a while to reel them in.

They seemed pleased to see Big Sister. I left them to talk together while Athumani and I prepared lunch. Over the meal, David and I tried to elicit the reason for their visit. We were taken aback by Big Sister's announcement: "We've come to take the boys with us to live in Dar es Salaam." I looked at the three boys. "Do all of you want to move to Dar?" They nodded. Well, that solved the problem of deciding their futures. Off they'd go.

Sis and husband wanted to take Gillie first. They'd decided the other two boys could come later. They left us out of the decision-making process. Gillie went with Big Sister the next day.

Some days later our headteacher came to us. "Mama Simba, why did you allow Gilbert to leave school without my permission? He will have trouble getting into another school without me signing his workbook."

I had no idea about such a requirement. Big Sister didn't check in with the headteacher, leaving me with an ordeal that lasted months. We wrote letters that got no replies, made phone calls that went nowhere. All our efforts to contact Sister and Husband resulted in frustration. These were the days before the internet.

Mzee Lenard

Communication between the coast and Mangola was like signaling a satellite with a flashlight. The headteacher of our local school pestered us with paperwork. We ended up financing his trips to the regional office. Finally, we got the right permissions for the boys to switch schools. It was November before we finalized plans to send Len and Sam away.

There was still a significant hurdle before the boys could leave, namely their father, Mzee Lenard. Custom demanded that his sons get his approval. I needed to see him in person. I thought of an inducement. I sent Athumani to offer Mzee Lenard a job doing thatching for us; he was the local expert thatcher. If he came, we'd have chances to talk. But Mzee Lenard refused the job.

I asked Athumani if he could explain to me why the man didn't take the job or just come over. Athumani sat down on the kitchen bench and sighed. I could almost hear him thinking he must explain very clearly. Mama Simba needed to understand the situation.

"Mzee Leonard is by far the best thatcher. But he won't come to help you here at Mikwajuni." He paused, giving me a chance to solve this riddle, but it only left me more puzzled.

"He won't come because he feels he would have to do the job for free. He feels indebted to you for raising his boys. But he can't afford to work for free. And he would be embarrassed to work here in front of the boys."

Well, I was glad Mzee appreciated the years we'd fostered the boys. But I needed his presence, not his gratitude. It was a busy time, and I was dealing with many different things, so we hired another thatcher.

However, I was adamant that Len and Sam had to see their father before leaving. I told them, "You both have to go to see Mzee in the village. He needs to know you are going to Dar es Salaam and when you are leaving."

I trusted they'd see their father, but days passed without their telling me anything. Several days before we were due to leave, Len and Sam admitted they hadn't yet talked with their father. This time I made a demand. "You *must* talk to your father. You cannot leave without doing this."

On the day before we were to leave, we were making the final preparations. Bags were packed, the car checked out, seats allotted to passengers, lists made, boxes of our books and things to sell, empty boxes for the supplies to bring back. I'd bought new backpacks and duffle bags for Len and Sam. They had packed their things. We planned to drop them at their mother's in Arusha and give them funds to go on to Dar.

At our main meal mid-afternoon, I asked Big Len in Swahili, "How did it go with your father?" Len's dark brown cheeks could not blush, but I knew by the long pause he was embarrassed. He looked down at the tabletop and pushed his fork to and fro. "We haven't seen Mzee," he told his plate.

My patience evaporated. "Len, I want you to go find Sam. Then the two of you walk over to the village to see your father. Tell him you are going to Dar tomorrow. Tell him goodbye."

Len got up from the bench and looked at me. We stared at each other. He frowned and said, "I don't want to go to Dar." I was so shocked, I just blinked. He looked close to tears, so humble and vulnerable that I felt close to tears, too.

"Why don't you want to go?" I asked gently.

"I want to stay in Mangola," he mumbled.

"Len, do you want to stay here with us?"

"Ndiyo, mama," he replied, looking at me directly and mustered a sentence in English. "Yes, I do want to stay here."

While Len went to look for Sam, I thought about what he'd said. I needed other reasonable minds, so went to find David and Athumani for an immediate parents' conference. We discussed why Len would change his mind at the last minute and what we should do about it. "Maybe it is time for the boys to choose their fates," David said.

Both Athumani and I agreed but were more concerned about Mzee Lenard. He needed to be involved in the fates of his boys. When Len finally returned with sour-faced Sam, we three elders looked at them: they looked back, resigned to whatever scorpions were going to ride on their backs as they tried to cross this river in their lives.

"Go to the village," I said. "Find Mzee Lenard. Tell him we plan to leave for Arusha tomorrow. You both asked to go to Dar to live with your sister. Now Len is changing his mind. You have to see your father before we do anything. Go *now*!"

They went but returned with the verdict: "Baba amekataa." *Father has refused.*

"Refused?" I grumbled, wondering if I could bear any more of this ambiguity. Athumani quickly asked the right question. "Len, did your father refuse to come here or refuse to let you and Sam go to Dar es Salaam?"

Len replied, "He says he cannot agree to us going to Dar. Mzee thought Mama Simba was taking us to a new school. He told us he would have agreed to that."

Sam added another detail. "Baba thinks they can't support us in Dar. He doesn't know what they want to do with us. He doesn't want us to live there."

This news, on the eve of our departure, ignited my flashpoint. "Well, boys, you had better work this out with your Baba!" I fumed, tired of all the turmoil. In a moment of anger, I added a threat I didn't know I could carry out: "If you two can't resolve this issue, you will have to leave us and go live with your father in the village. You need to be absolutely clear about what you want to do."

They came back with the news. Mzee Lenard agreed to see us the next day. Although I was stressed about having to discuss the boys' futures at the very last minute, I was also relieved their father was responding.

Father arrived in the morning. After greetings, Len and Sam nervously escaped to the shamba, suddenly remembering chores they needed to do. Mzee Lenard sat at the kitchen table looking much older and more shriveled than when I'd last seen him during the hassles about the boys' circumcisions. He waved away the offered tea and biscuits but did not avoid my anxious gaze.

"I refuse to let the boys go to Dar. I am angry Gillie left here with that sister. I did not give him my approval. The other two boys will not go. I do not trust that sister or her husband."

We sat and digested this in the ensuing silence.

"Maybe the boys should come to stay with you?" I offered.

Mzee stared at me. He nodded. "Yes, I will keep Lenard and Samwel with me. When you come back from safari, we will decide what to do."

We were relieved to have a temporary solution, a limbo for the boys that would give them time with their father. David sent Pascal to retrieve Len and Sam from the shamba. They came reluctantly, obediently collected their new luggage, told us goodbye, and followed their father along the river path back to the village. We watched them go, wondering if they felt rejected or relieved to leave Mikwajuni, happy or fearful of living with their father. It was all very disconcerting. We left for town and waited for further developments.

Len and the letter

Soon after we returned, Big Len came with a nicely written letter. I smiled as I read it, a sad smile bringing tears. He begged our forgiveness for any wrongs done us and asked to be allowed to come back. He wanted to live at Mikwajuni, to help with the work in our compound and on the shamba. As I read the letter, I felt the hand and heart of the father behind the words, even though Len had written and signed it.

"Len, thank you for your letter," I said, wiping tears away. "We will think about it. For now, help yourself to some food while I talk to David and Athumani." He sat at the kitchen table, looking a bit strained. I decided I would welcome Len back. But I wasn't clear on what terms. Len had to do something to show his sincerity about returning. David and Athumani humored me by reading Len's letter.

"Yes," said Athumani, "it is a good letter."

"Very polite and contrite," agreed David.

"So, now what?" I asked them.

Both men offered ideas but no clear suggestions. At last, David handed back the weighty task. "It's really up to you."

I went to sit on the dock by the river and pondered the options. I liked Len; I wanted him back. But he had to earn the chance. He'd need a new rank or position. But it might be better for him to go to Arusha. Or live with his father. Or maybe get a job in the village. Finally, a worthy idea poked up from under the debris of discarded scenarios. I ran my scheme by my advisory panel. They agreed it was an excellent solution.

By the time I got back to Len at the kitchen area, he'd washed all the dishes and was stacking firewood neatly by the outdoor stove. I tried to look neutral, which probably looked grim to Len. I beckoned him to sit on the bench with me. "Len, we're happy you want to stay," I said in careful Swahili. "But you will have to pass a final examination to show us you are ready to work and live here. I want you to prove you have learned some things while living with us." I paused and looked at him. He met my gaze and nodded, his shoulders hunched, worried. I let him sit through a long pause before speaking.

"Here is your test: You will plan and build a small house over on the shamba. We want you to build a house with two rooms and an outside toilet. We will pay for the building materials. You have to specify everything you'll need, draw a plan, put on the measurements, and calculate the expenses."

I paused to give Len some time to absorb the many aspects of his test. "Once we approve your plans and list of materials, we will hire someone to help you build. Meanwhile, we'll continue to provide you with a room, meals and give you basic pay. When you are finished building, you can stay in your house all by yourself or with a friend. You can continue to do other work for us. Now, go back to Mzee

Lenard and tell him what we have decided. If he agrees, come back and move into your old room." Len moved back later in the afternoon. His father had agreed to the test and conditions.

About a week later, Sam arrived with a letter begging forgiveness and asking to come back, too. Although the message was almost precisely the same as the one Len brought, it didn't have the same impact. Sam brought it with his usual sour expression, as though someone had twisted his arm.

We thought it over and decided we'd had enough traumas trying to cope with the father, the mother, the sister, the school. The boys were easy to live with, but not the indecision and worry. Len staying with us was enough; Sam could remain with his father in the village. And he did, for a while. After finishing primary school, he started his onion farm, but some years later, he died in a knife fight. Gillie visited us once a couple of years later, in the dark, leaving with some of David's power tools. We never saw him again.

Mzee Lenard and Len's shamba house

Although two of "our boys" moved away, Len lived with us for some years. He completed his project. He submitted his house plans, and we approved them with a few modifications. He worked hard preparing the foundation, cut and shaped the poles. He got everything ready to build, including the thatch for the roof. After the inspection, I told Len I'd hired a helper who had building skills and could teach Len. He'd be on the plot to start in the morning.

Several days later, on a bright day when the wind whipped the papyrus fronds and made them sound as though they were chuckling with secrets, I went down to the river. I could hear voices over on the shamba; I knew who was talking over there. The boat rocked as I stepped in and took up the paddle, gliding through the papyrus tunnel to the opposite side. Unseen, I approached our garden plot. The mystery helper hadn't been easy to hire for the job. Either his sense of the ridiculous or sense of responsibility persuaded him. Yes, it was Len's father, Mzee Lenard.

I could see Mzee Lenard and Big Len putting palm thatch on the roof of the well-built hut. I was delighted with the structure, and more so, the sight of the father and son, working together.

CHAPTER 19

DEATH DAYS
TREES, BLOOD, DEATH, AND BURIALS: 1990S

Ali and the boat

The Village Crier banged vigorously on a metal pot. *Clank, clonk, bong, clank.* The sound found its way through the papyrus screen that shielded us from the farms on the other side of the Chemchem Stream. He shouted news I couldn't understand. I hoped someone would come and interpret for me. I didn't wait long. Ali, the manager of our vegetable garden, paddled over to our side. He rammed the boat into the little dock David had built. I was there watering the baby trees that I wanted to plant. Ali got out and stood over me as I washed my dirty hands in the water.

"Well, Mama Simba," he said, "we can't plant those trees today."

I stood up, frowning. Today was planting day. I'd packed baby trees in boxes to transport across the river. Laboriously I'd carried them in batches from my tree nursery up the slope to stack them on the dock.

"Why not?"

"Mama Girardi died. Now there are three days with no work," said Ali raising his eyebrows and giving a little shrug.

I had no idea who Mama Girardi was. But her death meant that my tree-planting project might die, too. I'd spent years trying to get the villagers to agree. The plan was that we would all cooperate in replanting native trees on the village side of the Chemchem Stream.

We would be complying with an old law, probably colonial British, stating that there should be no farming or clearance of vegetation within 30 meters of the river. But farmers had wiped out most native plants alongside the stream on the village side, leaving ugly, weedy, and muddy bare ground.

Obeying the law wasn't the reason why I wanted to plant trees. Streamside vegetation—trees, bushes, and grasses—had value beyond their appearance. Vegetation along Chemchem Stream stopped erosion and nourished the soil; allowed people to fish, graze stock, collect firewood, building poles, and thatching grass. Trees along riversides also provided shade and places to hang beehives.

A shining exception to the barren streamside was our shamba. Mama Rama still had the lease on the parcel but allowed me to use it in exchange for another plot the village gave us. It was a mutually satisfactory exchange.

From our wild side of the river, we could take the punt across and a little way downstream. Gliding through an inlet lined with tall papyrus, I could hop out on the bank. Upslope, a giant old fig tree with outstretched leafy arms stood in welcome. A path led through bushes to our vegetable garden. Mama Rama had kept the streamside vegetation protected, and I followed her tradition.

To increase the vegetation all along the stream was our plan. The village council had agreed. We would start at the edge of our plot and plant right up to the source of the springs. I hoped the project would be a contribution to the beauty and long-term sustainability of our village. I had an ally in Adam Chorah, one of the powerful men in Gorofani. He also believed that restoring the vegetation was a good thing. As a religious leader and village council member, people listened to him. Through him, I had a more effective voice.

We'd campaigned with the village leaders to get people to stop cutting and cultivating along the Chemchem Stream. The leaders agreed, but nothing happened after the collective pronouncement. Almost two years after that brave decision, and many meetings, our village chairman, Julius, finally called together men to dig holes along the village side of the stream. The good news had arrived several days earlier. Julius wrote, "Men will come to dig holes and help with the planting on Tuesday next."

It was rainy season; the soil was ready. The baby trees were ready. too, already outgrowing their little pots. I had shovels, buckets, and other tools laid out. All was set for Tuesday. Then Mama Girardi died. The Three Death Days set in. No workers. No planting.

I told Ali, "Let me think about this change in our plans. Meanwhile, please finish watering all these pots. They might have to wait out the Death Days." I headed towards our kitchen area. I wanted to talk to Athumani, my social advisor, and ask him about the custom of death days.

He looked unusually grim as he intercepted me on the path from the riverbank. I knew immediately that some problem awaited my attention.

"What now?" I asked.

"I'm sorry, Mama Simba, but an old man has come from the far side of the village. He won't tell me why he came. He says it is a private matter and will only tell you. He seems very tense."

I was never pleased to see a stranger who wouldn't state what he wanted but heaved a sigh and went to meet the man. The emaciated man sitting hunched at the kitchen table. He returned my greeting, mumbled his name, and extended his limp, withered hand. It was cold and felt like leather, almost corpse-like.

The man was thin and wrinkled, dressed in ragged, soiled clothes. His hair was matted, and his arms looked as though dusted with powder. I concluded he was malnourished, old, and tired.

I asked Athumani to bring tea and slices of bread with honey. Sitting down on the bench opposite the man, I tried to learn what he wanted. He looked longingly at the plate of food but didn't touch it. I gestured to him to eat. He shook his head.

"Can I help you?" I asked in Swahili. "Tell me why you have come."

"There is a relative, very ill at my house," he said.

Oh no, I thought. I cannot give this stranger anything; it's too big of a risk. I was all too aware of the dangers, so immediately launched into what was by then my standard speech.

"I cannot provide you or your sick relative with medicine. The government forbids anyone but authorized medical people to give medicine. I am not authorized. I am not a doctor. Perhaps you can take your relative to the clinic in town?"

The old man just sat there.

I asked him, "Other than medicine, what can I do for you?"

He looked at me with sad eyes and stared quietly at the ground. "I need money to buy medicine."

I looked at him and sighed. I could not give all passers-by money for their sick relatives. My silence seemed to prompt him to speak.

"I have heard you help people for blood."

I was dumbfounded. I had never given anyone blood. I had no blood plasma, nor did I know how to get any in Mangola. I wondered if his statement had something to do with the reputation of some of our visiting researchers. They had come to take blood samples. They had a great deal of trouble, having to get special permits, visit multiple offices, and persuade bureaucrats. Blood was a sticky subject.

There were many local superstitions about blood, even a vampire-like belief in some areas that because white people were so pale, they needed to suck African blood. When I could, I asked people what they knew of witchcraft and beliefs about blood in particular. What I learned was disquieting.

A dear friend, a Catholic priest, told us, "Most Tanzanians have deep-seated beliefs about how blood and dead people affect the living. They have fears about all kinds of evil spirits. Many have taboos about the blood of menstruating women and a general fear of blood transfusions or bloodletting.

"Scratch a converted Christian here in Tanzania, and you'll find fear and super-stition," our priest friend told us. He pointed out the obvious: "I celebrate commu-nion with a wafer and wine, symbolizing flesh and blood of Christ. What could be more vampire-like or cannibalistic than that image? And to back it up, my religion has many mysterious rituals, plus a long history of infighting, inquisitions, torture, and bloody warfare! It's no wonder local people keep their fear and superstitions just under the surface. And the witchdoctors or shamans don't help."

It was clear to me that shamans or traditional healers, dubbed "witchdoctors" by British colonizers, still practiced in most villages. Some of them sacrificed animals ritually, and there were rumors of the use of human body parts, too. Mostly they dealt with illnesses thought to be caused by evil persons or spirits. A shaman might be hired by families to dispel evil, pains, hurts, and curses. We knew personally of such cases.

These "healers" and beliefs could be helpful, and they could be deadly. The local press in the Arusha region reported stories about children stolen or bought, then cut up for sale to people who believed the body parts would make them healthy or wealthy. Supposedly, the witchdoctors often drained their victims' bodies of blood. Such tales were so horrible that I dismissed a lot of them. But then we read in the newspaper and heard on the radio about albinos persecuted for sacrifice; pieces of their bodies hacked off and sold for their supposed magical qualities.

There were scary published reports by eyewitnesses of men in the Sukuma tribe near Lake Victoria, not far from Mangola, who killed old ladies because they believed they were witches. Witches were easy to recognize, they said, because of their red eyes. Thus, if you didn't like someone, and she cooked on a smoky wood fire inside her hut, you could easily finger her as a witch. Sorcery and the occult seemed to be especially strong in the rural areas around the fishing and mining regions at Lake Victoria.

Take my blood...

Obviously, there was an enormous reservoir of fear and superstition beneath the thin crust of modern education.

Now here was this man holding out his bony arm to me. Why? Did he think I had special powers? I stared at him; he looked so sad. I looked over at Athumani for help. He seemed as puzzled as I and took a few steps back towards the sink. Spooky.

The old man looked at me for a long time with his sad, dark eyes. He pointed to his arm. He said softly, "Take my blood; I have come to sell my blood to you."

I sat still, completely horrified. Wherever did he get the idea that I'd buy his blood? What could I say? With an effort to look deep into the man's sunken eyes, I said, "No, I do not buy blood. But I will give you a note to the clinic doctor who can help you." In my message, I asked the doctor to tend to the old man. I gave the doctor permission to dole out money in a discreet way, taking it from the special fund we'd set up to help people who couldn't pay.

The blood event troubled me profoundly. The combination of the Death Days impasse to tree planting with the horrifying request to sell blood made me pause. I tried to think through what our neighbors thought and did about deaths. What did I know about those local customs?

I knew that if someone died at home, there were rites and rituals. If someone died far away, the family had to get the body home. Transport had become harder as people became more mobile. Workers nowadays often lived far from their birthplace, and it was a considerable expense to get bodies back to home villages. Also, many people died in hospitals, of AIDS, malaria, and other diseases. No one wanted to handle a corpse that they thought might infect them. They hoped the hospitals would deal with it all. But most Tanzanians still felt that they had to take the body home. After all, who but the family would be motivated to deal with the burial arrangements?

Undertakers were rare or non-existent. In Nairobi, Kenya, there was a conspicuous street corner where black cars perched like sleek vultures, waiting to haul dead bodies somewhere. It was called "Corpse Corner."

We didn't have such a thing in Tanzania—yet. If someone without a car wanted to take a body home, they had to negotiate with the men who drove little buses or taxis or private vehicles. Those drivers didn't like the job, but they knew they could get a lot of money taking a body home for burial. Funeral rites were also costly, always involving food, the women having to deal with getting supplies, and cooking. Funerals surely added to a family's financial burdens, in addition to the loss of whatever income the dead person had contributed.

I wondered what it might cost a local family to buy a coffin. People who died in Mangola were typically just wrapped in a cloth and buried somewhere close, a simple "green" return to earth. That thought reminded me of the elaborate,

expensive burial process in my home country with purchases of burial sites, preparation of the corpse, embalming or cremation, planting people in concrete bunkers,
building monuments, as well as memorial services.

Dealing with dead bodies was familiar to every culture. The return of bodies
"home" was not just a Tanzanian imperative. I thought of all the dead soldiers
during wartime having to be flown home. I concluded that dealing carefully with
dead bodies was fundamental human nature. It probably had been so for thousands
of years. There were signs of respectful burials by our Neanderthal relatives and
even earlier ancestors.

Other animals seemed to recognize death, too: chimps and elephants touched,
groomed, and stayed with the bodies of their dead companions—I want to call
them their loved ones. For highly social creatures like humans, caring for dead
bodies was a part of life. Grieving and letting go of a dead loved one usually required
there be a body for focus.

I wondered if the three-day mourning period was also a norm or just a local
custom. I could see its value in earlier days when people lived in smaller, tighter
communities. For a whole village to take a "death break" may have been useful in
times when people were more closely related. Relatives and friends would stop to
mourn and mingle. The three days given over to burial and mourning was a gesture
of respect and a time to reinforce the group.

Trying to understand these customs, I explored the way our different cultural
groups in Mangola dealt with death. We had the foraging Hadza, pastoralist Datoga,
agro-pastoralist Iraqw, and the farming Bantu. Did they share three death days?
Other rituals?

Hadza Tribe: The Hadza were the oldest residents in the area. Mariamu,
a member of our extended household, was a Hadza woman. We had helped put
her and several other Hadza girls through secondary school. I asked her about the
customs. "Are three days of mourning a Hadza custom?"

"No," she replied. "If someone dies, the body is left or buried right there. Bodies
are left out for hyenas, to become part of the land with the help of scavengers.
Sometimes the person's hut is burned with the body inside. It depends on age and
disease. Then the rest of the group goes on with whatever they need to do."

I checked Mariamu's rendition with other Hadza friends and some anthro-
pologists. They confirmed what Mariamu said, and added that nowadays most dead
people were buried, sometimes with a broken gourd or ostrich feathers laid on

the deceased's grave. Nowhere did I find any mention of three days of grieving, or rituals performed for the Hadza dead.

Datoga Tribe: I rounded up information from our Datoga acquaintances, especially "know-it-all" Jumoda, plus current Japanese researchers who'd studied Datoga customs. We had personal experience with Datoga death rituals, too, and had even participated. The elaborate Bung'eda funerals of the Datoga were for esteemed male elders. The event of death involved complex rituals lasting over months, even years. The drinking, dancing, and feasting at funerals were an integral part of Datoga culture. They celebrated life during death. Mounds planted with tree cuttings sprouted and grew after the symbolic planting of the deceased. We still saw many living monuments to dead people in the area.

All those I asked agreed it was essential for the Datoga to remember and respect the ancestors. Some elders could recite the names of their male ancestors going back over 15 generations. The deaths of elderly women and other more "ordinary" people seemed to involve much simpler burials and no prescribed days of mourning or ceremonies.

Iraqw Tribe: My primary Iraqw informants were the two present occupants in our compound, Man Friday Pascal and nursing school student Ruth. I also consulted the current researcher studying the Iraqw.

Pascal was quite stern when he said, "The three days are custom for us; it shows respect." Ruth was less sure of the mandatory three death days. She told me, "I think that often after a death, people stop all work to organize the funeral, burial, and have a ceremony of some sort." She added, "Most Iraqw people believe the spirits of the dead can affect the living. We need to show respect to the ancestors and remember them through rituals such as pouring a small libation of mead or beer on the ground. Sometimes a small vessel of beer is left in a special location as an offering. Chickens or goats might be sacrificed. Music is a big part of most funerals."

I remembered the drumming and singing at Iraqw gatherings and easily imagined it lending comfort to those grieving, strengthening social bonds, as well as chasing away evil spirits.

Bantu Tribes: Finally, I consulted my primary representative of the many Bantu tribes in Tanzania—Athumani. He was from the Wasambaa, a Bantu tribe of the Usambara Mountains near the coast of Tanzania. "Taking the body back is necessary," he told me. "Also, the days after burial. At least three or more."

Later I did some more research on Bantu tribal customs and found a nugget in a long article about one particular Bantu tribe living south of Mangola, the Nyamwezi. I read that neighbors "are expected to refrain from agricultural work for two to three days after a death in the village, and they must visit a bereaved homestead to comfort its members by their presence and conversation." Similar statements about Bantu tribes led me to conclude the three death days may have come from the Bantu and spread. The three days of death allowed people to see and catch up with one another, increasing solidarity in communities.

All four ethnic groups seemed to have a routine for the correct handling of the dead, showing respect and at the same time dealing with spirits. Proper burial and activities during mourning periods brought peace to the dead as well as to the living. Some tribes had unusual practices like "widow cleansing," where a person from another tribe comes to have sex with the spouse of the deceased, emphasizing the pollution factor of death. Survivors, in general, needed to be cleansed by rituals and the corpse buried, burnt, or otherwise kept from polluting the living.

Burial without a casket was the norm, even though Mangola people worried about hyenas digging up the dead body. Often heaps of rocks were put on top of graves. We had seen many rocky burial mounds, not only in Mangola but much older ones, from centuries ago, in Ngorongoro and Serengeti. We'll never know much about ancient practices of mourning, but among modern folks, we seemed to be following the Bantu custom of what I was calling the Three Death Days.

When I learned that a three-day mourning period followed the burial, I grieved, not for the dead woman, but the baby trees. They were languishing in their pots, dying. No helpers would come from the village.

But then I had a maverick thought: I am Mama Simba, a wayward Mzungu, a foreign white woman. I am exempt from this local custom. Mama Simba does not have burial or funeral customs; she doesn't believe in ancestral spirits, nor an afterlife. I was a dust-to-dust person, rather keen to deal with dust and dirt.

I conscripted Ali, a Bantu representative who also had a maverick streak. We dug holes for some trial trees alongside the stream while the family of Mama Girardi dug the grave in the village.

I got Len, Sam, and Gillie to help plant baby trees: figs, yellow barked acacias, tamarind, and sausage trees. We planted a mix to see which trees grew best.

We checked each day to ensure they survived the following death days. Luckily, there came a drizzle of rain and overcast skies, perfect weather for mourning, as well as baby trees. The transplanted trees lasted through the funeral and grew well.

I felt good that we had planted something alive while the villagers planted something dead. It seemed an appropriate balance. But I also felt sad. My bonds were more with those trees than my human neighbors. I would probably leave my mark on the earth rather than in people's memories or hearts.

No one ever criticized my tree planting during the three death days. There seemed to be a general tolerance of differences in dealing with death, as there was for differences in religion. I was glad of that.

Eventually, some of my neighbors joined in planting trees alongside the stream. As I watched the trees grow, I often thought of the old woman and the three death days. I wish the world had a burial custom of planting trees on graves to commemorate deaths and births; they are more enduring than flowers, and they last longer than three days.

Bung'eda tower

CHAPTER 20
RUTH
A WOMAN OF GUMPTION AND GRIT: 1990 AND ON

Young Ruth

Ruth appeared while we were in the middle of building at Mikwajuni. We felt like those leaf cutter ants—scurrying and hurrying with big loads. So much to do. I didn't want to add more leaves to carry, but there she was. Athumani welcomed Ruth then came to pry me away from listing supplies.

"It's Ruth, from the village. She wants to see you."

"What about?" I grumped.

"She will tell you," said Athumani in his calming-Mama-Simba voice. Reluctantly, I followed him to the kitchen. A young woman sat primly with her hands folded under our outdoor kitchen table. Her pretty face was calm and sincere; her eyes warm brown. I guessed she was about 16–17 years old, a vulnerable age. As usual, my head filled with questions. Was she ill? Pregnant? Going to ask for a lift to town? Money?

I stood next to her, hoping to deal with her quickly.

"Hello, how can I help you?"

"Mama Simba, thank you for seeing me." Pause.

"Yes, Ruth," I said, "go on. Tell me why you have come."

"I am coming to ask for help." Another pause. Already my impatience was bubbling up like a geyser.

"Yes?" I said grimly, with a "go-on" nod. Spit it out, girl!

"I am Iraqw, from Mbulu. I am here in Mangola, working for my brother at his grain mill."

My mind's eye saw this demure lass sitting at the noisy, dusty mill in the village—not a job I would have chosen for her. I sighed and sat down on the bench opposite Ruth, waiting to learn more. I noticed she was relaxed enough to bring her hands into view.

She told me, "I do not want to sit all day at a mill." She paused, bowed her head, lifted her face, and looked at me directly.

"I want to go to nursing school. Can you help me? Please."

Such a direct plea prompted my desire to help. Even so, we were already putting Len, Sam, and Gillie through primary school, homeschooling another person, and helping five girls through secondary school. Could we realistically support yet another student?

I asked, "Ruth, why do you want to go to nursing school?"

"It is my dream since I was young. After primary school, I became very sick. They took me to Haydom Hospital, where I kept to bed for a month."

We knew about Haydom. It had been established by Norwegian missionaries to supply health care to the nomadic Datoga and settled Iraqw peoples in the highlands. Despite its remoteness, Haydom Hospital had an outstanding reputation as a hospital and nursing school.

Ruth continued, "One of the nurses became a friend. We kept in touch. One day I asked her what is the procedure to get admission to Haydom Pre-Nursing School? She told me to write an application letter. I wrote, but they said that to get admission, I had to be 18."

So, I thought, she is not old enough. She has some time to prepare.

"In a year or so, when I am 18, I can apply again. But I have not been to secondary school. I fear they will not accept me."

I asked a critical question, "Ruth, do you know English?"

"Only a little."

English was the language of instruction at Haydom. She would have to learn English and so much else. I could see the obstacles ahead. We talked. Ruth didn't know the entry requirements to nursing school. She understood no anatomy, let alone any physiology or medicine. She didn't know a body cell from a prison cell and had no books. Being the last born of seven surviving children to a man with four wives, she couldn't count on her family being of much help. And her brother in the village seemed to be actively discouraging her from applying to nursing school.

I sat opposite Ruth while questions spun around in my centrifuge mind. How could we help her? Was she bright enough? Did she have the will to enter the competition and stick with the program? She already showed courage by approaching us. That also showed shrewdness. Ruth knew we had outside connections and were keen to promote education.

Ruth's gumption was admirable, but I tried to rein in my urge to support her. Many others needed and wanted our help; we couldn't help everyone.

I took a good look at Ruth. Here sat a new challenge for me. She was pleasant, polite, and attractive. Both David and I would enjoy mentoring her. Ruth might be someone who could benefit from our knowledge, as frustrated teachers, as well as our language. Already we had learned that not all the young people we helped would make a significant contribution to their communities. Maybe Ruth could.

Ruth raised her head. Her nut-brown eyes spoke the silent question: Well?

"Yes, Ruth," I conceded, "We will help you. But you will have to work hard. You are starting now. First, you'll have to find out what the nursing school requires for admission. Second, you must start learning English right away."

"Please, Mama, yes, I know I need to learn English." She paused and added, in English, "I try."

Thus, began our deep involvement in Ruth's life. I gave her the language books I'd got from the British Council. They were graded from simple vocabulary upwards. I'd been using them successfully to teach our boys. Ruth soon learned how to use a dictionary and started working her way through the books in the series.

After several sessions learning English, I gave Ruth two essential books: *Where There Is No Doctor* in English and the Kiswahili version, *Mahali Pasipo Na Daktari*. Those two books helped Ruth to master two new languages: English and the terminology of health care and disease. She clutched them to her breast and left, saying shyly, "Mama Simba, I will try to read at the mill, but best I come here, too."

Working all day in the village and then coming to our place to study required real devotion and perseverance. Ruth's brother continued to try to discourage her, offering her land and help to start a business. But Ruth remained firmly committed to her dream, joining us at Mikwajuni several times a week.

During these early days, Ruth studied at the kitchen table under the old acacia tree. The people who hung around distracted her; she was a magnet to all our young lads. I decided that we'd have to move lessons to a more private space. To get her out of the chaos of the kitchen area, I led her to our quiet porch. Cowboy, our live-in youth from Texas, was there, sitting on the couch, trying to read an easy Swahili book. I introduced them, and an idea came to me: the two language learners could help one another. I chose a puzzle book with pictures that Ruth and Cowboy could read to one another. Immediately, they started sharing Swahili and English words. It was a breakthrough. Ruth seemed more relaxed as she and Cowboy laughed together at their mispronunciations and lousy grammar.

The next day, Athumani brought me a note from Ruth. In lovely handwriting, the note alerted me of Ruth's impending visit at 3:00 in the afternoon. Such a formal letter puzzled me. Had the session with Cowboy perturbed her? Did she want to come to tell me she had to quit?

Ruth came into the compound on time. She told me she only wrote the note to practice writing in English. I smiled with relief. She was staying the course. At dusk, when Ruth was heading back to the village, she stopped by the kitchen to tell me cheerfully in English, "Bye, bye, Mama. I thanks you for this day lessons." I chuckled, enjoying this young woman's special grace.

Ruth's lessons became something we looked forward to. She began asking questions: "Does cow dung help heal wounds?" "Is maize meal better to eat or rice?" "How can local women get help with contraceptives?" There were pauses when she had to tally bean harvests or run the maize mill. On the days when Ruth had to work at the mill, we joked that it was her "daily grind." Such simple puns seemed to help her mood as well as her English. Besides the work at the mill, she ground her way through books and lessons.

During those months, Ruth grew familiar with the Flying Medical Service team when they flew in for village clinics. She also met researchers who came to our place while they were studying various tribes, geology, genetics, or archeology. She met medical people who came because of local health issues and those at hospitals and clinics further away. All this helped Ruth get over her shyness and use her new vocabulary.

The day came to apply to the Haydom Nursing School. "Bahati njema," we said—*Good luck*—and sent Ruth off to do the entry exam. She went by local transport, which takes two days over terrible roads.

Ruth returned with good news. "Mama Simba, I passed the entrance exam!" she told me with pride. "There were 185 applicants; only 52 of us passed!" Ruth's happy face suddenly clouded as she added, "But I don't know if I passed the other test." She explained how passing the exam had only allowed her to confront the next hurdle—the dreaded personal interview.

"What did they ask you in the interview?" I prompted.

"They asked why I wanted coming to nursing school; what I expecting to learn." Ruth's face creased with worry as she recalled the interview. "I was nervous. I didn't speak well."

We worried with her; it was a tense time. Would Ruth get one of the 30 available studentships? She did. We were relieved. She was lucky, too, because it was the last year the school admitted students who had not completed secondary school. However, her lack of that qualification would cause us conflict later.

For now, we were happy she'd got into a worthy school, full of devoted doctors and marvelous teachers. By then, Ruth had become part of our mixed Tanzanian family. I thought of her as another of our foster children. On a higher level, we bonded because we had similar interests in health and education.

During her four years at nursing school, we gave Ruth money, clothes, books, and as much time and love as we could. I also tried to teach Ruth about finances. We set her up with a bank account and put money in for her living expenses. Keeping accounts was a struggle. Ruth could charm us into supporting her but found it very hard to write down her expenses. I had to shrug; we had the same problem!

During school breaks, we quizzed Ruth about her courses, teachers, and friends. Seldom did she express worry or hesitation. "Mama Simba, I am working hard. I will succeed." Such optimism and tenacity infected me, too. I bought children's booklets to help her learn biology and found it great fun to work together reading or coloring them.

From one book, we assembled a cardboard skeleton, learning the names of bones. We poked at the ulna and radius bones in our arms, smiling at the name "humerus" as we squeezed each other's upper arms. Another book had organs to punch out: lungs, a stomach and intestines, a liver, brain, and bits of the nervous system. We placed the organs on top of the bones and discussed their functions.

Ruth and I would dip into *Where There Is No Doctor* and go over her word lists. Some of the most amusing and enjoyable exercises were the quizzes we made up: What kinds of foods build cells? What's an enzyme, histamine, hormone, or insulin? If you were running a hospital with a budget of $2,000 for medicines, how many and which could you buy? When is a woman most likely to get pregnant?

One memorable day, we gave Ruth a practical anatomy lesson. Athumani, being a Muslim, could butcher an animal in a "halal" manner so people of any faith could eat it. I had him slaughter one of the goats we kept with our watchman's herd. We laid the animal out on a table in the shade. David deftly slit the carcass down the midline; we worked through the parts, teeth to testicles. Ruth covered her mouth in surprise when David attached a tube and blew into the goat's lungs: they inflated like balloons.

The goat dissection

Most goat parts are pretty similar to human parts, except it has four stomachs instead of one. We pointed out the differences and emphasized the similarities. The dissection was a great success, not only with Ruth but all our crew who hung about and watched. Athumani finally took the goat away to be skinned, dismembered, and cooked for lunch. You can't do that with a human cadaver!

From time to time, I felt the need to see how Ruth was faring. The urge meant a long trip over the hills behind Mangola, through the Yaeda Valley and up the back slopes of the Mbulu plateau. I brought things for her and the school: sacks of onions that would be welcome in the hospital kitchen, accumulated soaps or sets of crockery from the hotels of our friends, useful books.

Ruth always showed me around the wards and grounds. Thus, through Ruth, I learned more about the health care offered at the hospital. I also made some acquaintances that helped bind us to the thin social network spread over our remote region.

Ruth passed all of her courses. She especially loved working in communities and became superior at maternity care and midwifery. When she came to tell us she was graduating, she exclaimed, "They asked me to give the graduation speech! In English!"

Ruth's graduating class

Of course, we had to go to the ceremony. We arrived dusty and tired at Haydom, but the warm welcome from the staff rejuvenated us. A special treat awaited. We got to meet more of the original medical people, such as the Olsons, the family who had initiated Haydom hospital. They complimented us on Ruth's outstanding performance. That embarrassed us because we knew we hardly deserved even small part of the credit for her success. Ruth was the one with tenacity and intelligence, and the gumption I so admired.

We wanted to give Ruth a special graduation present. "What would you like?" I asked. Without hesitation, she said, "I want to go to Nairobi!" Her wish was a surprise, but we agreed on a date. A trip to the Big City of Kenya needed careful planning, lists made, items to sell, and our car to prepare.

Some weeks after Ruth's graduation, we three headed out of Mangola on the long journey to the metropolis. As David and I went about our chores in the city, we were amused to see what Ruth did.

"Mama, I want to go to the hairdresser." She got her hair done in a fancy style.

"Mama Simba, do you think I can get some new clothes?" She shopped far and wide and bought blouses and trim trousers.

"No dresses?" I asked.

"No, Mama, I like to wear pants, they are more practical."

We rode elevators up and down in big hotels, introduced Ruth to art and craft galleries. We took her out for meals at unusual places. She was amazed at the lacquer boxes and bowls for the food we got at a Japanese restaurant. Fumbling with her chopsticks trying to fish out the noodles at a Chinese café, we laughed, remembering our first time with those utensils.

One day we spent hours at the Nairobi museum with its many archeological and historical displays. Looking bemused, Ruth admitted she had information overload. Feeling somewhat sneaky, we offered Ruth a visit to the adjoining snake park, expecting her to cringe. Instead, she said, "Oh, yes, let's go." Although she shuddered when she touched the smooth skins of snakes, she joined us in laughter as we watched a writhing pile of baby crocodiles.

We had a great time together. Then Ruth had to go back to the hospital at Haydom, a place as different from Nairobi as two settlements can be. She stayed on for another year, learning more skills as a midwife and then the second year of contract work.

Ruth giving Jeannette a vaccination

During her time at home, Ruth helped with my usual local medical cases. It was good to have a proper nurse with me. She helped deliver babies, treat common illnesses, and deal with the symptoms of venereal disease. Ruth helped me treat a burnt Hadza child. She cleaned and bandaged the little girl properly. She even remembered to give her my "special magic potion," namely a rehydration drink. This foaming drink was always a winner: salt, sugar or honey, baking powder, and a squeeze of lemon juice in a big glass of water. It was not only restorative but looked impressive, too.

Finally, Ruth moved on from Haydom Hospital. But she soon found she could not advance to higher nursing education, status, or pay, without that secondary school diploma. Now a real problem developed between us. I could never get Ruth to keep proper accounts. I felt she hadn't learned to spend wisely or to justify her expenses. When she asked me for money to bribe her way into a particular private school, I refused. David and I just didn't do any bribing; it wasn't part of our culture. Local people accepted bribery as an unavoidable part of life. Ruth didn't understand why I wouldn't give her money to advance her education. She was hurt or disillusioned or both and stayed away for a time.

She came back, though, and we talked about the differences in our backgrounds and values. Eventually, we compromised and understood one another a lot better. I helped her to pay for a tutor. She worked through the courses necessary for the missing secondary degree.

All this time, I wondered if Ruth would fall in love or get pregnant. Marriage and children would have distracted her from her nursing career. Tanzanian men were still dominant in family affairs. Ruth would have had to move wherever her husband wished. Although Ruth could have married, the men she was attracted to were too old, or already married. The men attracted to Ruth were such a nuisance that she quit jobs to get away from them. Still single, she came back to Mangola and started work at a hospital established by Spanish priests in the sprawling neighboring town of Barazani.

Ruth learned while she worked, mastering the use of various machines in the hospital. I made a small contribution by volunteering for a lesson on the use of an ultrasound machine. Ruth, and the doctor supervising her, gleefully practiced scanning me for gallstones. During that time, more researchers came to Mangola. Ruth started working with visiting scientists and medical people. She eagerly took on any offer to accompany researchers and clinicians, getting blood samples, measuring the height and weight of children, monitoring heart rates or lactose intolerance, and giving immunizations and many tests.

Living relatively near us, Ruth often visited. I started teaching her how to use a computer. She also wanted to learn to drive. We gave her lessons. With David or me as an instructor, she seemed to do OK. But with anyone else, she became nervous and made mistakes. One day with our handyman Pascal, she rammed our car into a tree. We decided to put off driving lessons for a while.

As Ruth matured, so did her social conscience. Together we surveyed women about female genital cutting, a practice officially banned in Tanzania but still widely practiced locally. Virtually alone, Ruth started a project with the Hadza tribe, treating HIV disease. She went to Hadza camps, testing and bringing the worst cases back to the hospital. Her fundraising skills helped her acquire a motorcycle for her work. She goes places on the back of a little motorbike, roaring here and there. I watch in awe.

Beyond the years of this book, Ruth is still busy in Mangola running the health clinic she struggled for years to build. We often communicate, mostly by email. She has visited us in the USA. On our visits to Mangola, we go to see her. Often, she makes us our favorite dish, fragrant pilau, using chopped onions from Mangola, of course. She offers us a soda, a beer, or even a glass of wine while the meat, rice, and spices steam together.

While we eat, I look at her. She amazes me, this woman who bootstrapped herself into being a versatile, competent nurse and businesswoman. Surely, she was born with good genes, and she got some support at the right time, but the qualities that stand out are her tenacity and optimism, her gumption, her grit. Ruth is a woman still going strong, fulfilling her dream.

Ruth in 2016

CHAPTER 21
HOUSE BLESSING

A BUILDING CELEBRATION, FRIENDS, AND NEIGHBORS: 1990

Worker on main house roof

Mikwajuni, our home among the tamarind trees, hummed with people: four staff, the three boys, a stray or two, transient students, the two of us, as well as local and foreign guests. We gathered mostly at the hub of Mikwajuni—the baraza—the kitchen and common area with the guardian acacia tree.

We'd started building more than three years ago, living in tents with a prefab metal storeroom. We'd built six round houses and one rectangular house on our 10 acres. We'd started building our two-story studio, but we'd already done enough to reward ourselves with a celebration. We felt like people who'd been living together, raising many children without being properly married. Now we wanted the ceremony.

We proposed the idea to Saidi Kimaka, our former village chairman, now a trusted advisor and friend. We were sitting at the kitchen table in the acacia's shade, enjoying cups of coffee or tea, and eating sugary mandazi. Saidi had come to borrow tools for his own house. For our part, we were keen to solicit his ideas for a party.

"This party you are planning, how many people will you invite?" Saidi asked us.

"All the people who helped us build," said David. "Maybe one or two," he added with his I'm-just-joking-expression.

I ignored the comment and said, "If we ask the people here in Mangola plus our friends from Karatu and Ndutu, we'll invite at least 25 people."

David chuckled, saying, "Saidi, you and I know there will be more than 25. Mama Simba is underestimating as usual."

Saidi pondered numbers, then said, "Well, 30 or 60, or more, you'll need organization. And you'll need lots of help. He sat back like an ebony sculpture, dressed in a chic blue jacket with an embroidered white hat perched on his head, hands clasped on his walking stick between his knees. He scanned around the kitchen area where some of our helpers were busy.

He glanced at Athumani, who was kneading bread dough. I felt glad again that Athumani had agreed to come back to work for us. He made my life in Mangola less like bobbing about in a life raft on a stormy sea and more like fishing in a calm lake.

Saidi nodded approvingly at his friend Athumani then looked over at our boys. Sam and Gillie were washing their shoes in a bucket while Len stood at the outdoor sink washing dishes. Handyman Pascal came into view with a load of firewood, and we could hear our watchman Gwaruda and a local helper talking as they pumped water down by the stream. Cowboy and Jumoda sauntered through the kitchen area with the self-confident swaggers of healthy young men. They started hauling boxes from the kitchen store out to the car, getting ready for a trip to town.

Saidi returned his gaze to us, saying, "Well, you've got plenty of people to help, and I'm sure you'll have plenty of food. When you are ready with invitations, I will personally take them to friends in the village. I'll also arrange the House Blessing for you."

"House Blessing?" I asked warily. "What would that entail?"

Saidi smiled, lifting his eyebrows as though surprised that we were ignorant of such an important custom. He explained:

"Some elders and a band of children will come to Mikwajuni, right here, at your baraza. We will ask Allah to bless this compound for you. We will pray to make it a haven of righteousness, goodness, and blessings. Holding a feast now will be a happy occasion. It will also ward off evil."

I tried not to look at David at the final word in the sentence. Despite setbacks and traumas during our lives, we didn't believe in evil, a force in the universe out to cause harm to humans. We'd been raised in the Christian tradition, but had ceased to believe in miracles, resurrection, and original sin when we were young.

As adults we rejected most of the mysticism and constraints while keeping some of the customs.

We belonged to no organized religion but did appreciate social values and customs. If Islam had a tradition of honoring a new home, we wanted to take part in the ceremony. We liked the idea of a blessing and party. It would give us the chance to thank all who had made Mikwajuni a reality.

Saidi continued his explanation of the House Blessing: "They will come in the morning. They will sing. Lovely, their young voices. Someone will read the right passages from the Quran. It's an important ceremony."

Inwardly I worried how I would cope with more than 20 village children and elders while organizing the party, the cooking, and tending to guests. I quickly reassured myself that Saidi would make it work.

Athumani brought a fresh teapot to the table. I asked him to help us decide when to have the party. He immediately offered the obvious choice: "Next mnada day."

We all agreed. Having the party on the monthly market day would be a chance to buy fresh food for the event. The mnada would also allow our guests from distant places to buy things at the market as well. It was the perfect day to get lifts to Mangola. On mnada days, transport ranged from big cattle trucks and onion lorries to all types of carts and donkeys.

Saidi left with various tools tucked under his arm. We started to deploy our human tools. I looked around at the crew and paused before delegating jobs. I turned to David first. He smiled knowingly, saying, "Go on. Tell us what to do. I'll set up, invent, and improvise, but you'll need to remind me what to do."

I gave him a fake glare; he knew I disliked the boss role. Even so, we also knew I would have to organize the show. I'd learned a useful social skill from the fictional Tom Sawyer. He enlisted help by pretending a chore was the most fun job ever. The ploy didn't always work, but my enthusiasm usually helped push people along.

Without prompting, Athumani said, "I'll coordinate the kitchen work and cooking. Should we slaughter the livestock the day before? Or is it better to do that early on the day of the party?

"Probably the day before," I said. We'd need to round up some of the animals we kept with neighbors. I asked Athumani, "How many of our goats should we retrieve from Gwaruda's herd? And will we need to get some of our chickens back, too?"

"Yes," said Athumani, "I'll also check with Ali about vegetables and fruits from the shamba. I think the boys will have to cut back the papyrus in the stream so the boat can get over more easily."

Not only would the boys have to cut papyrus, a chore they loved, but they'd also have many other jobs to do for the party. I switched into Mama-the-Boss mode handing out praises and promises: "Len, you are our best mandazi maker, you'll have to make lots of them for the morning visitors. You can eat as much as you want. Check we have enough flour, fat, and sugar. You are chief boatman, too; you'll organize the runs over to the shamba with Ali and bring people over also. Sam, you're good at figuring out what and how much the cooks will need. You can help them prepare…"

I paused at his pout, knowing he would be bored with cleaning and chopping vegetables. I added, "Yes, you can play your radio while you clean the rice and do other jobs for Athumani."

"Gillie, you'll be head waiter and serve the food. Show people where the washbasins and toilets are. You'll all help set up and clean up. And yes, you can invite some of your friends to join in."

Cowboy and Jumoda got jobs to do as well. I put them in charge of sanding down, painting, and erecting a massive piece of plywood on trestles for our main table. Before and on the day of the party, they'd assemble chairs, mats, and blankets for people to sit on.

Night watchman Gwaruda and his helper got jobs tidying up the entire compound, checking the paths and fences, cutting back the grass, and clearing the site beneath the giant fig tree by the river. Pascal became our parking attendant. He would also tend the fire, help Athumani roast goat ribs, and make the enormous pots of stew.

I wanted formal printed invitations for the event. We carefully listed everyone who helped us in building Mikwajuni. Besides head builder Kefti, we had the carpenters, block makers, thatchers. and neighbors. We needed to remember the many people who'd provided tools, materials, places to stay, and moral support. Yes, it was more like 50 than 25 people and that didn't include whomever showed up unexpected on mnada day.

Mid-month, Saidi came to consult about the party.

"I will send over one sheep," he told me. "It will stay with Mama Rama's herd. She is contributing a goat. Issa will bring the two animals in the early morning the day before the celebration." I felt a rush of gratitude for our village friends.

"I've arranged for the children to come. They're preparing for the blessing ceremony. They'll come in the morning and leave before noon. It's mnada day, so they'll be eager to go to the market. After the feast, I'll give a little speech—if you like."

I not only liked the idea, but I was delighted. Of course, we had to have speeches, I'd forgotten this mandatory custom. "Oh yes," I gushed. "Saidi, we'd be honored, you always speak so well."

David winked at me. He was pointing out my use of what we called Ploy Number One: "You do… (fill in the blank) so well!" I looked back at him, putting on my most intense, honest face because it was true, Saidi did speak well. Even though his English was adequate, his Swahili was outstanding. He was used to giving talks to groups. Saidi would be the toastmaster if such a word applied to Tanzanian get-togethers.

"I can say a few words of thanks, too," offered David. Coming from my quiet partner, that was a noble gesture.

"Yes," nodded Saidi, "Mzee David giving a speech would be very appropriate." He stood and shook our hands, saying, "Mambo tayari!" *The matter is done.* He left for home alongside the Chemchem Stream.

David and I remained at the table. The basic plan was complete, but I felt something missing. Our party needed something special, not just feasting and speeches. I wanted a game of some kind, something fun that would get everyone involved, a memorable activity. An exciting idea swam into my mind.

"David, we could have a fishpond game!"

David wasn't the only one who looked at me as though I'd proposed something like a communal jump in the river. Of course, no one in Mangola had any idea what a fishpond game entailed. It reminded me of the time I tried to explain the Archery Contest with the Hadza.

Gathering the crew together, I described the game: A little booth is set up with a painted screen around three sides. On the open side, behind the screen, is a pile of goodies. Those are the "fish," the gifts hidden from view.

I looked at the puzzled faces of my audience. I forged on with the explanation. "We give each guest a long bamboo pole with a string and a hook at the end. The person throws the string over the screen. One of us hides behind the screen. When the hook comes over, we attach a prize. Then the fisherperson pulls up his or her surprise!"

David and Cowboy merely looked skeptical, perhaps trying to imagine a mixed bunch of locals, foreigners, young and old, playing this fishpond game. Athumani's face was blank, his mind considering what Mama Simba's idea might require. The boys looked mystified. I had the feeling no one quite understood the concept of a fishpond game. I trusted everyone would be more enthused when we were playing.

In the meantime, I started conscripting helpers: David would make the booth and paint the pond screen. Our neighborhood fisherman agreed to prepare several poles with hooks. The boys would haul the contraption to the site.

I needed to find more than 50 gifts. Our party guests, all from very different backgrounds and societies, would get small presents. I loved to imagine them as impromptu stars as they fished out their prize. Would the idea work? When I'd organized the archery contest for the Hadza when we first came to Mangola, it was first a goych, then a success. For the fishpond game, I hoped it would be a success from the start. Though some guests might feel embarrassed or awkward with my game, they could always decline to participate.

Group at kitchen. Standing: Msafiri (carpenter), David, Jeannette, Jumoda, Spitali, Athumani. Sitting: Issa, Rajabu, Kefti, Gillie. Front: Sam, Pascal, Len

The party day dawned bright and breezy. I took stock of the actors in our play day. Len was down with malaria, again, so Pascal had to take over making mandazi by the dozens. He and I made great bowls of leavened dough and put it aside. Later, he'd wrench out hunks and drop them in the hot sunflower oil.

All around, people were working. Ali, our garden man, was unloading the vegetables and fruits he'd brought over from the shamba. Athumani and Sam were cleaning and chopping them. Gillie was getting pots and pans ready. The rest of our gang was cutting grass, carrying chairs and mats, and setting up tables and stools.

I rushed around, checking on proceedings, greeting early guests. Athumani's wife and children arrived and pitched in, laying out mats under the tree. Ali ferried over our neighbors across the stream one boatload at a time.

Our shamba neighbor helped his wife and five children out of the boat. He approached me with a smile spread over his long, worry-worn face, holding out an old Afrikoko bottle. It was full of gold, crimson, and pink zinnia flowers, a real surprise. The flowers had spread from our vegetable plot to his, all descendants from one packet my niece Beth had sent me. They were a perfect symbol of us in our new habitat. We were also transient flowers from abroad, like the calla lilies at Chemchem.

I put the festive bouquet on the big table. The flowers accentuated the bright orange and yellow pumpkin design kanga cloths I'd laid out. I'd chosen them for color and also because of the motto printed on them: "Uzuri ya nyumba si rangi"— *The goodness of a home is not its paint*—a fitting motto for our unfinished but thriving homestead.

Festivities began when the young Muslims entered our compound, bearing the Quran, beating tambourines, and singing. Each one, from the tiny to the teenagers bowed, then arrayed themselves on the clean mats I'd put for them by the kitchen house. During the reading of the Quran, Saidi arrived on his yellow bicycle. He joined David and me on our mat.

We sat and enjoyed the songs, then the chanted prayers. I listened and looked up through the twisted twigs of the *Acacia tortilis* tree and felt charmed, truly blessed. The gentle and soul-restoring ceremony finished sooner than I wanted, but the choristers had brought us their blessings, and now it was time for their tea and mandazi. I gave the choir director a donation. We thanked each member of the choir and took photos.

We watched them set off to the village, from which we could hear the rumble of trucks and the roar of the crowd at the mnada. We were soon welcoming other guests. In came Hadza friends, some from distant Endamagha at the north end of the lake. I knew they had come not only for the party but also because it was mnada day. I bought all of Abeya's palm-leaf mats and put them to use immediately. The grassy area by the stream and tables needed more mats where people could sit. Abeya stood up, the leader of the pack, and told me, "We will come back. We join you later."

The choir at the house blessing

I turned to welcome Thatcher Men and Block Making Men. The men drifted around talking to other locals, and suddenly I remembered many of our village guests were waiting for a lift at Mama Rama's. I found Jumoda in the growing group of neighbors and gave him the car keys. He was out of the back gate just in time for the entry of a crowded Land Rover from Karatu.

Out stepped several dear friends from Gibb's Farm. I was quite out of breath, welcoming them. They told me more were on their way, as they went to the tables for refreshments. The next cars pulled in, and David shared my astonishment as more friends from Karatu piled out: six men who had helped us with supplies and building. Also emerging from the car was elderly Ambrosi, the astute farmer who was the model for the character of Akili in our book *Akili and Zuzu: A Story of Two Farmers*. We felt flattered, as pleased as could be—tea and mandazi for all.

Next came the car from distant Ndutu Lodge at the edge of the Serengeti plains. Aadje, my very best friend, had organized the trip, bringing along five more precious people, including Little John, her long-time cook at the lodge.

We beamed. What a mix! We never imagined so many would be able to come so far to celebrate our new home. Jumoda arrived with the car packed full of village people: Mama Rama, village officers, and supporters. Everyone spread out to investigate our buildings. Kefti and David gave tours while modestly accepting compliments on all our hard work.

People continued to arrive. Athumani took me aside, "Mama Simba, we are going to need more food. Perhaps we should get more goat legs to roast?"

I looked around and spied Cowboy and Jumoda. "Okay, off to the mnada! Buy eight more goat legs. And take Sam and Gillie with you so they can buy more oranges and mangoes."

People milled to and fro like a disturbed ant colony. Now was the time to orient them to the site of the feast. We rounded up the guests, herding all strays to benches, chairs, stools, and mats under the big fig tree. They settled down here and there 'til the grassy sward looked decorated with outlandish clusters of bright flowers with the hum of voices like bees above.

The cheerful chaos calmed when David started to make a welcome speech, alternating between Swahili and English. He thanked everyone and told them to stay as long as they liked and eat as much as pleased. He paused, then said, "But please don't swim across the river. We don't want anyone to drown from all the food in their bellies or too many beers!"

People chuckled and laughed. They raised their hands to receive drinks and plates from the boys circulating through the crowd. The delicious smell of spices and roasted meat wafted over everyone. Gwaruda, dressed in a black ngorori, what Cowboy called his Grim Reaper cloak, came by pushing a wheelbarrow. Instead of reaping grimness he brought joy in the form of a giant cooking pot, full of Athumani's prize pilau.

We passed around platters of roast ribs and meats. We ladled out scoops of sheep stew and spinach cooked in coconut milk, a bit of curry, onions, and tomatoes. There was also salad, a mix of crisp cabbage and sliced tomatoes with fresh lime juice and oil and, of course, sweet slices of big Mangola purple onions.

When everyone had a plate of food, I went to the kitchen to summon Athumani. He was talking animatedly to Little John, his fellow cook from Ndutu Lodge. I told them they needed to eat, too, so they went to join the throng. I saw the Hadza returning along the streamside path, their finely-honed foraging skills drawing them unerringly to the feast. They collected their food still on the fire, and I directed them to join the party under the fig tree.

The crunch of roasted goat ribs and the slurp of drinks punctuated the murmur of voices while kids tipped over their plates, and adults tripped over spread out legs. Children screamed with delight as they swung on the ropes we'd hung from the limbs of the fig tree. Lucky for us, the monkeys and baboons didn't come to join the party.

There were mercifully brief speeches by various officials and guests. Then the fun began: time for the fishpond game.

"Gie," David said, "Please step up to be our first fisherman."

Gie was a ranger who boldly tramped the Ngorongoro highlands catching poachers and wood thieves. He was the best person to model what we had in mind, because he was unafraid of new things and a bit of an actor, too. Fifteen generations of chiefs in his Iraqw ancestry prepared him for the stage.

David positioned Gie at the right distance from the booth. He gave him the fishing pole. Gie swung the line around so everyone could see the hook. He tossed it over the screen with its painting of a pond and leaping fish. I was hidden behind the screen, seated on a stool. I grabbed the hook and tied a flashlight to it, then jiggled the line up and down. With one tug, Gie pulled the gift up and over the screen. He was delighted and flashed the light around on the audience. Everyone laughed and clapped.

Per Kullander plays "fish pond" game

In turn, each guest tossed a line into the "pond" where Cowboy or I put a gift on the hook. Block-man Pili threw the line three times before I could grab the end and tie it to a concrete block. He struggled to pull it up, so, crouching behind the screen, I thrust it up and over the edge. He jumped back in surprise as it thunked on the ground. I peeked through a hole in the screen and watched Pili's face go from shock through bewilderment and then delight. He laughed, and others joined in: he'd understood the joke.

I whispered to David to make him try again. This time I tied on an envelope containing two framed black and white photos of him with his blocks and machine. He was so proud. Of course, Master Block-Maker Ebrahim also caught a block as well as other goodies.

Mama Rama got a bag with batteries and packets of tea; neighbors fished out matches, scarves, soap, sewing kits, boxes of buttons, or sacks of sugar. Workers got new shirts, flashlights, pictures, or pocketknives; children got balls, beads, or balloons. David had contributed packets of his wildlife greeting cards, welcome prizes for those friends who could use them.

The funniest moment was the look on our guard and livestock keeper Gwaruda's face when he pulled up a cardboard cow from the pond! The other cattle herders all got paper cows, as well as more useful items. Finally, it was David's turn. We had agreed he would get a large paper fish with THE END printed on its tail.

Sated silly, effervescing with soda or beer, people stretched out on mats, chattering in clusters and lounging on the chairs. It was time for more speeches. Saidi's promised speech was flattering and short. Ambrosi's was full of praise for our writing a book about him. David thanked everyone for coming to celebrate.

I finalized the event with an extra gift. I called our Master Builder Kefti to the forefront. He came reluctantly, always shy and uncomfortable when singled out. He accepted our thanks, and I gave him the photo album I'd made. He held it and stared at the cover. I opened the album to show him the first page. The first, full page, photograph showed him in front of our kitchen house. I stood back to watch as he slowly turned and studied the pages.

I'd put in many pictures of the building of Mikwajuni, illustrating the incredible amount of work he'd done. The album also included photos of each of his helpers, including us. Kefti seemed genuinely surprised and pleased, mumbled his thanks, clutched the album to his chest. He retreated to the table to take a closer look at his book.

In the moment of calm, following, Block Maker Pili stood up rather unsteadily. He said in a loud, slurred voice. "Thank you, Mama Simba. Thank you, Bwana David. We worked hard for you. Now, I am saying how pleased we are. You have remembered even us, your block-makers!" Pili bowed. Much clapping and cheers resounded in the clearing.

Pili wobbled and straightened, then stretched his hand out to me. When I reached forward to shake it, Pili stumbled, pushing me off balance. I stepped back. David caught me from behind and pushed me upright. The three of us teetered back and forth, laughing. General laughter continued as we completed the shaking of hands and disentangled ourselves.

The party started to break up. Suddenly, we were saying goodbye to a stream of cheerful people. They hoisted sacks of onions on rooftops or squeezed them into their cars. Vehicles left one by one, stuffed with people, gifts, and goods from the mnada. Tired and happy, we watched the sun closing curtains over the abandoned stage. It settled behind a peach-colored, glowing cloud bank, another goodbye. Most of our crew was assembled at the outdoor kitchen table, eating leftovers as though starved.

David and I sat at the empty table under the fig tree, watching big-eyed bush babies bound from limb to limb. A bright blue kingfisher flew by, a fitting symbol of the wildlife along the river. Papyrus fronds rustled in the background, saying relax, enjoy this peace. We felt satisfied and comfortable, contemplating our celebration of years of building in this wild corner of East Africa. Owls started a soothing hooting. We knew we had been thoroughly blessed.

Bush-baby

EPILOGUE
PEELING THE ONION

In this book, *Spirited Oasis,* we tell stories about how we got to Mangola and what it was like to live there. We've tried to share the place and people we came to know so that you might have a feel for this stunningly beautiful and culturally unique part of our planet.

Part of our aim is to impart a feel for and knowledge about Mangola's four major ethnic groups: Hadza, Datoga, Iraqw, and Bantu. We hope that providing portraits of specific individuals gives an impression of their traditions, relationships, lifestyles, and a bit of history. These peoples are fascinating in their diversity and interactions, all in the context of a demanding environment.

We tried to paint mental pictures of the landscape, as well: the papyrus fringed, spirited oasis; the pink- and purple-toned volcanic mountains; the rocky and mysterious granitic hills studded with baobab trees, and the dry, windswept shores of Lake Eyasi. Some stories portray our rural village, the region-wide markets, and pleasing or traumatizing events.

Our second book, *Safaris of Song and Stone,* peels other layers from our onion-like Mangola experiences. We tell stories about visitors from near and far, happenings that affected us, our adventures, and safaris. As we said in our prologue, we offer these stories to tempt you to feel, smell, taste, and hear what life was like in a distant part of East Africa: a place where onions thrive, rocks sing, people mix, and scorpions sting.

Jeannette and David

ACKNOWLEDGMENTS

First, we thank Tanzania for allowing us to live and work there from 1974 to 2003. More distantly, we acknowledge our *Homo sapiens* ancestors who evolved in East Africa and gave us our genetic heritage. Some of those people left Africa, migrated north and populated the rest of the world, where we were born. Living in Mangola was like coming home; we are grateful for that privilege.

Second, there are so many people who have helped us on this book project that we feel unable to list each one. Our list of characters at the start of this book names most of the people we would like to acknowledge because they are the main ingredients in our stories. We thank family, friends and neighbors who read early drafts.

Most recently, we acknowledge the critical input by David Belden, who read an early version of the manuscript, causing us to rethink the challenge of presenting our views of life in East Africa. Our diligent editor, Julie Johnson, must be mentioned because she improved our attitudes as well as the text, leading to the publication of *Spirited Oasis* and *Safaris of Song and Stone*.

The Hadza archer on p.41 was drawn from a photo by Carl Palazzolo, with his kind permission.

ABOUT THE AUTHORS

Jeannette Hanby has taken on jobs ranging from working with abused and abandoned children in Los Angeles County to placer gold mining in the Sierra Nevada mountains. After completing her Ph.D. dissertation in Oregon on monkeys, she went to Cambridge in England for further study of primates—one of whom, David Bygott, became her husband.

David Bygott began observing wildlife and drawing as a child exploring the countryside of southern England. He was finishing his Ph.D. thesis on wild chimpanzee behavior when he met Jeannette, his partner in field research, conservation, and business for almost five decades.

The couple studied lion biology in Tanzania's renowned Serengeti National Park and Ngorongoro Conservation Area. They have worked as conservation educators, university lecturers, safari guides, writers, and artists. Together, Jeannette and David have produced numerous guidebooks, educational booklets, activity books, and museum displays in both English and Swahili.

They now live in an intentional community in Tucson, Arizona, still learning about primate behavior, as well as continuing to travel and explore the world.

CPSIA information can be obtained
at www.ICGtesting.com
Printed in the USA
BVHW080223250221
601054BV00008B/160